To the ones who
discipled me —
Mom & Dad
With all my love,
Paul

Discipling
the
Young
Person

Discipling the Young Person

GATEWAY COMMUNITY CHURCH
1235 "E" Street
Washougal, WA 98671

Barry St. Clair
Becky Pippert
Bill Stewart
Josh McDowell
Dawson McAllister
Daryl Nuss
E.V. Hill
...and others

PAUL FLEISCHMANN, Editor
FOREWORD BY CHUCK KLEIN

DISCIPLING THE YOUNG PERSON

Editor, Paul Fleischmann

Published by
HERE'S LIFE PUBLISHERS, INC.
P.O. Box 1576
San Bernardino, CA 92402

HLP Product No. 951004

Library of Congress Cataloging in Publication Data
Main entry under title:

Discipling the young person.

1. Church work with youth — Addresses, essays, lectures.
2. Youth — Religious life — Addresses, essays, lectures.
   I. Fleischmann, Paul, 1946-
   BV4447.D57   1985   259'.2   85-5856
   ISBN 0-89840-093-7

Unless otherwise indicated, Scripture quotations are from the New American Standard Bible, ©The Lockman Foundation 1960, 1962, 1963, 1968, 1971, 1973, 1975, and are used by permission. Other Scripture quotations are from the Living Bible (TLB), ©1971 by Tyndale House Publishers, Wheaton, Illinois, the New International Version (NIV), ©1978 by New York International Bible Society, and the King James Version (KJV).

FOR MORE INFORMATION, WRITE:

L.I.F.E. — P.O. Box A399, Sydney South 2000, Australia
Campus Crusade for Christ of Canada — Box 300, Vancouver, B.C., V6C 2X3, Canada
Campus Crusade for Christ — 103 Friar Street, Reading RG1 1EP, Berkshire, England
Lay Institute for Evangelism — P.O. Box 8786, Auckland 3, New Zealand
Great Commission Movement of Nigeria — P.O. Box 500, Jos, Plateau State Nigeria, West Africa
Life Ministry — P.O. Box/Bus 91015, Auckland Park 2006, Republic of South Africa
Campus Crusade for Christ International — Arrowhead Springs, San Bernardino, CA 92414, U.S.A.

DISCIPLING THE YOUNG PERSON
Table Of Contents

Commitment

FOREWORD

When an entire nation, or, for that matter, even a small group of individuals, becomes aware of its spiritual needs and turns to God's leadership, we have a phenomenon that often is called "spiritual awakening." People "wake up" to the spiritual facts of life. Sin is confessed, people receive Christ, lives are changed, and values are reformed. Obedience to God becomes the norm.

But as great as awakening is, the fact that it is needed so desperately is a sad commentary on any nation, especially one in which Christ's gospel can be expressed so freely. So it is with America. By and large we are a nation still caught in deep spiritual slumber, drugged by our technological and material successes, deadened by our clever philosophies.

But God is poking the ribs of America, and it is exciting to watch as He goes about His agenda. Being an observer of the student world, I first saw God's hand move in the late '60s as He stirred young people, first on the West Coast and then all across the nation. That awakening, however, slowed down during the '70s as Christians got caught up in the passiveness and hedonism of our secular culture.

Now there is evidence of a new stirring among our young. The ideal of giving yourself to something of significance is beginning to surface once again. Young people in the late '80s and '90s could become some of God's greatest ambassadors. The potential is certainly there.

But with this new stir among our young, there also comes a tremendous responsibility . . . who is going to lead them? Who is going to help establish them on a true biblical foundation?

There are a lot of people engaged in the battle for today's youth. The secular world, as well as the church, sees our young as our most precious commodity. And it is very likely that whoever stands up and leads them at this juncture of history is going to win this generation.

This certainly makes our role as Christian leaders a critical one.

There is a lot expected of us and the necessity of being properly prepared and equipped is perhaps more critical than ever.

The intent of this book is to help us with that preparation. The insights and the inspiration contained in these pages will help prepare us for the spiritual awakening our young people so desperately need. The prespectives of the men and women included in this book provide a wealth of biblical insight that will sharpen all of us for our critical tasks ahead.

Chuck Klein

ACKNOWLEDGMENTS

I would like to express my appreciation to all of the speakers who ministered at the National Convention on High School Discipleship. There were 48 different seminars presented. Though we could not include them all in this book, each of them could have added something unique. The 16 men and women selected represent a variety of perspectives from both church youth ministries and youth organizations. God has given each author an outstanding ministry in the area they have addressed. And their combined experience in youth ministry totals more than 300 years!

I also would like to acknowledge the contribution of my wife Toni and my two sons whose tremendous cooperation and support helped me carry the load of this extra project. I am also grateful to my typist Donni Lloyd who not only did a wonderful job on the manuscripts, but served as my "grammatical consultant" from time to time. I would like to thank the National Network of Youth Ministries and Student Venture for allowing me the opportunity to do this. In addition, I am very appreciative of the wonderful staff at Here's Life Publishers who have been so patient, helpful and encouraging along the way.

INTRODUCTION

Get ready for a feast! The delicacies presented in these chapters will nourish you in your ministry for years to come. I feel confident of that because of the impact these messages have had already upon the youth workers who first heard them at the National Convention on High School Discipleship. Held August 5-9, 1983, on the campus of Colorado State Univerisity, Student Venture's third youth worker convention drew more than 900 delegates from 30 denominations, 40 states and 5 foreign countries. The feedback from these delegates encouraged us to compile this book.

Here are some typical comments from people who already have experienced the content of these chapters through the Convention: "It was dynamic!" "This week really turned me around . . ." "In 40 years of attending conferences I have never been to one where the spiritual impact was so great."

I must admit this book has had a significant impact upon me — possibly in a greater way than the Convention itself. Though I was the director of the National Convention on High School Discipleship, I was usually too preoccupied to listen adequaterly and absorb the tremendous truth that was being communicated. I think the Lord wanted to make sure I wasn't "trafficking in unlived truth," because in the process of transcribing those messages I had the privilege of going over the content time and time again! My heart was deeply moved — sometimes even to the point of tears, and many times to the point of action.

My prayer for you as you use this book is that you likewise will be encouraged in your personal life and sharpened in your ministry to young people. The need for integrity and excellence in youth ministry has never been more imperative. That is why the purpose of this book is the same as the purpose of the Convention: to help accelerate the cause of reaching and discipling young people for Christ as never before.

This is a real possibility if we take our task seriously. If we treat youth ministry as a legitimate lifetime profession instead of a temporary stop on the way to something else. If we focus less on shortsighted programs and more on long-range disciple-building.

If we seek to communicate Christ and the Word of God to students in a culturally relevant manner. If we spend less time in our offices and more time in the students' environment reaching out to non-Christians. If we curb our tendencies toward provincialism and take advantage of the synergy that can come from networking. And if we keep our personal lives strong through intimacy in our walk with the Lord and in our relationship with our families.

These are some of the things that were emphasized at the Convention in the theme "Reflecting Jesus Christ in the Battle for Today's Youth." The sections in this book entitled "Spiritual Power" and "Commitment" are classic concepts which enable us to "reflect Jesus Christ" — the backbone of any hope we may have for successful youth ministry. The sections entitled "Evangelism," "Discipleship" and "Youth Culture" focus on essential principles for winning in "the Battle for Today's Youth." (Of course the sections are not all-inclusive. For further study on these topics you may wish to refer to another Student Venture book published by Here's Life Publishers, *Insights — Building a Successful Youth Ministry*.)

Allow me to offer one final suggestion. Knowledge not soon utilized will soon be forgotten. One of the reasons this book made such an impact upon me was that after studying each chapter, I tried to summarize the outstanding points and think specifically about how they could be applied to my life. You'll find those thoughts at the end of each chapter under the heading "Putting This Chapter to Work."

I believe that God will speak to you also as you take a few moments to respond on paper to these questions. It will move the chapter beyond general inspiration and help you decide specifically where you can start. You may want to use these application steps with your staff or volunteers for discussion, training and planning. As you apply these principles, I believe that God will draw you into a more intimate relationship with Himself. In so doing, He will enable you to discern how you can be a part of His plan to bring about a spiritual awakening among the youth of your church, your community, and throughout the world.

Paul Fleischmann

WHO IS STUDENT VENTURE?

For more than three decades, God has enabled Campus Crusade for Christ to participate in a worldwide harvest for His Kingdom. Started at UCLA in 1951 by Dr. Bill Bright, the ministry has grown to a movement of 16,000 full-time and associate staff serving in 151 countries around the world.

To help meet the great spiritual needs among teenagers, Campus Crusade began its outreach to high school students in 1967. Since then, Campus Crusade's high school ministry, now known as Student Venture, has been ministering to students in hundreds of communities throughout the United States. As a resource to the Christian community, Student Venture has sponsored Youth Congress '85 in Washington, D.C., and the an biennial National Convention on High School Discipleship.

Currently, Student Venture is reaching out to more than 100,000 students yearly. Working alongside local churches and other organizations, their faith goals include helping to establish ministries to students in 1,000 communities across the nation by 1995.

VITAL PEOPLE

VITAL People is a growing network of volunteers and affiliates reaching young people through the assistance of Student Venture. Youth pastors, lay leaders, school teachers, and many others are finding Student Venture to be a timely resource to them as they reach out to young people through their churches and in their communities. For more information about this exciting program, contact Student Venture today.

Student Venture
Campus Crusade For Chrust
Arrowhead Springs
San Bernardino, CA 92414
(714) 886-5224

VITAL People Plan

The VITAL People Plan offers five roles in which you can be involved:

V = Volunteer Leader

I = Intern (from colleges and seminaries)

T = Teacher (from local high schools)

A = Affiliate (youth pastors and other leaders)

L = Lay Leader (backers in the community)

SPIRITUAL POWER

1

THE POWER OF PRAYER IN YOUTH MINISTRY

by Dr. E.V. Hill

There is *power* in prayer. Much prayer, much power. No prayer, no power. And particularly for those who are working with young people, prayer is one of the most vital subjects that could ever be addressed.

One of the most tragic errors made by those who work with youth is that they underestimate the tremendous job they have in trying to direct young people to Jesus. Young people are the prize sought after by Satan. Thus, it is no secret that those who teach and work with the young people at the church where I pastor are, to my knowledge, the best-equipped people I have.

NO PIGS — NO PORK CHOPS

On the second Sunday of each month at our church, our children and young people give us leadership. Thus, it slows the service down, it is not as excellent in speech and operation as it is when the adults are in charge, and sometimes we have a few grunting and complaining people. But I have a slogan that our young people have kept going: "No pigs — no pork chops." He who loves pork chops must be diligent with his pigs.

Across this nation, we have not yet grasped what Satan is prepared to do, what sacrifices he has prepared to make, to get our young people — because he knows how important it is. Once a person passes the teenage years conversion is very difficult.

There is supposed to be a mold in the top of our head that closes at age thirty-four, and after that, nothing can enter into our minds! The old folk used to explain things by saying, "You know his

---

Dr. Edward V. Hill is pastor of Mount Zion Missionary Baptist Church in south-central Los Angeles. *Time* magazine named him "one of America's outstanding pastors." He is well-known for his ability to mobilize laymen in reaching the young people of his community for Christ. He and his wife, Jane, are parents of two children — a married daughter and a teen-age son.

mold is closed, so there ain't nothin' you can do." And they used to say, "Marry 'em before the mold closes!" Everybody who has good judgment and good sense, and who plans to do something knows — even industry now knows — that you've got to get hold of people while they are young. Yet Christians do not sense this. We have not grasped this. We just believe that somehow or another they will be preserved.

But this is not true. So the first thing that I would like to impress upon you who work with young people is that *you are the most needed workers we have.* More than the senior pastor, more than anybody else, you are at the cutting edge. You are the ones who will insure the kind of leadership, the kinds of husbands and wives, the kind of children that we're going to have in our churches in years to come. So straighten out your shoulders and try not to be too proud, but grasp the significance of the position you are in. Don't forget what Hitler did to the world by capturing the youth!

For those of us who are called upon to work with young people at this particular time in history, let there be no play, let there be no politics, let there be no foolishness when we come to dealing with the very lives and the futures of young people. Give them your best. Sometimes your best is not necessarily your purity; but sometimes it includes your mistakes that they so badly need to know you have made and overcome. Often I go down in the basement of our church where our youth choir meets, and I talk and talk and talk until late at night and let them ask me all kinds of questions. They generally go out of the room saying, "He's a human being!" That's always shocking to them — but to them alone!

BEYOND THE PROGRAM

Not only do youth workers often fail to grasp the significance of their task, but most of the time they rely too heavily on the machinery — the materials, the denominational instructions, the plays, the jokes and the programs that are written for young people. Now, to attract and train our young people, you have to have all that. You've got to have materials; you've got to have your programs outlined; you've got to have your books, your camps, your fun nights; you've got to have funny people. But so often we rely *only* on that, to the point that when it doesn't work, we never see anything wrong with us or the program — it's just these weird young folk!

So, I want to urge you to consider what you need *besides* your material, *besides* your program. There are young people who have come out of our own church — where we have had dedicated workers, where we have had materials, where we have sent them to camp; we've sent them to this, we've sent them to that, we've had rededications, we've had revivals — and yet we've missed them. You have to do all the other, but there is still something else that must be done.

One day in 1966, a year after the Watts riots, I was watching television when a special newscast announced that police had just raided the Black Panther Party's headquarters on Central Avenue. There was a shootout, and the police had arrested all of the Black Panthers. As the newscast showed them coming out, all of a sudden a great big lump came into my stomach, because I saw a beautiful kid looking very fierce and holding her hands over her head. She was the former president of my youth choir. I shall never forget that.

When I called around and talked to some of my young people, they said, "Oh, yes, Pastor, she's been gone about a year — and now she is the Black Panthers' secretary." This was a young girl who was brilliant. She was given a four-year scholarship in chemical engineering. She was so wonderful in our Sunday school. She was president of our youth choir. And here she was in there shooting it out with the police and walking out with her hands overhead. I called everybody together and asked, "What happened? Didn't we have lessons? Didn't we have camp? Didn't we have this? Didn't we have that? What about Fun Night? What about everything? How did she slip through? This brilliant young person, who I really thought loved the Lord — how did she slip through?"

THE MISSING INGREDIENT

I want to call your attention to Matthew 17:14-21:

> And when they came to the multitude, a man came up to Him [Jesus], falling on his knees before Him and saying, "Lord, have mercy on my son; for he is an epileptic and is very ill; for he often falls into the fire, and often into the water. And I brought him to Your disciples, and they could not cure him." And Jesus answered and said, "O unbelieving and perverted generation, how long shall I be with you? How long shall I put up with you? Bring him here to Me." And Jesus rebuked him, and the demon came out of him and the boy was cured at once. Then the disciples came to Jesus privately and said, "Why could we not cast it out?" And He said unto them, "Because of the littleness of your faith; for truly I say to you, if you have faith as a mustard seed, you shall say to this mountain 'Move from here to there,' and it shall move; and nothing shall be impossible to you. But this kind does not go out except by prayer and fasting.

There are several verses that I want to emphasize.

My daughter is now grown and married. But one day when she was still living at home, she came to me and said, "Now Daddy, I'm fixing a *special* cake for you — it's your favorite!" She went to a lot of work fixing it and putting it into the oven. Finally, she pulled it out of the oven, and it was as flat as a pancake. She cried, and I lied and pretended that that was the way I like cake most.

When her mother came in the room, she looked at it and asked, "Well, now, did you do this, did you do that, did you do this, did you do that?"

Our daughter said, "Yes, yes, yes, yes."

Finally, mother said, "Well, I just assumed — I didn't even tell you — that you would *know* to put some baking powder in it."

Our daughter said, "You didn't tell me."

And her mother said, "Well, that's the missing ingredient."

We do all that we can to help our young people — we provide literature, we provide books, we provide opportunities, we bring in speakers, we have young people's rallies, we send them to meetings and convocations. But the *baking powder* — the thing that will make it all work — is intercessory prayer. You have to do one other thing besides all that you are already doing. You have to pray.

NEEDS WHICH CAN BE MET ONLY THROUGH PRAYER

Consider the situation in Matthew 17:15,16. The man came saying, "Jesus, I have a child who's sick! He has all these seizures; he falls and hurts himself; he even falls into the fire. I knew You could help him, but I couldn't find You. But I found your disciples and I just assumed that they could handle the situation. But your disciples could not help him. I brought my son to your disciples and they could not help! My son is sick!"

And this is a word that's heard all over the nation today. Young people are being brought to our churches by their mothers and fathers, and some of them are coming on their own. They are seeking help; they are seeking something that they can hold on to, something that will bring them out of the muck and mire that they are in. There may be statesque buildings and fine educational institutions fully accredited and fully staffed. But so often the response is, "I brought my son to Your disciples' feet, and they could not heal him."

And so, in like manner, Jesus' disciples came to Him saying, "Jesus, explain this phenomenon to us. Explain why we, Your disciples, could not cast the demon out of this child. We're Your disciples!" And Jesus said, after rebuking them for their lack of faith, "This kind does not go out except by prayer and fasting." Someone has said, "Work as if there were no God, and then when you've done all that you know how to do, trust as if there were *only* God."

SUPERNATURAL RESULTS

I can think of many answers to prayer that I have seen, but one in particular comes to mind. My first year as a pastor I served at the Mt. Corinth Baptist Church in Houston, Texas. Sister Douglas called me and said, "Come. Brother Douglas is in the hospital and he's calling for you." So I made a "clergy call" to the hospital, as I had been trained to do. Brother Douglas was about 72 years old. Neither of his kidneys were functioning, uremia had set in, blood was coming out of his mouth, and his body was badly swollen. When I walked into the room he didn't even recognize me, but I said my "clergy prayer" and left. Sister Douglas said, "It's just a matter of time." The specialists had been there and had given him up. It was just a matter of moments before he would die.

I went back home and told my wife that we couldn't go to Los Angeles as we'd planned; I would have to stay because Brother Douglas would be dead by morning, and since he was one of my senior deacons, I would have to preach at his funeral. My wife is a registered nurse with a master's in health and a doctorate in psychology. And this woman who knows about sickness and dying looked at me and said, "Why don't you do something?"

I said, "As I mentioned, Sugar, the *specialists* have already been there and they've given up. He is 72 years old, and neither kidney is functioning. You're a nurse, and you know about these things. Neither kidney is functioning, and he is dying — it's just a matter of moments."

Again she said, "But why don't you do something? I understand all the medical part — I know medicine. But you're his *pastor*. You know *God*. You're his pastor."

I stood still. Then I decided to go back to the hospital — not as a clergyman, but as his pastor. As I walked into the same room, Brother Douglas asked, "Is that you, Pastor Hill? I'm glad you've come to pray for me."

And I prayed and said, "Lord, this is my first year as a pastor, and I don't know all that there is to know. I wouldn't even be here now if I didn't have a wife who has more faith. But I want You to do me a favor. I want You to acquaint me with supernatural power. If You have to take him week after next, give him back to me now."

I went home and told my wife to pack, and we caught the midnight flight to Los Angeles. The next morning I called Sister Douglas back at the hospital. She said, "Pastor, I've been calling everywhere for you!"

"How's Brother Douglas?" I asked.

She said, "How is he? He's drinking orange juice, he's sitting up in the bed, and his kidneys are working all over the hospital!"

That was prayer. Prayer is a live option! Prayer is not just a ceremonial number on a program — it's a live option. We can pray! Praise His Holy Name! Fix all you want to fix up. Have your Youth Council, your young people's pastor, your young people's program, your annual Watermelon Feed, your annual Hayride, your annual Splash, your annual Annual! But we can *pray*! We can *pray*! We can PRAY! That's a live option, not only to you — it's a live option to our nation today. If our nation makes it, it will be because God will again multiply the fish and the loaves — but He does that only in response to prayer.

YOUTH MINISTRY — NOT WITHOUT PRAYER

The disciples asked, "Why could we not cast the demon out? It was so embarrassing. We couldn't do it!" And Jesus said, "But this is a special kind — this kind does not go out except by prayer."

Today's youth is a special kind. This kind has never known a newspaper without a war headline. This kind has had the opportunity to see right on television open pornograghy and smut unknown to my age. This kind has seen sin unbridled and marching across our nation with "respectability." This kind has experienced the alternative lifestyle suggestion — Adam and Eve and Steve. This kind knows all about cocaine and marijuana and all about the drug culture. This kind knows all about disobedience and getting off with it.

This kind knows about mothers and fathers who take a vote before deciding what the children will do. I didn't have that privilege. I grew up in a home where Mama said, "Did you hear me?" I thought her vocabulary was limited to "No," "Maybe," and "I'll see." But this kind — my own teenage son and all of the others — has come up in a world of fear and woe, drugs and murder, mugging and promiscuity. This kind needs the programs and the paperwork and the plans and the jokes and the training that you offer; but this kind will be saved only through intercessory prayer. We have to pray for this kind. If we don't pray for this kind, the devil will ruin them. Place emphasis on prayer.

DON'T WRITE OFF PRAYER

Will prayer work? Let me give you just another illustration. I've licensed 87 men to preach the gospel. The first preacher that I ever licensed to preach from our youth group was Teddy Hart. Teddy Ray Hart — the cute boy, Teddy Ray Hart — the silk-suit-wearer, Teddy Ray Hart — the alligator shoes-wearer, Teddy Ray Hart — the mama's boy, Teddy Ray Hart — the one that all of the Hart family spoiled. And he was our first preacher — with power! There was nobody who could plead to sinners like Teddy Ray Hart.

After he got married, he said to me, "Preacher, I have to have some money. My daddy's dead now; I'm on my own, and I have to have some money."I said, "Teddy, you're going to go to college, finish it, and then I'm going to see that you go to seminary."

"No, no, no! Pastor, I'll see you later."

I said, "But Teddy, you are a preacher — you know the church, you love the church, you were brought up in the church."

He said, "Preacher, I'll see you later. I'm not going to be poor all my life. Preacher, I love the way I was brought up with the silk suits and alligator shoes. I *know* how to make money; I'm going to go out there and make me some. And when I get me a whole lot of it where I don't have to work no more, I'm coming back to church."

Teddy broke my heart. I visited him, but there came a time when I wrote Teddy off. Teddy got into gambling, Teddy got into dope. Teddy got into all kinds of money-making schemes. And Teddy forgot the church. He was an outstanding young preacher who ought to be a pastor now. But Teddy quit his wife, Teddy left his child, and I wrote him off.

But my associate, Ed Bass, and Gibson, one of the laymen of our church, never wrote him off — they just kept on praying. One day they told me that Teddy was in the hospital. He had been shot twice. One bullet had creased his skull and the other one had hit the side of his chest. The next Sunday morning as I was saying to the church, "We've got to pray for Teddy Hart," he walked in the door.

He said, "Preacher, I'm here today because God don't need to send anything else to me. I got the message loud and clear."

But three weeks later, Teddy was gone. He got back into it, and I wrote him off again.

But Bass and Gibson, who are not pastors, kept on praying. And about a year ago, with no dramatic situation like a bullet in the head, I looked out in the audience and right in the middle of the aisle was Teddy Hart. I preached a sermon and he came down and said, "Pastor, I'm back home. And I want to thank you."

I said, "Don't thank me; I wrote you off. You thank Bass and Gibson, who never gave up on you. They kept praying."

Today Teddy is back preaching, Teddy has his family back, Teddy has his grandbaby praying at the church, *because prayer will work*. Don't do as I did; don't write folk off so quickly. God, in His own way and time, in response to prayer, will bring them in.

OUR ONLY OPTION

Do you need some personal testimony? I came from a broken family. My mother's income was $12 a week. We had no welfare, we had no Aid to Dependent Children, we didn't have anything but what we made during the summer by picking cotton and shaking peanuts. Five of us lived out in the country in a two-room log cabin.

We didn't have much, but we knew how to pray. Mama left me nothing that required a will, but she taught me how to pray at an early age. When there was no money for a doctor and no white doctors would see us in my county, my Mama laid her hands on me and prayed. When there was no hope that I should finish high school, my Mama said, "God's gonna send you through high school." And when I finished high school, my Mama shocked the whole community by saying, "Ed's going to college," and I did. I am the result of my mother's prayers.

PRAYER is a live option. It is not just a number on the program. It is not just being courteous to God, respectful to God. It is the appointed way that God has permitted us worm-like creatures to approach Him in Jesus' Name. Learn to pray. And pray, *pray*, PRAY, for fastly but surely it is becoming our *only certain* option.

PUTTING THIS CHAPTER TO WORK

1. If it were possible to take God's power out of your youth program, how long would it go on before you noticed any difference? Which programs would go on the longest?

2. Name three or more *specific* things which you would like to see God do in your life or ministry that, if they occurred, could only be explained by God's supernatural power.

3. If "this kind" — the youth of today — can only be reached through prayer, what are some of the specific needs of students you know which have been brought about by the culture they live in? Make a list of students with these needs, and write prayer requests which God shows you might help meet their needs.

4. How can you incorporate this kind of prayer more effectively into your ministry?

2

POWER TO MINISTER IN A SECULAR WORLD

by Bill Bright

You and I as believers are chosen and ordained of God. As we are indwelt and empowered by the living God, we can do all things through Christ who strengthens us. Today we are faced with a great battle — probably the greatest battle this nation has ever known in the arena of ideas. Our world has become increasingly secularized. Yet you and I do not need to look upon the challenges of this day with fear or timidity. We are men and women of destiny. There is royal blood in our veins. We are members of the Kingdom of Light, ambassadors of the living God. And no one can stop us if only we set our faces like a flint to obey God and trust in Him. We have the promise of our Savior that the gates of hell shall not prevail against us.

A TIME TO STAND

I was talking not long ago to the Superintendent of Schools of a great city system. He told me that almost daily the ACLU intimidates them with telephone calls and letters, threatening them with all kinds of lawsuits if they allow any kind of religious activity on the high school campuses. Don't be intimidated by those who would try to blackmail you. We stand on our First Amendment rights to freedom of speech and religious exercise. We, too, are citizens of this great Republic, and we shall pay whatever price to exercise our freedoms and our liberties. It may cost us, and we have to be prepared for that.

Dr. Martin Luther King, Jr. believed that black Americans had constitutional rights which were being neglected. He was willing to

---

Dr. William R. Bright is the founder and president of Campus Crusade for Christ International. He leads a staff of 16,000 ministering in 151 countries of the world. He has written many books, pamphlets and articles. He has two grown sons and resides in San Bernardino, California, with his wife, Vonette.

go to jail and to die for what he believed, even though he knew he was breaking the law. Though he eventually sacrificed his life, because of his leadership blacks today are enjoying many freedoms which they deserved long before. The time is coming when you and I are going to have to do the same thing for the cause of Christ, for a handful of men and women are trying to rob us of our God-given heritage.

I believe that God is giving you and me an opportunity to do something in this hour of crisis to reverse the whole course of history. We have a responsibility, since I believe that the reason we are faced with the problems that plague us today is that we who are Christians are guilty of disobeying our Lord. He has called us to be His witnesses, and we have remained strangely silent.

Where are the Christians?

Not long ago, a *Wall Street Journal* article shocked and sobered me. This was the gist of the editorial: "Where are all these born-again, evangelical Christians when there is an epidemic of crime, an epidemic of teenage pregnancy, an epidemic of divorce, an epidemic of drug addiction, an epidemic of alcoholism, an epidemic of venereal disease?" The list went on and on. "Where are these Christians who are the salt of the earth and the light of the world?" The writer seemed almost to plead, "Please come out of hiding and get into the battle — there is a world that is disintegrating."

So I come to you with a call to revolution, a call to spiritual revolution, a call to a revolution of love. I remember talking with one young student in the 1960's who was demanding the overthrow of our government. I said, "Look, I'm a revolutionary, too. Your revolution is shallow and superficial. I am a part of a revolution that changes the lives of men. I encourage you to join the *true* revolution that can change men inside and make a better world." And that is still true today. When enough people are changed in a community, that community is changed; eventually the nation and the world are changed. Jesus is the greatest revolutionary the world has ever known.

THE BIG DIFFERENCE

You and I move onto the high school and college campuses and into the various facets of society representing the peerless, incomparable Savior. *But we must do so only in the supernatural power which He has made available to His followers.* You remember that the disciples had been with Jesus for three and a half years. They had heard Him teach as no man had ever taught. They had seen Him perform many miracles. After such close association with the greatest person who had ever lived, you would think they would have been spiritual giants. But what happened? They deserted Him at the cross. One of them betrayed Him and committed suicide; the others ran away, fearful for their lives.

Now Jesus knew this was going to happen. As recorded in the sixteenth chapter of John, He said:

> "I am going away to the One who sent Me; and none of you seems interested in the purpose of My going; none wonders why. Instead you are only filled with sorrow. But the fact of the matter is that it is best for you that I go away, for if I don't, the Comforter won't come. If I do, He will — for I will send Him to you, and when He has come, He will convince the world of its sin, and of the availability of God's goodness, and of deliverance from judgment...He shall guide you into all truth...He will tell you about the future...He shall praise Me and bring Me great honor by showing you My glory (John 16:5-8,13,14, TLB).

Do you know this incomparable Holy Spirit whom Jesus sent at Pentecost? It was the Holy Spirit who filled these weak, defeated, frustrated, fruitless disciples on the Day of Pentecost and transformed them into men of God. Every one of the eleven remaining died as martyrs getting the message through to the world, except John, who died in exile after being burned in oil for preaching the gospel.

What made the difference? What changed weak men into powerful men, men who were timid and afraid into men of courage and boldness? What — or who — made the difference? The same Holy Spirit of God who dwells within you and me. And He wants to do in and through us all that He did in and through them. Do you believe that? Why, then, are we so weak and impotent as a body of believers? Because most Christians do not understand the ministry of the Holy Spirit.

Three Kinds of People

We read in 1 Corinthians 2:14 — 3:3 that there are three kinds of people in the world:

(1) *The nonbeliever* (the natural man) who doesn't understand the things of God. Even a brilliant person with several doctorates doesn't understand unless he receives Christ as Savior and becomes a humble servant of God.

(2) *The spiritual man* who understands all things. The same Spirit of God who inspired holy men to record the truths of God's Holy Word begins to speak to him giving him understanding.

(3) *The carnal Christian*, who, as Paul writes, is like a baby and doesn't understand the things of God either. He is always causing discord and conflict.

Back to the Basics

Through hundreds of thousands of surveys we have taken all
over the world, we have discovered that 50 percent of the body of
Christ does not have assurance of salvation and 95 percent do not
understand the ministry of the Holy Spirit. This is the answer to the
Wall Street Journal article that asks, "What's wrong with today's
so-called Christians?"

A minister came to me after hearing those statistics. He was a
little angry with me and said, "I don't believe those statistics are
true."

I said, "Why don't you take the surveys and survey your own
people?" He agreed. He had been pastor of his church for fifteen
years. His 1,500-member congregation was very prestigious, with
many scholars and professional people in the church. After he
took this survey, he came back to tell me that *75 percent* of his
members were not sure of their salvation. I'm amazed that he told
me, but he had the courage to acknowledge he needed help.

So the next Sunday morning, he passed out copies of The Four
Spiritual Laws booklet to all of his members, and that was his sermon. He read the booklet, and as he came to the prayer he said, "If
you don't have Christ in your life and you want Christ in your life,
pray this prayer aloud with me and receive Christ." Almost everybody prayed. The next Sunday, believing these statistics by now,
he passed out our little blue booklet, which explains the ministry of
the Holy Spirit. He read that from the pulpit as each of the members held a copy in his or her hands. Many prayed, appropriating
the filling of the Holy Spirit. In the weeks and months to follow, the
church "went into orbit"!

This is what the body of Christ needs! And you are in a position
to influence it. The power to minister in a secular world is available
to you and me. But we dare not go into the front line of battle depending on our own resources. I've been serving the Lord on the
campus for over thirty-two years, but I wouldn't venture in service
for Christ for one second without drawing upon the supernatural
resources of God that are available to me.

Romans 7 Christianity

Romans 7 gives us a little insight into what the average Christian is going through:

> I don't understand myself at all, for I really want to do what is right, but
> I can't. I do what I don't want to — what I hate. I know perfectly well
> that what I am doing is wrong, and my bad conscience proves that I
> agree with these laws I am breaking. But I can't help myself...I know
> that I am rotten through and through so far as my own sinful nature is
> concerned. No matter which way I turn I can't make myself do right. I
> want to but I can't....

It seems to be a fact of life that when I want to do what is right, I inevitably do what is wrong. I love to do God's will so far as my new nature is concerned; but there is something else deep within me, in my lower nature, that is at war with my mind and wins the fight and makes me a slave to the sin that is still within me. In my mind, I want to be God's willing servant but instead I find myself still enslaved to sin (Romans 7:15-23, TLB).

I would challenge those of you in youth ministry to be alert in at least three major areas of concern: pride, sex and materialism. These are constant threats to anyone who represents the Lord Jesus Christ. Frankly, some of the most godly men I've known — men who have had great popularity in the pulpit, people who have been extremely effective in their youth work — have fallen because they have become involved in immorality or materialism. They are captured by the things of this world instead of by the living God, or they become so consumed with their own importance that they get their eyes off the Lord and onto themselves. This is the Romans 7 kind of Christian. The world is full of Christian leaders, youth workers, pastors in great churches — I counsel some of them — who admit they are living in the Romans 7 experience. The apostle Paul describes their dilemma — and their delivery!

So you see how it is: my new life tells me to do right, but the old nature that is still inside me loves to sin. Oh, what a terrible predicament I'm in! Who will free me from my slavery to this deadly lower nature? Thank God, it has been done through Jesus Christ our Lord. He has set me free (Romans 7:24-25, TLB).

Paul continues this great message of hope in Romans chapter eight. I hope you'll memorize it.

So there is now no condemnation awaiting those who belong to Christ Jesus. For the power of the life-giving Spirit — and this power is mine through Christ Jesus — has freed me from the vicious circle of sin and death.... So now, we can obey God's laws if we follow after the Holy Spirit and no longer obey the old evil nature within us (Romans 8:1,2, 4, TLB).

The Christian Life Is Not Difficult — It's Impossible!

I have walked with the Lord for over thirty-eight years, but I am still so weak that I cannot walk one second in my own strength. Jesus said:

Abide in Me, and I in you. As a branch cannot bear fruit of itself, unless it abides in the vine, so neither can you, unless you abide in Me. I am the vine, you are the branches; he who abides in Me, and I in him, he bears much fruit; for apart from Me you can do nothing (John 15:4,5).

I can do NOTHING. Now you'd think that after all these years maybe I could earn some brownie points or could build up my spiritual muscles so I would be able to say, "Lord, why don't You help some of the new Christians? I'm okay." I want to assure you, I'm *not able* to live the Christian life in my own strength, and neither will you ever be. If I live to the ripe old age of a hundred years of exalting Christ, I will still be as dependent upon the Lord Jesus Christ as I am today.

That is because the Christian life is *supernatural.* No one can live the Christian life in his own strength. For years I fasted, prayed, begged and pleaded with God for His power. I memorized Scripture and went through all kinds of self-imposed disciplines. One day I read this passage, and it absolutely liberated me. Think of this:

> Following after the Holy Spirit leads to life and peace, but following after the old nature leads to death, because the old sinful nature within us is against God. It never did obey God's laws, and it never will (Romans 8:6,7, TLB).

I was trying to serve God in the energy of my own effort. But Bill Bright is not able to live the Christian life, nor are you.

SPIRITUAL BREATHING

If I had only one message to give to the whole Christian world, it would be this message. The best and most important thing that one can understand as a believer is a concept that I like to call "Spiritual Breathing." *Exhale* by confessing your sins. *Inhale* by appropriating the fullness of God's Spirit.

Exhaling — Cleansing by Confession

The word "confess" literally means "to agree with." If I agree with God concerning my pride, my jealousy, my lust, my dishonesty — or whatever it may be — I am saying to God at least three things. First of all, Lord, I know that it's wrong; it's sin. Second, I know that Christ paid the penalty when He died on the cross and shed His blood for my sin. And third, I repent. If I repent, I change my attitude. And if I change my attitude toward my sin, I must also change my action. A person may say, "Lord, I goofed, I'm sorry. I hope I do better next time." But unless there is repentance, there is no true confession.

The Bible says, "If we confess our sins, He [God] is faithful and just to forgive us our sins and to cleanse us from all unrighteousness" (1 John 1:9, KJV). God cannot use impure vessels. If there is any unconfessed sin in your life, I'd like to suggest that you take a sheet of paper and write down everything the Holy Spirit shows you. (Writing it down helps keep you focused and specific.) If you have a grievance toward anyone — you're not getting along with your husband or your wife or your parents or your children or your neighbors or your friends or your pastor or your choir director or your Sunday school superintendent or whomever — if you have resentment toward *anyone*, write it down and say, "Lord that's sin; I confess it." It may be a sin in the area of pride or lust or materialism. Whatever it is, God will show you. Tonight, before you go to bed, make that list. After you've confessed, destroy the list so that no one else will ever see it. Destroying the list is also a graphic reminder that if you sincerely confess, God will forgive you and cleanse you according to His *promise* in 1 John 1:9. That which took place on the cross two thousand years ago where Christ forgave *all* of our sins — past, present and future — becomes a reality in your experience.

This concept of spiritual breathing has been the most important truth I have ever heard or experienced. As you experience the freedom and joy which comes in *knowing* that your sins are forgiven and forgotten, I think you'll understand why I would make such a statement.

Inhaling — Fullness by Faith

Now you have "exhaled." How do you "inhale"? Simply appropriate the fullness of God's Spirit by faith. This is not a once-and-for-all experience; rather it is a moment-by-moment walk. At the moment of spiritual birth, the Holy Spirit — who enables us to be born again — comes to dwell within us. He baptizes us into the body of Christ, and at that moment, we are filled with the Holy Spirit. There is one baptism, but many fillings. And that is the reason the concept of spiritual breathing is so important. We walk moment by moment, day by day, in the fullness and in the power of God's Spirit.

Search Me, O God

You may feel that you understand this, but let me ask you to hold before you as a mirror Ephesians 5. In Ephesians 5:18 we are admonished, "Be not drunk with wine, wherein is excess, but be filled with the Spirit." Now when one is filled with the Spirit, certain things happen. As we read this passage, continuing with verse 19, we see that the Spirit-filled person talks much about the Lord. His mind is saturated with the things of God. He quotes psalms and hymns; he sings and makes melody in his heart to the Lord. He has a thankful spirit, always giving thanks to God for everything. He honors Christ by submitting to others — the husband loving his wife as Christ loved the church; the wife submitting herself to her husband's leadership and loving him; the parent loving the child; the child honoring and obeying the parent; the worker serving as unto the Lord. All of this is part of what it means to be filled with the Spirit.

As you look into that mirror, do you find it easy to talk about the Lord? By nature, I'm a reserved person. I'm the kind of person who would be very happy to retire to some lakeshore or mountainous area, read good books, listen to good music, be alone with my beloved wife and a few close friends, and let the world go by. By nature, I am that kind of person. But the Holy Spirit gives me a boldness.

One morning recently I was at a seminar in Colorado Springs. As the seminar was progressing, I observed a hotel staff person assigned to record the messages, and the Holy Spirit said, "Go talk to him." So I went to talk to him, and I said, "Are you a Christian?"

He said, "No."

I then asked, "Would you like to be?"

And he said, "Yes."

I said, "Do you understand how?" And I went through the gospel presentation in the Four Spiritual Laws booklet with him and, miracle of miracles, he said he would like to receive Christ! So we had prayer together. The Holy Spirit first gives you the discernment, He tells you what to do, and then He gives you the power and the wisdom to do it. And there are millions of people like this young man all waiting for someone who cares enough to tell them how they can know the Lord Jesus.

UNDERSTANDING THE MINISTRY OF THE HOLY SPIRIT

Today, you can *know* you are filled with the Holy Spirit if you want to be. Jesus said, "Blessed are they who do hunger and thirst after righteousness; for they shall be filled" (Matthew 5:6, KJV). You can be filled if you want to be filled. And I want to tell you how. There are several things you need to know about the Holy Spirit.

The Holy Spirit's Role

First, who is the Holy Spirit? He is God — an equal part of the Trinity. He is no less God than the Father or the Son. He possesses all the attributes of deity. Why did He come? To glorify Christ, to lead us into all truth, to empower us for witness, to empower us to live holy lives. In fact, as we think about it, everything that happens to us in the Christian life — from the moment of our new birth until we go to be with the Lord — involves God the Holy Spirit.

The Average Christian's Blindness

Why, then, is the average Christian not filled with the Spirit? Because, as our surveys revealed, he doesn't understand the ministry of the Holy Spirit. Let me illustrate how important this is.

My brother lives in west Texas. On my first visit there, he took me out to see some incredible oil wells. A little town in a desert area is the site of one of the biggest oil fields in all the world, apart from the oil fields in the Middle East. This land was originally owned by a man named Yates, who used the land as a sheep ranch during the Depression years. In fact, he was having such difficulty making his payments on the ranch that he was about to lose everything he had. He had no money for food and clothing for his family; he was depending on government subsidy to stay alive.

Then one day an oil crew came by and told Yates, "We believe there is oil on your property." After doing seismographic tests, they asked permission to drill a wildcat well. Yates agreed. A few days later, they discovered oil. At that time, it was the largest oil well ever discovered, bringing in 80,000 barrels of oil a day. The second well came in at 180,000 barrels a day. Imagine how valuable that land was! Eventually there were hundreds of wells. In fact, when I was there, I saw oil in a creek flowing through the community. An enterprising oilman took a skimmer, pumped the oil into trucks, shipped it away and made a fortune. That's how plentiful the oil was.

Think of it! For years this man lived in poverty, and yet he was probably one of the richest men in the world. He was worth billions. The government tested one of the wells recently, and it was still producing 125,000 barrels of oil a day. Yates had owned it all. The day he purchased the land, he received with it the oil and mineral rights. Why was he living in poverty? Because he didn't know the oil was there. He owned it, but he did not posses it!

The same is true with us as Christians. The moment we receive Christ, we become men and women of God. All the supernatural resources of God are available to us. But most Christians never make this discovery, so they go through life living in a Romans 7 experience — never knowing how to draw upon the mighty power of God.

THE PROMISE OF THE SPIRIT'S FILLING

What does it mean to be filled with the Spirit? It means very simply to be filled with Jesus, the Son of God, because the Holy Spirit came to glorify Christ. If I am filled with the Holy Spirit, Jesus Christ walks around in my body. He thinks with my mind, He loves with my heart, He speaks with my lips. He seeks and saves the lost through me. I don't have to make things happen in the flesh.

How can one be filled with the Spirit? This is the big question. I used to beg God for His fullness. I would fast and pray for days at a time, begging with tears, "Oh, God, I'm defeated. I'm miserable. I need help. Show me where I can touch You and You can touch me, and somehow I'll be different. I want to be different; I want to love and serve You with all my heart." Nothing seemed to happen. I would make decisions, commitments, resolutions, only to break them. And then God, in His wisdom, love and grace, showed me how simple it is. "As you therefore have received Christ Jesus the Lord, so walk in Him" (Colossians 2:6). How did you receive Christ? By faith. How are you filled and empowered with the Spirit of God? *By faith.*

Two Crucial Words

There are two words that are crucial to an understanding of how to appropriate God's spirit by faith. The first word is "command." Ephesians 5:18 (KJV) says: "Be not drunk with wine wherein is excess; but *be filled with the Spirit.*" Literally this verse means "be ye being filled" as a way of life, moment by moment, day by day. All the days of our lives we are to be filled with the Spirit. It's a command of God. Not to be filled with the Spirit is to disobey God.

The second word is "promise." 1 John 5:14,15 says: "*If we ask anything according to His [God's] will, He hears us.* And if we know that He hears us in whatever we ask, we know that we have the requests which we have asked from Him." Is it God's will that you and I be filled with the Spirit? It's not only His will, it's His command. If you and I claim the fullness of God's Spirit, will He hear us? He says He will. Will He answer us? It's a promise.

Three Essential Prerequisites

Though we are filled by faith and faith alone, there are three important things to consider by way of heart preparation.

First, hunger and thirst after righteousness. Jesus said, "Blessed are they who do hunger and thirst after righteousness; for they shall be filled" (Matthew 5:6, KJV). God will honor the person who sincerely wants to be filled with the Spirit. The person who is casual and indifferent and says, "Look, I want to do my own thing, I'm not ready to be filled with the Spirit" will not be filled. To conjure up some kind of emotional experience is not what we're talking about here. Feelings are wonderful, but they come and go. They are the by-product of faith and obedience. Seek the Giver instead of the Gift.

Second, turn from all known sin. God does not fill impure vessels. "If we confess our sins, He is faithful and just to forgive us our sins and to cleanse us from all unrighteousness" (1 John 1:9, KJV).

Third, make Christ the Lord of your life. It is impossible to be filled with the Spirit if you insist on running your own life. Christ must be Lord. The apostle Paul was a great example. In Romans 1:1, he calls himself "a slave of Jesus Christ." One of the greatest things my wife, Vonette, and I ever did was to sign a contract with the Lord more than 30 years ago in which we became His slaves. We literally signed off all of our rights, saying to the Lord, "We don't want to seek honor or praise or applause or money or materialism."

Both of us had experienced some of the so-called "good life" when I was in business. But God showed us, "What does it profit a man to gain the whole world, and forfeit his own soul? For what shall a man give in exchange for his soul?" (Mark 8:36). We discovered that seeking first the Kingdom of God was the greatest challenge that had ever been placed before us. Our attitude then, and now, was that if we had to live on bread and water the rest of our lives to serve the Lord Jesus Christ, it would be worth it.

That absolute, complete, irrevocable surrender to the lordship of Christ was, I believe, the beginning of the great adventure we have known now all these thirty plus years. In fact, it was only a few days later that God entrusted me with the vision that we now call Campus Crusade for Christ. I'm sure that had there not first been that complete surrender to the lordship of Christ there would not have been the vision which now embraces 151 countries and is helping to reach the lives of millions of people all over the world. To God be the praise and glory.

BE FILLED WITH THE SPIRIT!

Are you filled with the Spirit right now? Does your life reflect the qualities we reviewed in Ephesians 5? Do you talk about the Lord wherever you go? Do you saturate your mind with the Word of God? If you're not filled with the Spirit, you can be right now. Claim the fullness and control of the Holy Spirit by faith. He has *commanded* us to do so, and He has *promised* that if we ask any thing according to His will, He will answer us.

It's Contagious!

A layman who was a volunteer youth pastor came to me one day. He was very popular with young people — some called him "a pied piper." He had an outstanding personality and a real way with kids. Hundreds of students loved him and followed him. Nevertheless, he came to me empty — very, very hungry for God. So I shared with him about the ministry of the Holy Spirit.

Then I asked him, "Do you believe it is God's will that you be filled with the Spirit?"

He said, "It's God's command."

"Do you believe that if we were to bow right here and pray and you would, by faith, claim the fullness of the Spirit, God would hear you?"

He said, "Yes, He would hear us."

"Would He fill you?"

He didn't answer that; he got on his knees and began to pray. And when he stood to his feet, he thanked me — no emotion, no great ecstatics, but he knew he was filled.

Six months later, he wrote me a letter telling me that every day since he had been filled with the Spirit was more profitable for God than all the previous years of his life as a very active layman. Those in the church noticed the difference. One leader said:

> I've seen a change take place in this young man. I remember when he was a "pied piper," and the students followed him and worshiped him instead of the Lord. After he was filled with the Holy Spirit, he became a humble servant. Though the students still follow him, now they follow him as he follows Jesus. He is beautiful, and something wonderful happened to him. I want what he has.

Your church will come alive if you demonstrate those Spirit-filled qualities Many senior pastors don't understand this great truth. (I say that on the basis of our surveys.) Most of your laymen in the church — sincere, wonderful people — don't know why they feel like Romans 7 Christians. Nobody has ever explained to them how they can be filled with the Spirit.

ALL OR NOTHING

As you surrender your will to the Lordship of Christ and by faith claim the fullness of God's Spirit, He will equip you with power to minister in this secular society. Campuses will come alive; churches will come alive. And I can tell you from experience, there is no substitute for the Holy Spirit. Organizations, strategies, plans and all the ideas of men are just wood, hay and stubble apart from the Holy Spirit. Nothing of value will ever be accomplished in the lives of your young men and women, or in their fathers and mothers, apart from His power.

However, with His power and enabling, we can confidently expect supernatural results. Personal lives will bear the rich fruit of the Spirit. The reaching of the eighteen million high school students in the United States becomes possible, and spiritual awakening will begin to sweep the campuses, the churches and the communities of America and the world.

For this and much more, the Holy Spirit now waits to fill and empower you.

PUTTING THIS CHAPTER TO WORK

1. *Exhale* — Claim Christ's forgiveness for any unconfessed sin. As Dr. Bright suggested, make a list noting the specific sins the Holy Spirit shows you. After confession, destroy the list as a symbol of God's permanent forgiveness.

2. *Inhale* — Claim the fullness of God's Spirit by faith. According to His command and promise, *believe* that you are filled. You may want to pray a prayer like this:

   > Dear Father, I need You. I hunger and thirst after righteousness. I have confessed all my known sins. Thank You for forgiving me completely. Fill me with the Holy Spirit as You commanded me to be filled and as You promised in Your Word that You would do if I asked in faith. Thank You for filling me with the Holy Spirit right now.

3. *Demonstrate your Faith* — To solidify your experience, tell someone else what you have done. Review why you *know* you are filled with the Holy Spirit right now. Writing these things down also may be a good way to express your faith.

4. *Keep "breathing"!* Keep a "short account" with God. If you become aware of an attitude or action that is displeasing to God, confess it immediately — breathe spiritually — and continue walking in the Spirit. Begin to look for the fruit of the Spirit to become more obvious in your life.

3

THE AUTHORITY
OF THE BELIEVER

by Josh McDowell

Thousands of students are being reached for Christ today. We're seeing churches and organizations work together as never before to meet the needs of students. Youth workers are taking the Great Commission seriously, but we are not making the impact that we could due to one very important factor. In Matthew 28:19 Jesus said, "Go, therefore...." Do you realize what the "therefore" is there for? It is a transition from verse 18 in which Jesus said, "*All authority* has been given to Me in heaven and on earth. Go, therefore...." Many of us in youth ministry may be going with the message, we may be going in the power of the Holy Spirit, but many of us are going without the authority of the believer.

One Easter week, I was at Balboa Beach in California. Typically, thousands of students go there to spend their spring break, and that Easter, Campus Crusade for Christ sent many of their students and staff to present Christ and hold some special meetings. We had André Kole, the illusionist, appearing at a big ballroom called the Supper Club. The Goodyear blimp advertised the events, and the Supper Club was packed out eight or ten times a day. We had so many people coming to our meetings that nobody was showing up at the bars. The people who owned one of the bars got a little upset, so they decided to come over and try to break up our meetings. They knew that if they could break up one meeting, they could break them all up.

One fellow drove up in his big, new, souped-up car. He stopped right at the front door of the Supper Club and started to rev his engines to a deafening level. Then he popped the clutch and screeched down the street. Of course, everybody turned around

Josh McDowell is the author of numerous books, including the best-selling *Evidence That Demands a Verdict*. As a traveling representative for Campus Crusade for Christ, he has spoken to over seven million students and faculty at 600 universities in 62 countries. He received degrees from Wheaton College and Talbot Theological Seminary. He is currently a professor at two California schools — Simon Greenleaf School of Law and the Julian Center. He, his wife, Dottie, and their three children live in Julian, California.

and André had to get their attention again. The driver came around a second time, stopped right at the front door, revved the car's engine loudly, popped the clutch and screeched off again down the street. By this time, people were standing up and looking around.

I turned to Gene Huntsman, who was the Youth Pastor at Scott Memorial Baptist Church in San Diego. I said, "Gene, I think Satan is trying to break up this meeting. Step out the door with me, and let's exercise the authority of the believer." We stepped into that doorway and prayed a 30-second prayer, the basis of which I will be explaining to you. The man came back around the block, stopped right at the front door, revved his engine even louder than before. He popped the clutch, and then "Ka-poom!" — he blew the rear end of his car all over the street! As Gene and I went out to help push his car over to the side, we were reminded that all authority is given to *us* in heaven and on earth!

Recently I was speaking in "Mecca" — that is the name of the town auditorium in Milwaukee, Wisconsin. It was the second night. We had a huge crowd out, and I was speaking on the subject of maximum sex. I always like to get to a meeting early just to go around and meet people. As I was walking around talking and getting acquainted, I felt a strange coldness — an unusual atmosphere for this crowd. All of a sudden some people walked up behind me and started saying quietly, "We're going to kill you; we're going to destroy you tonight. We are going to wipe you off the face of the earth." And everywhere I went for thirty or forty minutes, they were right behind me. I tried not to pay much attention to them.

Finally it was time for me to speak. As I walked up to the front and started to speak, before me sat one of the coldest audiences I had ever faced — absolutely zero response. I had never seen anything like it. Then I looked over to the right. About twelve Satan worshippers sat in the second or third row, and they were going through some motions. Ten or twelve minutes into the talk I realized what was happening, so I reached down and turned off my radio mike. Then, out loud, and though most of the audience couldn't hear me, I exercised the authority of believer. It was just as though a combustion took place in the whole auditorium. As soon as I finished the talk, people started coming up asking, "What did you do? Did you see what happened? All of a sudden the whole crowd just exploded!" And then I was able to explain the authority of the believer.

This truth can make the difference between defeat and victory for you, the difference between enthusiasm and despair. It is vitally important because of the power that it confers upon the believer who is filled with the Holy Spirit by faith. Satan has done everything possible to blind believers to the authority that we have. Even very few mature believers grasp the authority of the believer.

WRONG CONCEPTIONS OF AUTHORITY

Often, to explain what something is, it is best to explain what something is not.

Filling of the Spirit

Some people say that the authority of the believer over Satan is being filled with the Holy Spirit; that is, if you are filled with the Holy Spirit, then you have authority over Satan. Certainly I believe that every individual ought to walk every moment of his life filled with and controlled by the Holy Spirit. But the filling of the Holy Spirit and the authority of the believer are totally distinct from one another.

Gift of the Spirit

Other people believe that the authority of the believer is a special gift of the Holy Spirit conferred upon a certain group or certain individuals with spiritual maturity. This gift, then, endows them with power over Satan. True, God gives spiritual gifts, but the authority of the believer and spiritual gifts are totally distinct from one another.

Prevailing Prayer

Still others believe that the authority of the believer is prevailing prayer; we go to our knees and we pray something through. God, I believe, leads all of us to prevailing prayer. But prevailing prayer and the authority of the believer are totally distinct from one other.

CLARIFYING AUTHORITY

Then what *is* the authority of the believer? To explain what it is, I need to show you the difference between authority and power. In the King James version, Luke 10:19 reads, "Behold, I give unto you power to tread on serpents and scorpions, and over all the power of the enemy: and nothing shall by any means hurt you." The New American Standard Bible renders the Greek more accurately, I believe. "Behold, I have given you authority [not power]...over all the *power* of the enemy...." There are two different Greek words here. We have not been given power over the power of Satan; we have been given *authority* over the power of Satan.

Let me illustrate what that means. I used to live in Argentina. There was one street, Corrientes, that was about three blocks wide. One day I was walking with another Campus Crusade staff member, and when we came to the corner of Florida and Corrientes, a very strange thing took place — yet it had a very common explanation. There was a lot of traffic, so we stopped at the corner. Out in the center of the intersection was a pole. On top of the pole was a platform. A policeman was standing on the platform directing traffic. He looked over and saw us ready to cross the street. He blew his whistle, put out his hand, and *immediately* all those cars came to a screeching halt. Then he motioned for us to walk across the street. What's the explanation of that? He had no personal power over those cars. With all the strength that he had, he couldn't have stopped a Volkswagon. What's the explanation of it? He had something far better than personal power — he had authority. He was vested with the authority of the Police Department and the State of Argentina, and the drivers of those cars recognized that delegated power. Authority is delegated power. We do not have power over Satan; we have delegated authority over Satan.

I'll share another illustration. When I lived in Mexico, I saw a very strange happening. They have what is called a "glorietta" — the center where a number of streets converge, like the hub of a wheel. In the center, there is often a traffic cop going through certain motions to direct traffic. All he does is put up his hands and everything stops. A mother was down on the street with her son, who was probably about seven or eight years old and seemed to be very infatuated with what the policeman was doing. It so happened that the traffic policeman stepped off the little box and walked across this glorietta. At that moment, the little kid broke away from his mother, ran out in the center of the glorietta, jumped on the box, put out his hands, and the traffic stopped!

Obviously the drivers didn't respond to the boy's personal power; they responded to the authority of that position. The moving crowds recognized the delegated power that gave the person authority in that situation. In other words, if authority is delegated power, then *its value depends upon the force behind its user*. The believer who is fully conscious of the divine power in him and behind him and at the right hand of God can face Satan without fear or hesitation. He has the authority.

THE SOURCE OF AUTHORITY

The source of the authority of the believer is found in Ephesians 1:19-23:

> And what is the surpassing greatness of His power toward us who believe. These are in accordance with the working of the strength of His might which He brought about in Christ, when He raised Him from the dead, and seated Him at His right Hand in the heavenly places, far above all rule and authority and power and dominion, and

every name that is named, not only in this age but also in the one to come. And He put all things in subjection under His feet and gave Him His Head over all things to the church, which is His Body, the fullness of Him Who fills all in all.

When Jesus Christ was raised from the dead, the act of His resurrection, ascension and seating at the right hand of the throne of God was probably one of the greatest displays of God's power in all of history — even greater than creation. It was so great that the apostle Paul had to use four different Greek words for power in verse 19 to describe this work of God. "The surpassing greatness of His *power*" — "power" is the Greek word dynamis — we get our English word "dynamite" from it. "In accordance with the *working*" — "working" is the Greek word energeia — from it we get the English word "energy." "Of the *strength*" — "strength" is the Greek word kratos. It means utilizing tremendous *strength* as you work. "Of His *might*" — "might" is the word ischys, which means a great summation of power. You can see how the combination of these four words illustrates the magnitude of the great work God performed in the resurrection, the ascension and the seating of Jesus Christ at the right hand of the throne of God — "far above all rule and authority and power and dominion and every name that is named."

Why? Why such an exertion of the authority and the power of God? Primarily because the last thing Satan wanted was for Jesus Christ to be resurrected, to pass through the power of the air and to be seated at the right hand of the Father. At the moment Jesus was seated at the right hand of the Father, Satan was defeated. This is the source of our authority.

Having been buried with Him in baptism, in which you were also raised up with Him through faith in the working of God, who raised Him from the dead. And when you were dead in your transgressions and the uncircumcision of your flesh, He made you alive together with Him, having forgiven us all our transgressions....When He had disarmed the rulers and authorities, He made a public display of them, having triumphed over them through Him (Colossians 2:12,13,15).

Peter says in 1 Peter 3:22 that Jesus, "is at the right hand of God, having gone into heaven, after angels and authorities and powers had been subjected to Him." The source of our authority is the right hand of the throne of God where Jesus is seated.

AUTHORITY CONFERRED UPON THE BELIEVER

When did this authority over Satan become operational in the life of the believer? When was it conferred upon you and me? Note that in Ephesians 1:19 there are four important words that relate:

"toward us who believe." All of this unleashing of the power of God was intended for you and me! This power enables us to overcome right now — not just down the road. We can overcome *right now* in our daily lives and ministries.

Co-seated at Salvation

You can see this more clearly as you look at Ephesians 2, which focuses on believers overcoming the evil one and living victoriously. Since Ephesians 1:21-23 is a parenthetical clause, there is a direct link between Ephesians 1:20, which talks about Christ being raised from the dead, and Ephesians 2:1-7, which talks about believers being "made alive together with Christ" when we were dead in our sins. Paul clarifies the link even further in Ephesians 2:6, "and raised us up *with* Him, and seated us *with* Him in the heavenly places, *in* Christ Jesus."

In other words, at the moment we confess Jesus Christ as Savior and Lord, God the Holy Spirit places us into the body of Christ. We are totally identified with Him. At the moment of salvation, in the eyes of God, we are co-crucified, co-buried, co-resurrected, co-ascended and co-seated with Jesus Christ at the right hand of power — "far above all rule and authority and power and dominion and every name that is named." At the moment of salvation, it was conferred upon every one of us.

The basic problem is that God and Satan know this, but the believer usually doesn't. I did not know this for the first ten years of my Christian life. This is not some special gift given to a certain spiritual group or individual; it is the birthright of every true believer in Jesus Christ. You don't climb some ladder of faith to get there. Every believer, from the moment of salvation, has the authority because he has been co-resurrected, co-ascended, and co-seated at the right hand of the Father (cf. Hebrews 8:1, Matthew 26:64).

Exercising Authority Brings Boldness

What does that mean to us today? The right hand of the throne of God is the center of the authority over Satan. We have been elevated by the grace of God to that very position at the right hand of God in Jesus Christ, and we now have the privilege of exercising what Christ earned for us when He defeated Satan on the cross.

In Matthew 28:19, Jesus said, "Go therefore and make disciples...." As we mentioned, "therefore" refers to verse 18 in which Jesus said, "All authority has been given to Me in heaven and on earth"; and because of that, *you* can go and make disciples. You even can exercise this authority over Satan *right now* in your own life, in the lives of others, in witnessing situations and in your ministry.

I wish I had learned this concept of being co-resurrected, co-ascended and co-seated the first day I became a Christian. Sadly, very few believers understand it. It is sad because there is such victory when the concept is applied to our daily lives and circumstances. Colossians 3:1-3 says:

> If then you have been raised up with Christ, keep seeking the things above, where Christ is, seated at the right hand of God. Set your mind on things above, not on things that are on earth. For you have died and your life is hidden with Christ in God.

I am not sure about you, but I know my personality. If I get in a very delicate, tense situation and I set my mind on the earthly circumstances around me, I will be defeated. If I am in a witnessing situation, and the people start to gang up and it gets a little hostile, if I set my mind on circumstances, I'll start to back off. I'll start to become apologetic, I'll start to become subdued and timid. That's my personality. But once I learned that I have been co-resurrected, co-ascended and co-seated with Jesus Christ at the right hand of the throne of God, far above all rule and authority and power and dominion and every name that is named, I became bold.

Let me illustrate. I was at Colorado University in a building that was packed. I had just finished speaking on prophecy when five men came running to the front, just screaming. They stood right there, nose to nose, and damned God, damned the Holy Spirit, damned Jesus and damned me. I appreciated the fellowship! I said, "Who are you?" And they said, "We were born to be disciples of Satan, and by free choice we have become them." And they let me have it! Let me tell you, if I had set my mind on the circumstances around me, I would have backed off. But I set my mind at the right hand of God and realized that I had been co-resurrected, co-ascended, co-seated, far above all rule and authority and power and dominion and every name that is named. Every time they opened their mouths, I quoted Scripture. They'd say something else, and I would quote Scripture.

Finally, after fifteen or twenty minutes, they started to walk away, and the leader of the group turned around and said, "Mister, we're going to meet again, and the next time the tables will be turned."

Let me tell you, if I had set my mind on the circumstances around me, I would have thought, "Fine. I just hope we never meet again!" Instead, I set my mind at the right hand of the Father, realizing I had been co-resurrected, co-ascended and co-seated far above all rule and authority and power and dominion and every name that is named, and I looked back at them and I said, "Oh, no, they won't be."

He said, "How can you say that?"

I said, "Mister, because I have confessed Jesus Christ as Savior and Lord, and I have been co-resurrected, co-ascended and co-seated at the right hand of the Father, far above all rule and authority and power and dominion and every name that is named. There is nothing you can do to hinder the gospel of Jesus from going out when I preach it. Come on back tomorrow night!" All authority! I realized that since I had set my mind at the right hand of the throne of God and was filled with the Holy Spirit, I now could become bold instead of settling on the circumstances around me.

QUALIFICATIONS FOR EXERCISING AUTHORITY

You need to understand that the authority of the believer is not some special gift. Even the newest of believers has the same authority as Billy Graham. It is ours simply to acknowledge and exercise.

Knowledge

You need to know that at the moment of salvation you were co-crucified, co-buried, co-resurrected, co-ascended, co-seated; that you are right now co-seated with Christ at the right hand of the throne of God. You need to know that. You need to realize that when Jesus Christ was resurrected, when He passed through the power of the air and sat at the right hand of the throne of God, Satan was defeated. If you don't know these things, how can you ever exercise your authority as a believer? To me, this is part of the victorious life of Romans 6, which says, "Do you not know?" "Know this." "Know that." The problem is that so many believers don't. Realizing your position in Christ is the first step in the victorious Christian life.

Belief

The New Testament concept of belief is literally "to live in accordance with." True belief is not merely mental assent. It involves action. We do not truly believe unless our convictions are manifested in our lives. If we *believe* that God has raised us up together with Christ and that we have been co-resurrected, co-ascended, co-seated, far above all rule and authority and power and dominion and every name that is named, we will be *bold* in Christ. When I wake up in the morning, one of the first things I do is acknowledge my position in Christ at the right hand of the Father, praying something like this, "Lord Jesus, take my position of authority that I have in You at the right hand of the Father, and make it a reality in my experience today." You talk about space-walk! People say, "This guy is so heavenly minded he is no earthly good."

I say, "Until you are heavenly minded, you are no earthly good!"

Until we realize our position in Christ at the right hand of the Father, we are going to see defeat after defeat. That simply is not necessary.

Humility

With knowledge and belief goes humility. Our belief in Jesus Christ introduces us to our place of authority *in* Christ at the right hand of the Father. Only humility can ensure that we will exercise our authority continually. Even regenerated men and women seem to think they can live the Christian life apart from the resources that God has provided. Humility, to me, is not going around saying, "I'm nothing, I'm nothing, I'm nothing!" Humility is not self-negation. Humility is knowing who you are, knowing who made you who you are, and giving God the glory for it. (John the Baptist was such a man; cf. John 1:19-23.) Unless you have these things straight and exercise the authority of the believer, when you see God do some unbelievable things through your life and ministry, you'll get your eyes off Him and your position, and immediately there will be defeat.

Boldness

To me, true humility leads to true godly boldness. When God has spoken, to hold back is not humility, it's sin. What we need today in the exercise of the authority of the believer is the divine Spirit-filled courage that fears nothing but God — not even the U.S. Supreme Court's jurisdiction over our high schools. And we need to realize that when we are filled with the Holy Spirit, when we understand our position in Christ, and when we exercise the authority of the believer, then there will be a spirit of humility and godly boldness.

Awareness

The last qualification for exercising the authority of the believer is the most important. It is the awareness that the place of every blessing at the right hand of the Father is also the place of the greatest spiritual conflict. Once you start practicing the authority of the believer, Satan will do every thing possible to discourage you personally, in your family life and in your ministry — I'll guarantee that. You will become a marked man or woman. The last thing Satan wants is a Spirit-filled believer — especially a Spirit-filled believer who knows his throne rights. So I need to warn you, based on hundreds of letters I have received over the years, that there will be a spiritual battle.

THE PRAYER OF AUTHORITY

Let me share with you how I exercise the authority of the believer. Once I realize that Satan is defeated and that I am co-resurrected, co-ascended and co-seated at the right hand of the Father, then I pray — usually out loud. I always pray "in the name of the Lord Jesus Christ." When I use those three specific titles, I am reminding Satan that the Lord Jesus Christ disarmed him and sat down at the right hand of the Father. Because I have no power over Satan, I am actually just letting him know that he is already defeated. My whole authority depends on the power behind me — Jesus Christ, resurrected, ascended and seated at the right hand of God.

Second, I always refer to His shed blood on the cross. I often say, "Satan, in the name of the Lord Jesus Christ and His shed blood on the cross, I command you to cease your activity in this area," or "Satan, in the name of the Lord Jesus Christ and His shed blood on the cross, I acknowledge that you are defeated and that victory in this situation goes to God." I have no *power* to do that — but I have the *authority*.

Discern If It's Really Satan

Whenever I pray to exercise the authority of the believer, I want to make sure that it's really Satan working. Sometimes when I speak, other Christians will say, "Boy, Satan is trying to do everything to destroy this."

I've often answered, "No, Satan is not working; you are just totally disorganized."

Sometimes you need to exercise the authority of the believer over the believers! Satan often gets a lot of blame that he doesn't deserve. Sometimes you don't need to exercise the authority of the believer, you just need to get your act together!

However, there are several ways to determine whether or not Satan is working. First, know the Scriptures. Do not be ignorant of the "wiles of the devil" (Ephesians 6:11). Be aware of what the Scriptures say about how Satan works. He is pretty consistent.

Second, get the counsel of spiritual believers. There is great wisdom in much counsel (see Proverbs 15:22).

Third, be aware of a sense of spiritual conflict. If you are working with youth, I'm sure you have sensed at various times an intense spiritual battle.

Pray ONCE — Then Walk by Faith

When I exercise the authority of the believer in a situation, I do it only *once*, and then I walk by faith. I need to realize that God will act in His timing and in a way that will bring the greatest honor and glory to Him, not me. Sometimes I have had to wait six to nine months to see how a situation would turn out to the glory of God. But I can honestly say that in the fourteen or fifteen years that I have understood the concept of the authority of the believer I don't think I have ever been in a defeated situation.

But be willing to wait; God knows what He's doing. Let me illustrate. I was invited to the University of Uruguay — a very intense university with a lot of violence at that time. I was the first American who had spoken on campus. I had taken over a free-speech situation, and a Marxist student didn't appreciate it. The room was jammed — seven hundred were crammed into a room that should have seated three hundred. My back was against the wall, and the only two exits were way at the back. The rows of chairs were packed right up to the front, and people were standing in the back, crammed together. Right in the front sat some of the Marxist students. They crossed their legs, and as I started to speak, they kicked me right in the shins with their pointed boots. In fact, I still have a large bump from that night. I was black and blue. They kicked me and then waited for me to react.

There were professional agitators in the audience. When a person like me is not fluent in the language, the agitators try to twist everything he says. As I was speaking, the agitators stood up and said, "You filthy capitalist American. How can you come down here?" One would throw an accusation, and I'd try to answer and go on with my talk. Others would jump up and challenge me again, and I'd answer and go on with my talk. The situation got so bad that I wanted to get out of there. It got to the point where I'd mention the name of Jesus Christ, and people would break out laughing. Now that hurts. I prayed and exercised the authority of the believer, and the situation got worse! If I could have gotten out of that room alive by leaving early, I believe I would have gone. But it went on for forty-five minutes — to the point that I was embarrassed for the Christians who had invited me. They had asked me to the University of Uruguay to get contacts for them to help get the movement going, and the first night the effort was destroyed — or appeared to be. I kept exercising the authority of the believer, and I got upset with God. I asked, "God, why aren't You doing something?"

At the point where I was almost crying, a woman jumped to her feet, and the entire audience grew silent. I thought, "Oh-oh, here it comes." She identified herself as the secretary of the militant group of Marxist leaders. She said, "Mr. McDowell, if I became a Christian, would God give me the love for people that you have for us?" And instantly it was like a revival. An unbelievable spirit spread throughout the audience. More than fifty people came to Christ that night. God taught me then that He acts when it brings the greatest honor and glory to HIS Name, not mine. I learned to the greatest honor and glory to HIS Name, not mine. I learned to exercise the authority of the believer just once, then walk by faith, believing that in His time and in His way, He will act. I can honestly say that in the years I have understood this concept I have always found that to be true.

"All authority has been given to me in heaven and on earth. Go therefore and make disciples of all nations."

PUTTING THIS CHAPTER TO WORK

1. Do you feel you understand how to exercise the authority of the believer? Attempt to explain it to someone else today. That process will help to solidify this vital concept in your own mind.

2. List some situations in your life or in the lives of others in which you need to exercise authority over Satan. For each situation, acknowledge that Satan is defeated in the name of the Lord Jesus Christ and by His shed blood which has seated Him at the right hand of God.

3. Consider offering this prayer of thankfulness and faith:

    > Lord Jesus, thank You that You are resurrected, ascended and seated at the right hand of the Father. Thank You that Satan is defeated and that at the moment I confessed You as Savior and Lord I was co-resurrected, co-ascended and co-seated with You at the right hand of the Father, far above all rule and authority and power and dominion and every name that is named. Take my position of authority at Your right hand and make it a reality in my experience today. Amen.

YOUTH CULTURE

4

YOUTH MINISTRY AND THE HIDDEN DYNAMICS OF SECULAR CULTURE

by Wes Hurd

God has given us so much — and part of what He has given us includes the many advantages of the culture in which we live. Sometimes, however, in the midst of those material and technological advantages, we get lost, we break down, we become confused by the very things we wish to take advantage of. We live in a country that does not have just one culture, but many, many subcultures within it. One of those subcultures is made up of the young people for which you and many others are pouring out your lives. We all desire to understand them, minister to them, and reach them for Christ. However, it has become very clear to me over the years that unless I understand the milieu within which they operate, I am like someone who is trying to play "doctor" but who hasn't gone to medical school. It is important to understand what is going on.

In 2 Corinthians 4:1-6, the apostle Paul gives us a theological perspective of culture and how it operates.

> Therefore, since we have this ministry, as we have received mercy, we do not lose heart, but we have renounced the things hidden because of shame, not walking in craftiness or adulterating the word of God, but by the manifestation of truth, commending ourselves to every man's conscience in the sight of God. And even if our gospel is veiled, it is veiled to those who are perishing, in whose case the god of this world has blinded the minds of the unbelieving, that they might not see the light of the gospel of the glory of Christ, who is the image of God. For we do not preach ourselves but Christ Jesus as Lord,

---

Wes Hurd is the founder and director of the McKenzie Study Center, a college-level training program in Eugene, Oregon. He was on staff with Campus Crusade for Christ's high school ministry for five years, serving in various parts of the United States and in London, England. He served as a youth pastor for four years. Wes received his B.A. from Southern Oregon College, his M.A. at Western Baptist Seminary, and has completed doctoral studies at the University of Oregon. He and his wife, Carol, have three children, two of whom are teenagers.

and ourselves as your bond-servants for Jesus' sake. For God who said, "Light shall shine out of darkness," is the One who has shone in our hearts to give the light of the knowledge of the glory of God in the face of Christ.

I think that when Paul refers to "the god of this world" and the blindness that occurs to those who are caught up in that world, he's talking about the enemy who actively rules our culture. God made us in such a way that we are unique creatures. On the one hand, we are spiritual creatures: we have a transcendent spirit; we are made in the image of God. On the other hand, we are material creatures made up of "stuff" that God made; we have a psyche — mind, emotion, and intellect — that is connected to our material nature. This is what we refer to as the cultural side of our existence. Culture is that godless realm that Satan now rules, and we need to understand how that realm operates, if we are going to live *in* it but not be *of* it. We need to be able to "read" our culture in the same sense that a physician reads the disease of a body and understands what is involved.

I would like to approach this by first giving you a simple overview of how modern secular culture has come into existence. Then I will define what culture is and talk about how it works. Finally, I will suggest some ideas to help you counter the hidden power of culture. The focus here is not so much on how-to techniques but rather on gaining a better understanding of the environment which affects us and the young people we are committed to reaching.

INSIGHT FROM HISTORY

There was a time in western history when the church's ideas about the world and the universe were dominant. After the period of the life of Christ and the burgeoning of the church, the church became established in western culture. The Roman Catholic Church dominated Europe and the then-known world — the Roman Empire. If you were doing a man-on-the-street interview during that medieval period and you stuck your microphone under the nose of the average serf, you might have asked him, "What is ultimate reality? What's the most important thing you can think of?" His answer would have included words like: God, spiritual things, heaven, hell, demons and angels. His world, his understanding, his symbolic universe would have been canopied by the church and Christianity. Now, he might not have been a believer in the sense that we understand authentic belief, but the grid through which he looked at reality would have been determined and structured by Christianity So then, in the medieval period, ultimate reality was defined in spiritual terms.

A Shift Toward The Earth

As we move to the renaissance period (roughly A.D. 1300-1500), we notice that there was a major shift in consciousness. It happened subtly, but definitely. Here we see the church taking into itself a new emphasis on man and mankind — we could call it a "new humanism." Primarily because of the resurgence of classical Greek thought, religion and philosophy, the church began to alter its world view as evidenced by its focus on the work of Thomas Aquinas. As a result, we see a shift toward the earth — a shift from viewing reality in the heavenly realm only, to an understanding of reality that included man as a more direct subject and object. We can see this in the arts, in the work of people like Leonardo da Vinci and Michelangelo.

There was a new emphasis on man's autonomous mind and its ability to discover "secular" truth which occurred as Greek philosophy and church theology began to blend. This emphasis became even more blatant during the Enlightenment period, which occurred during the 18th and early 19th centuries. Until that time, the church's theological ideas had remained dominant, but then cracks began to develop in the world view grid. With the growing emphasis on man and on the things of the earth, people subtly began to vent their criticism about the things the church was doing wrong. The institutional church was doing some gross things; people began to notice and started to doubt its credibility. During this time, the "new humanism" of the Renaissance was developing into a "new secular humanism." Enlightenment thinkers like Voltaire encouraged people to move away from the church, to move completely away from spiritual answers to reality. They wanted to be rid of the dominance of the Catholic Church and the church in general.

Reality is Material

This spirit of the Enlightenment lives with us today. It is the shift to the earth, the shift to the things of the earth, the shift to material reality that we live with today. If you took your microphone and interviewed people today as you interviewed the medieval serf, most people would talk about ultimate reality being something found in the physical universe, in the "stuff" of creation, in material substance. And in the process of this shift, man has placed himself in a box — a box that, in effect, is a closed-universe box. There is no God — God does not exist, He is not necessary. Reality is material. What exists is a product of matter plus time plus chance. We are an accident.

It is this kind of thinking, characterized by a philosophy of naturalism and evolutionism, that dominates our culture today. Most people operate according to this philosophy. But many don't realize its implications. If you happened to ask a fish what water is, even if it could speak it probably would not be able to answer. In the same way, most of us are very fuzzy in our understanding of our environment, our culture, because it's so much a part of our everyday life. But, like the fish, we are still greatly influenced by its impact.

The Emptiness of Existentialism

When I was in high school, I can remember walking to school one morning with a pile of books under my arm, thinking to myself, "What is this? Who am I? Where am I going? What is life all about?" As the thoughts, beliefs and assumptions of my culture inundated me in the classroom, through my friends, and in the secular society that I lived in, I struggled with the questions of identity, meaning and truth. I couldn't articulate them; they were affecting me at a deeply subconscious level. I can remember sitting in my living room with my parents and weeping. I did not know why. I think I was fearful about where I was going, what I wanted to do, how I would survive in this world. I was experiencing internally — in the very guts of my being — the emptiness of that closed universe.

That's the world in which the young people with whom we work are living. It is predominantly a philosophical materialism — but we are not just talking about wealth. When someone in this kind of a universe is struggling with the questions of identity, meaning and truth as I was, he soon realizes that those ultimate kinds of answers cannot be verified, in any absolute sense, in a closed, empty, accidental universe. Because the canopy of meaning that overarches our society is one of materialism, he has to find answers within the "closed box" of a physical universe. Then, because there are no infinite, transcendent answers, he must look within. So those are the two things that happen within a material culture: We seek to manipulate the culture — to control it, to change it, to use it, and to find our security in doing that; then we turn from meaning and truth to the inside, existentially.

Existentialism is a response to this predicament. It is that view of reality which says, "Yes, it *is* an absurd universe, it *is* a crazy place, there *is* no sense." But I have to face this bravely and realize that I am my own god, and then create my own meaning. Out of my radical freedom, I must choose my own meaning and identity. That's the heart and spirit of existentialism. We can see that today in the music scene. Sometimes my teenage daughter and I watch a little of the video rock station on TV. We talk about what the music means, what the punk nihilist is saying. What is that kid who looks like a basket case saying? He is saying, "My universe is a basket case. So what else is new?" That's the response of a materialistic culture to the search for identity, meaning and truth.

CULTURE DESCRIBED

Culture is an arena, a place, an atmosphere, an environment. It's like water to a fish. We can never escape culture — we are culture-bound creatures. Originally, we were created to function within a godly, perfect environment. So culture is not intrinsically bad; it is a fact. The challenge is to learn how to work within it.

Man Creates Culture

So what is culture? And how are cultural trends created? Two of the great fathers of sociology — Max Weber and Emile Durkheim — set up two schools of sociological analysis which have been vying for dominance ever since their day. Weber said that culture is created by man. I believe this is consistent with the first chapter of Genesis. When God created man to rule over the earth, culture is implied. So then, the first characteristic of culture is that it is an extension of man's being. It is a creation of man, and through it he creates ideas and things — *ideas* like language, symbols, communication, thought, poetry, and art; and *things* like machines and other objects that he can use.

The second characteristic of culture is that it takes on its own independent existence — it produces an object of its own being, it becomes a fact to itself. For example, I made a language, and now it exists. I made a machine — say, an automobile — and now it exists out there apart from me. I made a piece of art, now it exists. Culture, then, can become something other than mankind, something that exists on its own.

Culture Conforms Man

The third characteristic, which is the one that's most critical, is called "internalization." Internalization is the culture acting back upon the creator — man. And this was Emile Durkheim's sociological theory — not man creating culture, but once culture comes to exist corporately in the human race, it begins to shape man. So we have these two ideas. I'm trying to demonstrate that both are actually true. The way God put us together, we create our culture, and then culture acts back on us — it shapes us and molds us.

But from a biblical perspective, culture does not have ultimate power over us; it has only influencial power. That is why the

apostle Paul exhorts us in Romans 12:2, "...do not be conformed
to this world...." Now, modern sociological theory would say it has
total power. But God has given us volition — the ability to
choose — so that we can always act within our culture. But culture
does have a tremendous impact on us; we are very malleable. And
the young people we are working with are the ones who are *most*
vulnerable of all.

The Hidden Dynamic of Culture

There are two ways that culture can act back on a human being.
It can act back in a known way. We are aware that culture is influencing us, even by something so basic as our language, for
example. Or try to think of a world without automobiles. There are
many obvious ways that culture shapes us. But there is a hidden
dynamic, an unknown way that culture can act back on us at a subconscious level. I call that the "taken-for-granted level."

Let me illustrate this. My wife, Carol, and I lived in England a
number of years ago ministering to teenagers. There were certain
things about English culture that really seemed strange to me. For
example, the first day I walked into the flat where we would be living, I went into the kitchen and looked for the refrigerator. It was so
small, I couldn't believe it — about 4 feet by 2 feet. My whole conscious fabric was violated by the fact that they didn't have a refrigerator as big as the one back home. In this culture, they would
walk down to the village store, which was not far away. There was
a social, cultural community created by the fact that people go
shopping every day or so to get what they need because they just
have small refrigerators. I took it for granted that everyone had big
refrigerators. I didn't realize it was so important to me, but I found
that my emotions were really affected when I could not understand
their rationale for doing something so differently.

Near where we lived in London, there was a road that ran the
length of a long hill. Right at the top of the hill was an oak tree —
planted in the right lane! Traffic always had to pass single-file, so
you can imagine why it was no place to be at rush hour! The first
time I got caught in that traffic, I couldn't believe it! They were letting this *tree* block a major thoroughfare. In our American culture,
we would never have allowed that to happen. It was foreign to my
way of thinking to realize that these people *like* tradition, they like
"oldness," they like the way it was. That tree had been there
forever, and that's the way it was going to stay. Well, my modern,
fast-paced culture couldn't absorb that. I was being violated down
at this taken-for-granted level. There was nothing wrong with leaving the tree in the road. But my taken-for granted level of cultural
experience said, "Cut that thing down."

Culture, then, is able to act back at a level that is subconscious. In other words, we all have unexamined assumptions and beliefs that lie deep within us, and we have simply assimilated them from our culture. Many of these beliefs are unbiblical and have become rooted in at the subconscious level. We, as youth workers, must be aware of these beliefs because this is where we must minister. We want to be able to penetrate at that level because, as we look at the canopy of culture that exists over youth today, we can see that it has caused the kind of blindness previously mentioned in 2 Corinthians 4. It has blocked out "the Light," giving Satan the opportunity to reign as the "god of this world" for the majority of this country's youth. We must attempt to understand these hidden dynamics so that we can more adequately reflect the Light to the many who are groping in darkness.

CHARACTERISTICS OF TODAY'S YOUTH CULTURE

We have discussed what culture is and how it operates, and we have observed that there are many hidden assumptions within it. Let's examine the characteristics of our American culture so that we can have a better idea of exactly what assumptions we are dealing with.

Answers Found Only in the Physical Universe

First of all, for today's youth, reality is material. Although this has been mentioned before in the context of history, this philosophy lives at the taken-for-granted level of youth in our culture today. We've got to be aware that it is deeply ingrained. When you use language, when you try to penetrate their assumptions with ideas of spiritual reality, such as the gospel, you've got to be aware that to them reality is only material. Meaning, identity and fulfillment are material. You need to be praying that God will break into that culture because that is the only hope of getting through.

Romans 1:20-23 points out the tragic conflict of these two world views:

> For since the creation of the world His invisible attributes, His eternal power and divine nature, have been clearly seen, being understood through what has been made, so that they are without excuse. For even though they knew God, they did not honor Him as God, or give thanks; but they became futile in their speculations, and their foolish heart was darkened. Professing to be wise, they became fools, and exchanged the glory of the incorruptible God for an image in the form of corruptible man and of birds and four-footed animals and crawling creatures.

Man was created in the image of God to follow His leadership and to utilize God's interpretations of reality in his life and environment. Instead, man rebels and claims to be autonomous and is still in the position of needing identity, needing to know what the meaning of existence is, needing to know what truth is — and all those other related questions. But man has chosen to try to answer those questions outside of the realm of God's existence, since he has ruled Him out from the very beginning. He feels the stress; he has to find answers. But he is trying to find them in a material universe, in a material way. So what do we see going on today in the most advanced, wealthiest, fat-cat society that's ever existed on the face of the earth? We find people scrambling everywhere to manipulate, use, control, or find something in the "stuff" of material reality to satisfy themselves. It is tragic, but it's a taken-for-granted in our culture.

Do-It-Yourself Identities

Second, man must create his own identity, and because he has placed himself in a closed-universe box where there is no God, he must find the answers to these things within himself existentially. This is an empty experience, and there are thousands of kids who are feeling deep stress at this taken-for-granted level. They haven't got a clue as to why they are hurting and what they should do about it. Of course, that's where the gospel goes to work.

Private Values Separated from Public Life

Third, the life of modern man has been split into two categories. The process of secularization, which started with the Enlightenment period in terms of western culture, slowly but surely has pushed the notion of a transcendent creator God out of the realm of existence. Secularization is the process that removes the notion that God is real and that He is relevant. It has caused western man to split how he views reality into two worlds — the private world and the public world.

In other words, he is a modern schizophrenic at the most fundamental levels of his own consciousness. First of all, there is the private world of home, hobbies, leisure, personal values, etc. Modern technological society says, "All that is *your* domain — that's *your* little kingdom." But then there is the public domain — industry, marketing, commerce, bureaucracy, institutions, education, law, etc. Secular culture tells us that these two worlds must keep their distance.

When religion and a transcendent spiritual view of man were eliminated, all that was left was the natural, the material world. This, then, is the *real* world — that's where the movers and shakers are, that's where things really happen, that's the world of politics, that's the world of control. On the private side, you can go back to your home and believe and do what you want. "Hey, do your own thing." Just don't bring your personal beliefs and values out here into the real world because they don't count. What counts in this world is being able to measure it, quantify it, control it, manipulate it, use it, scientifically manage it — that's the *real* world, not what you do in your private world. This is the world our kids live in, and it splits them right down the middle. They lack wholeness in their lives. They can't put personal meaning and identity together with these two worlds divided.

So we end up with a culture which is, on one hand, therapeutic in the private realm and dominated by technology in the other realm. Therapy and technology — that's where kids are going for the answers today to search for meaning, identity and truth. They can either go to the material world — the workplace, the shopping centers, the video arcades, computers, education — or come back to their private world and look for therapeutic help to find meaning within themselves. When young people don't have Christ, they must draw their answers from those two realms, and we need to be aware of that.

SUBSTITUTES FOR GOD

There are some things we can do to overcome some of these cultural blocks to the gospel. But before I offer a few brief suggestions, it would be helpful for us to realize some of the things that the secular world has substituted for God. They have produced substitutions for God's interpretations of reality, for His truth, for a relationship with Him, for identity, meaning and fulfillment. First of all, there is a need for commitment, and the secular culture has tried to replace it with consumerism. A commitment to truth has been replaced by a compulsion to buy everything. I do battle with my junior high son, trying to get it into his head that he can have some things and can't have other things. But kids are at the place where they have to be *saturated* with things. They go from one thing to another thing to another thing, and pretty soon that transience translates into relationships. Relationships become trivial. So, then, there is the need for commitment — something to believe in, ideals, truth — as opposed to consumerism where security is found in possessing and controlling the material world.

Second, there is a need for release from guilt, and the secular culture tries to replace that need with drugs, materialism, technological answers and therapies. "Hey, what can get my act together for me?" "Tell me something that will make me feel good!"

Finally, there is a need for community. The secular world has substituted that with the media. Again, all these substitutes are coming from the realm of a naturalistic universe — a culture where you can either produce it technologically, chemically, or you can dream it into existence in your own mind and heart.

OVERCOMING THE CULTURAL BARRIERS

How, then, can we overcome some of these hindrances and complexities of our modern culture?

Make the Gospel Clear

First of all, we must clearly communicate the message of the gospel. That means that you must understand the gospel carefully yourself. I have been greatly disturbed over the last few years to see how "technologized" the gospel has become, to see what a marketable product it has become, to see how trivialized it has become. We need to understand the profundity of what God has done for us such that it grips the core of our beings, that it is our sole hope. And when we *believe* that, when God has put that into our hearts and minds, we won't walk away from ministering the gospel because it will possess us. So we need to understand the gospel and make it clear.

Develop Some Basic Questions

Second, we must develop questions. I'm not giving you a list of the questions; it's best for you to think them through yourself. Develop questions that reveal hidden culture. In other words, think of questions that will get students to reveal what the assumptions in their lives are, and penetrate those assumptions. Ask God to use your words, your mind, and your heart to get down to that sub-conscious level where they are not aware of that taken-for-granted reality in their lives. Use films, media, magazines and music, and then throw it back to them. Look at it together, talk it through with them. Ask them, "What does that mean?" "What's the assumption underlying the lyrics in that music?" "What is that guy in the film really saying?" "What does he believe?" Use those things creatively.

Challenge Their Assumptions

Third, challenge their beliefs at this taken-for-granted level because they have never asked themselves these questions. They have simply adopted them by a process of osmosis in their culture. In order to challenge their beliefs, you need to come up with the questions — the major presuppositional questions that they are going to be asking. What is ultimate reality? What is the origin of life? Who is man? What happens after death? Where does morality come from? James W. Sire's book, *The Universe Next Door* (InterVarsity Press), has the world-view questions in it that you can ask anyone.

Build Relationships

Fourth, you and I know that what gets through in the long run with the gospel is relationships. *Build relationships.* I run into people from my past whom I've worked with and trained and helped and struggled with — and those relationships are absolutely incredible. You will run into those students years and years later. One caution: Build relationships, not a subculture. We don't want to build a Christian ghetto. We don't want our students to remove themselves from the culture. We want them to understand culture. We want to disciple them and apprentice them into the world so that they can deal with their culture.

Deepen Your Christian World View

That leads to my final encouragement: Develop your Christian mind. Ask God to give you His wisdom about the culture, about the world. It's possible to have a committed heart and to have a very secular mind. One of the greatest struggles I have at the University of Oregon is with the incoming freshmen we work with. Many of them come out of their youth groups with a Christian world view that has dealt with the basics — home, family, girlfriend/boyfriend, hobbies, sports. Then when they get to the university, all of a sudden they have to deal with Marxism and other ideologies that they don't understand. The world has exploded in front of them, and they don't have a world view that can encompass it. They simply are not equipped. We must develop a Christ-mind about as much as we can and pass that on to our young people.

GOD IS NOT LIMITED BY OUR CULTURE

In conclusion, let me urge you: Don't trust methods and techniques; trust God. Use them, develop them, but don't *trust* them in the way that you trust God, because God is like Aslan, the lion, in C. S. Lewis's *Chronicles of Narnia.* He is not tame. God wants to do things outside of the realms and the methods and the techniques that we can come up with. Give God the freedom to do it. It's our only sure way to penetrate this twisted culture with the life-changing gospel of Christ.

PUTTING THIS CHAPTER TO WORK

1. Hurd says that in our secular culture, security is found in possessing and controlling the material world. In what ways do you see that philosophy manifesting itself in your young people? in your family? in yourself?

2. In what ways does society tell you and your young people that personal beliefs don't count in the "real world"?

3. What are some secular assumptions the young people you know have absorbed at their taken-for-granted level?

4. What are some basic questions you could ask which would reveal unexamined, unbiblical assumptions?

5

COMMUNICATING ABSOLUTES — RELATIVELY SPEAKING!

by J. Dennis Miller

We live in a generation in which young people have been taught more about the Bible than any generation in history. The average student in a youth group today — even if he tends to be rebellious — has heard more spiritual information than the average student years ago. Today many of our materials are Bible-based, discipleship-centered and youth-oriented. Our publishing houses have given us a wealth of options from which to choose. But the real tragedy is that kids today have heard more and used less than any generation I know of. Why is that? Despite all that is available to meet their needs, why is the message apparently not getting through? The key measure of our effectiveness is not what we do and say; rather it is how our students' lives *change* as a result of what we do and say. Your teaching may be "slick," but do your kids make use of what they learn?

RISKY ASSUMPTIONS

2 Timothy 4:2 says, "...preach the word; be ready in season and out of season; reprove, rebuke, exhort, with great patience and instruction." Now you may say, "But I've been faithful to preach the Word. It's God's responsibility to bring about a response from the kids. I'm just supposed to preach the Word." Yes, we are supposed to preach the Word, but there are certain dangerous assumptions that we need to be aware of.

First, we assume that students are information-oriented — that they have a tendency to react, in their lifestyles, according to the information they understand. And so we teach them very dili-

---

Dennis Miller is founder and president of Church Youth Development, a training and consulting ministry to youth pastors founded in 1977. He has written *The Youth Worker's Guide to Discipleship* and *A Practical Handbook for Youth Ministry.* He is a graduate of Multnomah School of the Bible in Portland, Oregon, and has had nineteen years of experience working with youth. He lives in Edina, Minnesota, with his wife, Kristi, and their three children.

gently — appealing primarily to their mind, their intellect, expecting change to occur. But educational research shows that teaching is not telling, and learning is not merely listening.

Second, we assume that students are skilled in listening. Do you know that the attention span of the average teenager has gone down, not up, in recent years? It is currently considered to be only about *eight minutes*. That means that about eight minutes into one of your best talks, your average student is already saturated in his ability to listen.

Third, we assume that students are going to remember and use what they hear — that they are going to accept automatically that precious pearl from the Scripture, remember it, and use it the rest of their lives. Research has shown, however, that we remember only about 10 percent of what we hear.

What am I trying to say, that preaching is no good? Throw it out and do something else? Of course not. But I am trying to say that we must use our preaching in a way that will effect *change* in the lives of kids.

ACTIVE PARTNERS WITH THE HOLY SPIRIT

There is another passage we sometimes hide behind. John 16:13 says, "But when He, the Spirit of truth comes, He will guide you into all the truth; for He will not speak on His own initiative; but whatever He hears, He will speak; and He will disclose to you what is to come." I've heard people argue, "Well, you see, it doesn't matter about my teaching method; that's the Holy Spirit's responsibility. He is the one that takes truth and puts it in the life." Yes, the Holy Spirit is ultimately responsible. But we have been given the privilege of working in *partnership* with the Holy Spirit to see that accomplished.

Are you doing that, or are you just throwing things out and hoping He will pick up something and use it? It's like the difference between shooting a shotgun and shooting a rifle. If you shoot a shotgun at a target, a few pellets may make little holes in the bull's eye. But if you hit the bull's eye with a rifle bullet, there isn't going to be a bull's eye left! Likewise, when you are throwing truth out at random, it is not possible for you to make the kind of impact that you could make when you work in partnership with the Holy Spirit. Don't act as though the Holy Spirit doesn't care what you do. He can work in spite of you, but He'd rather work through you!

Also, though the Holy Spirit promises to "guide us into all the truth," we cannot assume that students are open to His teaching. They may not even recognize the teaching ministry of the Holy Spirit in their lives when it occurs. If they were open and aware, we would see more changed lives.

CREATING AN APPETITE

Another passage that is used frequently when we talk about teaching young people is Proverbs 22:6. It says, "Train up a child in the way he should go and when he is old he will not depart from it" (KJV). A number of parents have said to me, "Well, I know my son (or daughter) is not walking with the Lord right now; I know that he's rebellious; I know that he's contributing nothing to the cause of Christ right now. But we have had him in Sunday school all his life, receiving all this spiritual information. I'm sure this training will eventually bring him back to God."

It all depends on how much of the training "got through." Let's look at Proverbs 22:6 more closely. In the first phrase, "Train up a child," the Hebrew word used for "train" is a word that conveys the ancient process of weaning a baby. Specifically, a little piece of date was placed on a baby's palate and the fruit's sweetness would make the baby suck and wean itself from the breast. The process had nothing to do with verbal instruction — it was all about creating an appetite. In other words, the verse could be translated, "Create a sweetness in a child's life concerning the things of God, and when he is old he will not depart from it."

The second phrase, "in.the way he should go," refers to a person's "bent." The word "way" describes a tree that is shaped by the wind. Have you ever seen a tree like that? I picture one standing on the edge of a cliff, sculptured by the wind that blows over it. That's what the word means. Train up a child — put sweetness concerning spiritual things in a child's life when he is young — yet according to his *uniqueness*, his "bent." And then, "*even* when he is old he will not depart from it". The verse does not mean: Cram a kid's mind full of spiritual information when he is young — *make* him act like a Christian — and when he is old, he'll turn out okay. God has something far more wonderful in life than that! He wants us to "remember also our Creator in the days of our *youth*" (Ecclesiastes 12:1).

ABSOLUTELY NO ABSOLUTES!

I recognize that "training up a child" is no easy task — it never has been, but in recent years, the challenge has become more complex. Today, a young person's evaluation of truth is not usually based upon absolutes like the Bible. Rather, his evaluation is based upon his life experiences. Did you ever notice that? If you start talking about a spiritual principle with a kid, he may say, "Yeah, but Mike drinks, and he's a pretty neat guy — he's not an alcoholic." Or, "But what would my girlfriend think about us praying on a date? Man, she would flip out." Or, "Wait a minute. If I start talking about Christ, I'd lose every friend I've got." Truth is relative to their life experience.

Picture the student who comes up through church fights and hears adults arguing all the way through his childhood. He sits through 500 boring, ill-prepared Sunday school lessons, and by the time he graduates from high school, we're expecting him to be "turned on for Jesus." Instead, he's looking at his life experience and saying, "Do I know *anyone* who lives like these people preach? Anybody? I don't know anybody."

Relative Thinking

The average student is taught to evaluate truth from this premise: Everything is relative to his experience. If his life experience dictates that he *needs* spiritual input in his life, he's there. If it doesn't dictate that he needs spiritual information and interest in his life, he's not there. From his life experience, discovery of attitudes and actions take place.

One classic example of this is the drug information program that went through our schools. All the medical reasons were given to show why kids shouldn't take drugs. The information was good, but I saw many kids respond, "I have 50 friends who take drugs, and not one of them has a single symptom that they talked about."

And you say, "Yeah, but 40 years down the road...."

"Man, I don't know if I can live forty years. What do I care?"

You see, these authorities came in giving information at one level (cognitive), while the students were receiving it at another level (experiential).

Attitudes and actions begin to form out of life experience. Picture a student who walks into your youth group. Nobody talks to him. He sits there and listens to some spiritual mumbo-jumbo he doesn't understand and walks out. What has his life experience been? If I eventually go to that student and say, "You need Jesus Christ in your life," he's apt to tell me, "Nah, I don't think so." He's formed an attitude, and he's taking an action on the basis of his attitude. Out of those attitudes and actions he starts identifying certain things that he feels are true for him.

Prevailing Truth

One time I was talking about Christ with a student on a campus in California. He was so interested that as we were talking I felt that the Holy Spirit was really speaking to him. He was smiling and excited the whole time. But when I asked, "Would you like to invite Jesus Christ into your life?" he answered, "Hey, man, I'm just not into that."

I said, "Well, I'm a little confused. You were so excited and interested about what I was telling you."

He said, "Man, I was excited for *you!* But, see, I'm not into that. I'm just not into that."

In other words, he was saying, "Tremendous! *Your* life experience includes God, and I can see how it has helped you. But *my* life experience hasn't included God, and I'm afraid I just don't believe that stuff. I have identified certain truths out of my life experience that prevent me from accepting what you say." He had accepted a prevailing truth. Prevailing truth is the closest many young people ever get to an absolute today — "Hey, this is true every time I experience it, so I am going to believe this is true until I have an alternate experience." "Two plus two equals four — at least for now."

So you can see, absolutes in the youth culture today are viewed as relative in nature — a contradiction of terms to be sure! But if you think about it, you can understand why it appears that way to young people. Take a look at the string of things we have discovered throughout the last hundred years that have violated what our culture thought were absolutes. We used to believe that if you went over 22 miles per hour in a car, you would disintegrate. That was a widely held "fact" of science. And those are the kinds of absolutes our kids have been dealing with all the way along. It's only an absolute until the next discovery proves it false. Prevailing truth — it prevails today, but tomorrow, who knows?

CHRISTIANITY — BUILT ON ABSOLUTES

Think about that process for a minute, and then think about how you are teaching your kids. Most of us start with absolutes. We say, "Jesus is God." Period. Let a kid try to question that in your youth group sometime — or in front of your church. Watch how the people react! "You don't believe Jesus is God? What's the matter with you? All Christians believe that! I don't believe you don't believe that!" Maybe nobody says those things, but they would think them nevertheless. Why? Because most people raised in our churches have accepted that absolute as their presupposition. They are saying, "Hey, I have agreed that Jesus is God." Period. I don't question it. That's an absolute.

Assuming that young people still think that way today, we bring them in and say, "Here's an absolute you must believe." But what do they really think? They think, "Wait a minute. How does this fit into my life experience?" And if it's a contradiction, your message just doesn't get through — and, of course, their lives aren't affected. Why? Because they divorce the truth from their life experience and create what Clark Pinnock calls "the upper story." The "upper story" is the nonsense level of a person's brain where he stores anything that doesn't work in his life experience.

Many of our kids are taking the spiritual truth we are sharing and chucking it into the "upper story." Why? Because it doesn't fit with their life experience. They don't see the need for it down here where they live. Did you know that if a student is in your church every time your doors are open, you have him only 3 percent of his time? You're trying to influence him for eternity in 3 percent of his time! We had better do an excellent job of communicating to kids.

After establishing absolutes, what do we tend to do next? In effect, many of us say, "Because of these absolutes, here are the attitudes and actions that the Bible says you must demonstrate. Because this is absolutely true, you must act like this." But many of our young people are not buying what we are saying. They are saying, "Not so fast. I haven't met too many Christians who are 'together.' Most of them are just as hung up as everybody else. Frankly, I'm beginning to believe that there isn't too much value to this stuff [attitude]; I don't think I want to come to the group anymore [action]." We're saying, "Because Jesus is God, you be there." He's saying, "Sorry, that does not compute."

We are teaching kids from one perspective, but they are learning from another. Is it any wonder that we miss them altogether? Is it any wonder that we have a generation of kids who have more stored in the "upper story" and less evidence of life change than any other generation in history? How can we "connect"? How can we take the truth which is so important and translate it into their life experience?

SURFACING NEED THROUGH QUESTIONS

A few years ago, I went through the New Testament and counted the number of times Jesus asked questions and the number of times He gave answers. What do you think was the ratio of the two? Jesus asked questions *ten times* more than He gave answers. This was the Son of God, who had at least ten times more *answers* than questions! Isn't that ironic? God, in the flesh, comes to earth and lives among us, knowing the solutions, knowing the answers — yet He asks questions! One of my favorite examples is in Luke 20. Jesus was in the Temple on the Sabbath. The chief priests and scribes were trying to pin something on Him so they could crucify Him.

> And they spoke, saying to Him, "Tell us by what authority You are doing these things, or who is the one who gave You this authority?" And He answered and said to them, "I shall also ask you a question, and you tell me: Was the baptism of John from heaven or from men?" And they reasoned among themselves, saying, "If we say, 'From heaven,' He will say, 'Why did you not believe him?' But if we say,

'From men,' all the people will stone us to death, for they are convinced that John was a prophet." And they answered that they did not know where it came from. And Jesus said to them, "Neither will I tell you by what authority I am doing these things" (Luke 20:2-8).

What would you have done if you had been Jesus? Would you have opened your Bible and begun to give "proof-texts"? Would you have given an exegetical explanation of your messiahship? What would you have done?

Jesus asked questions — time and time and time again. The parables were just forms of questions; He'd create a question in the minds of His listeners. Isn't that amazing? And this was the Son of God, who knew everything! He could have created a manual for churches and told us what the perfect form of government was. He could have answered all the "gray areas" of the Christian life. But He didn't. He asked questions. Why? Because He desperately wanted the people to understand the *need* for the information that He did give them. We are so busy giving information that we often neglect to create the need for it. We are answering questions that have never been asked by our kids.

Have you ever tried to drink a quart of water when you weren't thirsty? Try it some time. You get about half of it down, and you begin to feel nauseated. On the other hand, maybe you've been in the desert all day; you come home, and you are just dying of thirst. Someone hands you a quart of water, and you polish the whole thing off without a breath. What is the difference? In one case, you didn't need the water. In the other case, you did. We must keep this distinction in mind when we teach truth to our young people. We must think through carefully how we can create the need for the information we are giving our kids. That's as important as the information itself.

This, then, is the solution for our dilemma. If our youth don't have a life experience that validates the truth, give them one. That's what Jesus did. Do you remember the woman at the well in John 4? Jesus made some outrageous statements to her. First of all, He asked her for a drink. The woman knew that was highly unusual since Jews did not mix with Samaritans. Then, He said He'd give her living water that would spring up to eternal life. She must have been saying to herself, "What?" She wasn't looking at it theologically as we do. We might say, "Isn't that a precious thing that the Lord is saying here?" Well, yes, it is a precious thing, but it wasn't precious to her. She probably thought He was nuts! And I think she begins to ridicule Him at this point. "Oh, living water, huh? Well, then give me some."

Why did He ask these questions and go about it all so indirectly? Why didn't He just go up to the woman and say, "How do you do. I'd like to introduce myself — I am the Messiah you've waited for so long." Why didn't He do that? Because He knew that if this lady was not thirsty for the things of God, she wouldn't listen. She already had a whole string of relationships that had dulled her sensitivity; she was living with a man right then who was not her husband. Jesus had to get her attention — and you must admit, He was successful. Our kids are the same way. Why do we expect them to accept spiritual truth if they aren't thirsty for it?

STIMULATING THIRST FOR TRUTH

What, then, are some practical things that we can do to create this thirst for truth within students?

Life Experiences

First, I would encourage you to involve your young people in some biblically oriented life experiences. We need to be putting our young people into some life experiences where they see the need of spiritual power in their lives. Most of us have it backward. We want them to get the spiritual power *first*; then we help them apply it to their life experience.

I have a friend who became youth pastor of a large church. Out of 3,400 people in the church, only 40 teenagers were involved in youth activites. Most of them had been through Christian grade school and Christian high school. The majority were totally turned off to spiritual things. Their attitude was "teach me something I don't know." The first night this youth pastor was there, one of the kids took him out beyond the building and tried to beat him up. Needless to say, this was a tough group! That first night he went back to his office, got on his knees, and said, "God, what do I teach these kids? They don't want to know anything. They are not curious about anything. What do I teach them? What do I do?" He prayed fervently, and God gave him an idea.

There was a retarded children's home in this city, and this youth pastor took his group to visit the children. Some of these kids were so retarded they couldn't speak. Many couldn't sit up by themselves. Some had no mental capacity whatsoever. The pastor and his group took these kids to a rodeo, and all day long they took care of them. The students had to hold them on their laps in the buses. They did everything for the children all day. When they got back on the bus to return home, the youth pastor said, "Kids, I'm so proud of you. You did a wonderful thing today. It was so exciting. But I have a question. How many of you are grieved that many of those children may never think a normal thought in their lives?" Every kid raised his hand. It was impossible not to be grieved. And he said to them, "I grieve, too. But I am more grieved because you are just as retarded to God as those kids seemed to be to you." He sat down, started the bus, and drove back to the church.

No one sang "Ninety-nine Bottles of Beer on the Wall" that afternoon on the bus! It was quiet. When the youth pastor got back to the church, he made an announcement to that group of kids — still shy, carnal, uninterested, and rebellious — but some of them were thinking. He said, "Next week we are going to talk about how to experience the love of Jesus Christ in your life. If you are interested, I encourage to you show up."

Forty kids were on the bus, and the next week 70 kids showed up at the meeting — more kids than had ever come in the previous four years. Why? Because, for the first time, they saw the *need* for what he was going to talk about. Why did they see the need? Because he put them into a life experience that helped *them see* the need.

Let's take an example from the life of Jesus. In John 11, Jesus gets the news that His good friend, Lazarus, is very sick. Nevertheless, Jesus decided to stay where He was for two more days. Now, can you see those disciples? If they were like us, I'll bet it went something like this:

"What? Two more days? Lazarus is sick! We gotta go right now!"

"No, we are going to stay here."

"But Lazarus is going to die."

"Lazarus won't die."

"Okay, if you say so, Jesus...."

A couple of days later Jesus announced, "Well, it's time to go to Lazarus. Come on, men."

They get down the road a little way, and somebody runs up to them saying, "Jesus, Lazarus is dead."

You can see those disciples. "We tried to tell Him. He wouldn't go. He stayed right where He was. We don't know why."

They get about a mile from that crypt, and they begin to hear the mourning — the wailing, the tears, the lamenting — wafting over the winds as they walk down the road. Can you imagine what those disciples are thinking? "Why didn't He go? Why didn't Jesus go?"

And before they even get there, Martha runs out to meet Jesus. "Lord, if You had been here, Lazarus would not have died."

Then Mary comes and says the same thing. The disciples are saying, "That's right, that's right. If Jesus would have left when He found out...."

People are mourning, wailing — can you picture the scene? John 11:33-35 reports that Jesus was "deeply moved," and that He actually wept. I don't think that Jesus was weeping about Lazarus. Lazarus was going to be resurrected in a minute or two. I think He was weeping over the unbelief of His disciples. He used this entire life experience to teach them about belief, and as a result, many more believed in Him (John 11:45-48).

Suppose He had stayed with His disciples in that same city and had said, "Men, today is the day that we learn about resurrection."

These men probably would have said, "But, Lord, what do we need to know about it? We know it's going to be great in the last day — we are all going to live forever in the Kingdom!"

"Remember when I told you that I was going to die?"

"Lord, don't say that — we don't want to hear that."

That was their attitude all the way through. He even rebuked them for saying it — they just wouldn't have understood. So Jesus allowed a life experience to develop which put them in a position where they could really learn about resurrection.

Life Simulations

A similar method that helps create this appetite for spiritual growth in our students is life simulation. One of my youth pastor friends had a group of young people who were spiritually interested but who were very immature in the area of personal Bible study. He told them that they should have their quiet time, but they wouldn't do it. Yet many of them were considered the "spiritual leaders" on campus.

He had a real burden to help them establish this important habit. So he took them on a retreat, and there he set up a life simulation. He brought a Bible cover and put a dictionary in it. It looked just like a Bible, with gold edges and everything. He stood up to speak and opened his "Bible." About halfway into his talk the kids began to get restless. You know how it goes — Fred is punching Mary and Mary is giggling; Jim is snoring against the back wall, and so on.

My friend waited until just the right moment, and then he said, "Well, it doesn't appear to me that anybody is interested.... If that's the way you want it — okay." He shut the "Bible" and *threw it into the fire*! Now this was only a dictionary, but the kids didn't know that! And as that dictionary opened up and began to burn, those kids came to attention.

They said, "Why did you do that? That was the Bible!"

"Oh, that shouldn't make any difference to you. Most of you don't read it, anyway."

"But that was the Bible. You can't throw a Bible in the fire!"

"Well, why not?"

"Because...it's the *Bible*!"

And so they had a lively discussion about what the Bible really is and why it is so important to spend time in it regularly. That's a life simulation — an experience you create as opposed to a real situation that teaches truth.

Questions

Another way to bring truth home to young people is through the use of well-conceived questions. Many youth workers have told me, "You don't understand — I'm not creative; I can't do that." But as they've learned to use questions, as everyone can, they have seen their young people grow in a way they had never imagined.

Ask the kinds of questions that matter. We need to think through what qualities we want to develop in the lives of our students and then integrate related questions as we work with them. Ask questions that make a difference. Instead, we tend to ask questions like, "Well, what do you think this passage means?" Deep! Or, "Can't you just sense God speaking in this passage?" That's so deep I don't even know what it means! Ask the kinds of questions that relate to their development, that relate to where they live. If you want to learn more, study the Gospels and discover how Jesus used questions in such a masterful way.

Drama

A final method that brings truth to life for kids — though there are many others — is skits or role plays. One youth pastor I know was having real problems with his kids in the area of sex. Many didn't see anything wrong with petting — or premarital sex, for that matter. He taught them on the subject several times, but they weren't getting it. So at the next youth meeting, he set up a screen on the stage and put a mannequin behind it. During the meeting a student sat down in front of the screen and began reading a paper. A little girl ran up and started bothering the man reading the paper.

"Dad, can I play with the chain saw?"

"No, of course, you can't play with the chain saw. That's stupid."

"Please...I can handle it."

"No, you can't play with the chain saw."

"Come on, Dad, all my friends play with chain saws."

"Well, okay, you can play with the chain saw, but *be careful*. All right? I just want to read this paper."

So she skipped around behind the screen, and someone started up a real chain saw. (They were in the sanctuary and almost blew out the stained-glass windows!) Pretty soon, as the chain saw was idling, the arms and legs of the mannequin started flying over the top of the screen. When the man looked over his paper and saw what he thought was his dismembered daughter, he jumped off his chair, fell to his knees, and cried, "But you said you could handle it!"

The meeting went right on without comment. When the youth

pastor got up to speak, he said, "Now I have a question. How many think that this father should have let his little girl play with the chain saw?" Nobody thought that. Not a single kid.

"But she said she could handle it."

Someone answered, "Oh, I know, but that was stupid; he should have known she couldn't handle it."

"Really!" the youth pastor continued, "Some of you are telling me that you can handle premarital sex. Should I believe you or not?"

What followed was a very meaningful discussion as the kids drew upon the picture provided by the skit.

There is no substitute for well-placed skits. One time this same youth pastor had two girls get in a fight in front of the group. It was a "screamer." Before someone stopped them, they were almost tearing each other's eyes out! The whole group froze in their seats, looking on. Then the youth pastor got up and said, "I want to know something. We have had a very bad situation occur in our group tonight. These two girls have acted in a very unchristian manner, and I'd like to know what you think we ought to do about it. How many think we should send the girls home?" Several hands went up. "How many think that they really ought to come to my office and receive a rebuke after this meeting?" More hands went up.

Then one mother who happened to be there — and she wasn't part of the act! — spoke up and said, "I was prepared never to let my daughter come back to this group again."

The youth pastor then opened the discussion by saying, "You know what was really interesting to me? None of you seemed to care enough for these two girls to help them. You just sat there. Who is worse — you or they?"

The point is this: We need to create a thirst and a curiosity in the lives of our young people if we expect them to adopt and live by biblical absolutes. That's the way they think. They need it. It's not optional. They need it desperately.

Ask God to use you to create a thirst for Him in the lives of your young people — one that will bring changed lives for His glory.

PUTTING THIS CHAPTER TO WORK

1. In what ways do any of your youth ministry programs violate Miller's "Risky Assumptions"? List each program, and state the problem.

2. Since the ministry of the Holy Spirit is such an important ingredient in effective communication, when was the last time you were aware that He was teaching *you* something? How can you help your young people be more sensitive to the Holy Spirit's teaching ministry?

3. What spiritual absolutes do you think may be "in question" in the minds of your youth?

4. List several qualities you want the Holy Spirit to develop in the lives of your students. Suggest some possible life experiences, simulations, etc., which might stimulate their thirst for growth.

6

THE ROLE OF THE FAMILY IN SHAPING TODAY'S YOUTH

by Dick Day

Several years ago, some students asked me to speak in the open-air quadrangle at the University of California at San Diego. The students had a good music group to help draw the crowd, and before long about 500 students had gathered. I gave my talk, and as I was getting near the conclusion, I started sharing experiences from my own life. I mentioned that my wife and I were about to celebrate our 30th wedding anniversary, and instantly 500 students burst into applause. In fact, it was the only applause I got all day! But it was very interesting to me that, to university students today, if you have been married 30 years, you're a super hero. That's quite a commentary on our culture, isn't it? What I believe those students were saying to me was, "That's great. I wish I could do it, but I doubt if I will." The tragedy is that, if statistics hold true for them, their doubts will be confirmed, five out of seven marriages today end in divorce.

I had the privilege of being involved in Amsterdam '83, a conference for 4,000 itinerant evangelists gathered from 134 countries. It was interesting to see the emphasis that the Billy Graham organization put on the family, not only in the plenary sessions but in personal counseling. I was a part of a team of 20 individuals who were there to be available to counsel with those who came. Out of the 4,000 delegates, over 1,000 of them requested counseling. The majority had needs in the area of the family.

THE DETERIORATION OF THE FAMILY

There is no question that there is something happening in our

---

Dick Day is the director of the Julian Center, a discipleship training environment located in a mountain community near San Diego, California. He is a licensed marriage and children's counselor with a graduate degree in psychology from Azusa Pacific University. Dick graduated from Talbot Theological Seminary and served on the staff of Campus Crusade for Christ for 12 years. He and his wife, Charlotte, have six children and three grandchildren.

families today. The family system is breaking down, and as the family system breaks down, it has a tremendous impact on the individual. Urie Bronfenbrenner from Cornell University is one of today's foremost children's psychiatrists, and he said,

> Children need people in order to become human. We are experiencing a breakdown in the process of making human beings human. And, in summary, whether in comparison to other contemporary cultures or to itself over time, American society emerges as one that gives decreasing prominence to the family as a socializing agency.[1]

Statistics give us a picture of what has happened in the area of divorce. Over 100 years ago, in 1872, for every 32 marriages in a given year, there was one divorce. Twenty years later, for every 12 marriages, there was one divorce. Twenty years after that, at the conclusion of World War I, for every nine marriages, there was one divorce. In 1938, at the closing of the Depression, for every five marriages, there was one divorce. In 1958, in the post-World War II era, for every four marriages, there was one divorce. In 1978, for every two marriages, there was one divorce. And today, as noted before, it is now estimated that for every seven marriages, there will be five divorces. In the *Report to the President*, it was said:

> American families and their children are in trouble — trouble so deep and pervasive as to threaten the future of our nation. The source of the trouble is nothing less than a national neglect of children and those primarily engaged in their care.[2]

I am not a pessimist nor a "Doom's Day" person, but I firmly believe that if there is not a significant change in the family, culture as we know it today will not exist in 10 or 15 years.

To the casual observer, the religious profile of America could be puzzling. In the last 15 years, the majority of American people have moved away from a liberal theology to a more conservative theology. Gallup polls tell us that approximately 55 million people in the United States profess to be born-again Christians. Yet, despite these seemingly positive trends, historians are telling us that in the same period of time we have moved from the Christian era into the post-Christian era. I believe this has happened not because we have been short on information, but because we're short on relationships.

RELATIONSHIPS BRING STABILITY

Today we are blessed to have the Bible. The average person has at least one. But did you realize that probably 90 to 95 percent of all the Christians who have ever lived never had a Bible? Even if they had had one, they wouldn't have been able to read it because they were illiterate. One of the primary means God used to propagate the church of Jesus Christ was *relationships*. Christianity is not only a theological phenomenon, it is a sociological phenomenon. And if the sociological aspect of it breaks down, the dynamics of Christianity break down.

In the Church

It's interesting to note that the fastest growing churches today are rooted in the sociological principle of support groups, of family systems. We didn't even know that the Church of China existed until China was opened up recently. We thought that when the missionaries and others were removed after World War II the church would die out — the buildings were taken over, the Bibles were confiscated, and the teachers and pastors were taken away and imprisoned. The churches were turned into warehouses. But do you realize that today it is estimated that there are between 30 and 50 million believers in China? It has all come about with home cell groups.

At the turn of the century, less than 2 percent of the population of Korea was Christian. Today, it is approximately 38 percent Christian, and it is estimated that by the turn of the century, Korea will be over 42 percent Christian. One of the keys to this growth has been home cell groups. Relationships. People supporting each other. Coming together. God meant for the family to be that way, and when the family doesn't function, breakdown occurs — as persons and as a society.

In the Home

I was a counselor in our local school district for a time. I was hired by the School Board to work with children in kindergarten through eighth grade, in the areas of self-esteem, behavioral problems and family problems. The teachers referred them to me upon approval of the parents. By the time the year was over, one-tenth of the student body had been referred to me. Eighty percent of the students who came to me were struggling due to broken families, situations with "live-in" fathers, or general family stress. Once again I am reminded that what happens in the family is so significant.

On the Mission Field

Henry Brandt, the prominent Christian psychologist, was at the Julian Center recently. He is on several mission boards and often helps to review new applicants. Dr. Brandt observed: "Ten years ago, one out of every three applicants was accepted for the mission field. Today, it's one out of ten. The primary reason for rejection is a family background which adds up to unstable, immature people who are not able to cope with relationships and stress."

THE ECOLOGY OF THE FAMILY

I believe that in God's economy He is a great ecologist and that He has an ecology for His whole system — that is, there must be balance. We certainly see it in the natural realm in the balance of creation; we use it as one of the arguments for the intelligence of the Creator. I believe that God also meant for there to be an ecology of the family.

Maintaining the Right Balance for Development

We see this as early as Genesis 2:24 when it says that "a man shall leave . . . and cleave." Adam and Eve were created in a mature state, and, had they remained in that maturity without moral sin, they would have created an environment for their children which would have brought them to maturity also. The children would then have become ready to "leave and cleave" and start the process all over again. That is the function of a family. But with the Fall, that ecology was thrown off. Many teenagers today are very anxious to "leave" — and in some families it might not be such a bad idea! But if a person's family has been detrimental in his personal development, "cleaving" prematurely will only continue to throw the ecology of the family out of balance. If there is something missing from the input to their lives, there can be devastation in the future chain of family relationships.

I believe that God, in His ecology, uses two primary principles to develop a mature and healthy person through the family: the principle of *love* and the principle of *limits*. This is the way He prepares someone to function in the world successfully. Picture with me, if you will, a balanced teeter-totter. On one end of the teeter-totter is love; on the other end of the teeter-totter is limits. Now on the love side, you have another teeter-totter balancing *acceptance* and *appreciation*. On the limits side, you have a teeter-totter balancing *obedience* and *form*.

I think you can see from the teeter-totters that it can get complex. Life is complex. Though the solutions are quite often simple, it's the implementation that becomes complex. And that is the reason we don't see more balance in the families around us. Balance certainly is an impossible goal without the indwelling power of Christ within each of us.

Marriage and Intimacy

The person who has a fair degree of the above ingredients in a balanced form is the person who, I believe, is mature enough to "graduate" from the nest — he or she is ready to leave and cleave. But if those ingredients are not being built into a person, he will not have a healthy sense of identity, and if a person does not have good identity, he cannot handle intimacy. I believe that the major reason for the breakup of families today is the inability to handle intimacy caused by the lack of strong, personal identity. If I don't really know who I am, I'm going to be threatened by you. I am going to be afraid to let you into my life, because if I don't like who I am, how can I risk exposing myself to you? You may see what I'm really like and then you won't like me either! And so the family breaks up because we never developed good enough identities to allow ourselves the freedom to become really close.

Another result of an imbalance and lack of identity is becoming absorbed with the materialism of our culture. I have found that when people do not find security in relationships, they endeavor to find security in possessions. I spent five years in marriage and family counseling in Newport Beach, California, one of the more affluent communities in the United States. The affluency of many of the people was amazing to me — their homes, their habits, their cars. I saw a car with a bumper sticker that proclaimed, "My other car is a Porsche." But that bumper sticker was on a Rolls Royce!

And yet these people would come in for counseling, and despite their affluency, the moment they ran into financial difficulty, their marriages began to break apart. You show me a couple who are secure in their relationship, and when they go through financial reversals, despite the stress and tension, when the crisis is past, their marriage will have grown and they will have grown as individuals. But you show me a couple who are not secure in their relationship, and when they go through financial reversals, I will show you candidates for divorce.

People Need People!

The goal of a family is to develop people who can move, ultimately, from dependency into *interdependency*. The dependent person says, "I need you; I have to have you." The independent person says, "I don't need you." The interdependent person says, "I have something to give to you, and you have something to give to me." That's God's plan — to provide that kind of home environment where true development can take place.

Remember comedian Bill Cosby's monolog on Noah? One of his closing lines as the thunder starts to crash is "Jes you'n me, Lord, jes you'n me!" Now that's great humor, but it's poor theology. Barbra Streisand is much closer to biblical theology when she sings, "People who need people are the luckiest people in the world." After God created us, He said, "It is not good for the man to be alone" (Genesis 2:18). God created us as sociological beings, and we need to live and develop in the context of people. The man or the woman who is an island unto himself will never know himself. We come to know ourselves in the context of relationships, and the first of those relationships starts in the family.

THE PRINCIPLE OF LOVE

Let's take a little closer look at how to produce the kind of relationships in our families that will develop people to their full potential. As mentioned earlier, the first principle God uses to develop us is love, as expressed in acceptance of the person (bringing positive self-identity) and appreciation of his actions (bringing self-esteem).

Acceptance Brings Self-worth

First, let's look at self-identity. In the *Report to the President*, it was stated:

> Identity is the totality of one's thoughts and feelings about the universe, one's self, one's surroundings, others in the unknown. As a child develops, he or she will become more aware of and relate to more and more a personal universe. The child will develop a positive, healthy identity only if capacities to think and feel are guided toward knowledge and love. Knowing and loving must expand with awareness, and a child must come to know and to love self and others. Only if these capacities continue to expand will the child be able to fulfill his or her human potential and become his or herself. If his expansion of knowledge or love is frustrated or blocked, the child will remain unhappy, unsatisfied, even disturbed.[3]

In *Human Development: The Span of Life*, the author stated:

> In today's society, it is becoming increasingly difficult for the young adult to find his self-image. He stands rather alone in an unstructured moral climate. He is not given guidelines or standards to contemplate by which to pattern his life. Emphasis is on being free and "doing your own thing." With lack of background, how can he know what is most desirable for him? He proceeds, timidly, by trial and error or by imitating those who seem to know what they are doing. But do they know?[4]

A child needs to develop that security of person. A key to this is the area of acceptance within the family. There must be an emphasis on the worth of the person.

Mark 9:33-37 reports that the disciples had been discussing among themselves which of them was the greatest — arguing over their worth based on accomplishments and credentials. Jesus exhorted them by setting forth the principle of servant-leadership: "If any one wants to be first, he shall be last of all, and servant of all." Then Jesus went on to illustrate what He had said. He took a small child, seated him on His lap, and said, "Whoever receives one child like this in My name is receiving Me; and whoever receives Me is not receiving Me, but Him who sent Me."

Now what did Jesus mean by that? In the context of these men discussing which of them was the greatest, Jesus was saying, "Gentlemen, your worth to me is not based upon what you have done; it is based upon who you are. Your worth is in your *being*, not your doing." The small child He was holding was His object lesson — the one person who did not have any credentials based on *doing*. He was saying, "Your worth is in your *being* because back before creation, it was pleasing in the mind of God, in His sovereignty, to choose to create man in His image." Why? To have fellowship with Him. I don't know why God wanted that. It's a mystery of mysteries. But His *agape* love chose us nonetheless. We are the object of His unconditional love based on who we are, not on what we've done. Talk about acceptance and worth!

Appreciation Brings Self-Esteem

Love is also expressed by appreciation and encouragement which leads to self-esteem. Because we are behavioral beings, we spend a lot of time "doing." And as we express appreciation for the actions of our young people, we can assist in developing their capacity and potential.

Remember that we are not working for perfection, but for improvement. We live in a day and age that gets all caught up in competition. If we don't understand how to use competition, it can be devastating — not only to our sense of worth but also to our sense of self-esteem. Essentially we should use competition, not to beat down another, but to maximize one's potential and uniqueness. In order to do that, we must know ourselves.

An important part of the ecology of the family is raising young people who understand their own uniqueness. Unfortunately, in the growing process, we get all kinds of expectations thrown upon us by our parents, peers, culture and church. Probably most of them are not realistic expectations. When these things are taken too seriously, they hamper one's ability to value his own uniqueness. We must communicate appreciation for the progress that is being made and, by our encouragement, help our young people to build their sense of self-esteem as they grow.

Creating a Desire for Guidance

Proverbs 22:6 gives some practical insight, "Train up a child in the way he should go, even when he is old he will not depart from it." The word "child" used here refers to a youth anywhere from birth all the way to the stage of maturity. The words "train up" come from a root meaning that pictures creating a desire for guidance. In one case, the root of that word is used to describe the method used to stimulate sucking in a newborn child.

It was also used to describe the bridling of animals. Now, if you've ever been around livestock, you know that if you put a bridle on too tight, the animal will buck because it hurts. The bridle should fit comfortably, not applying enough pressure to cause bucking, but just enough to give guidance. And that's what is meant in this portion of Scripture, "Train up a child to maturity so that you are creating within him a desire for guidance."

"In the way he should go. . . ." It's beautiful to see how this word "way" is used in parallel passages. In Proverbs 30:18, the writer says:

> There are three things which are too wonderful for me, four which I do not understand: the way of an eagle in the sky, the way of a serpent on a rock, the way of a ship in the middle of the sea, and the way of man with a maid.

That same word for "way" that is used in "train up a child in the way" (Proverbs 22:6) is now used here. I think it will give fresh insight about encouraging and guiding our young people in a way that will build their self-esteem.

Guidance That Allows for Uniqueness

I live in the mountains of California, in the back country of San Diego County. Julian is a little town of about 1,500 people, a former gold mining town. We have lots of mountains and rolling hills. I love to get out and run in those hills, and often I see hawks and owls and even eagles. When they're in flight, they habitually use the air currents. And as they go on their way, there is a tremendous amount of freedom of expression in their flight. It's beautiful! You can see why the writer marveled at "the way of an eagle in the sky."

He also marveled at the "way of a serpent on a rock." Now sometimes we don't like serpents. Every now and then I run on the high desert, not too far from us. When it's hot, it's not too uncommon to come across some reptiles. It's fascinating to watch them. When a snake goes across the rock, it conforms to the rock and wiggles and slips across. It's beautiful when you stop and analyze it. There is direction, but there is freedom to it.

And then we come to the "way of a ship." I used to live in Newport Beach, which is a great sailing harbor. When you get out on a sailboat, there is a direction to it. But at the same time there is the freedom of going with the wind and the roll of the waves.

And then the passage refers to the "way of a young man with a maid." Have you ever noticed how weird some high school guys act when they are trying to impress a girl? Or how wonderful they can act when they are really "in love"? Recently we were coming out of a restaurant at night in a little lonely part of town. A group of eight of us were walking along joking and making noise. I looked across the street and there were a "young man and a maid." Despite our noise, they didn't even know we were on the street. This young guy was all eyes for this young lady, and she was all eyes for him. The "way of a young man with a maid" takes a direction all its own.

In another usage, "the way" is described as an archer's bow which is bendable, flexible. A bow has its own uniqueness, and a child must be raised up in his or her own uniqueness. We all need to understand that. All too often we find ourselves wishing that God would make us like so-and-so. In effect, we are asking God to make us to be something that He didn't create us to be. That quenches the Spirit. One of the greatest ministries we can have to young people today is to help them come to grips with their own uniqueness.

Communicating Love Through Encouragement

In that context, we need encouragement. I don't need anybody to dump on me. You know why? I do a thoroughly adequate job myself! How about you? We need encouragement. The purpose of the body of Christ is to edify (Ephesians 4:11-16). So many kids have grown up with such discouraging feedback — even in the church and more often at home. Their worth has been constantly negated by their environment. Kids don't need criticism, they need encouragement. They need somebody who will get behind them and say, "Hey, I believe in you!"

I remember when I was working at the school, I had one student who was going through tremendous problems. I concentrated on building him up, continually encouraging him. He was so changed by it that his mother started coming in to see me. Before long, we were able to get into the spiritual dimension. Why? Because her child got encouragement in the midst of a family that was breaking up.

THE PRINCIPLE OF LIMITS

So, then, on the one side of the teeter-totter is the principle of love with its emphasis on acceptance and appreciation. But to balance the teeter-totter on the other side, we have the principle of limits, which involves obedience and form. We must help our children to come to grips with obedience. It has been wisely said that the person who does not have enough willpower to submit to someone else will never have enough willpower to submit to himself.

Obedience Builds Self-discipline and Self-image

In Ephesians 6:1, Paul admonishes: "Children, obey your parents. . . ." A child's ability to respond properly to authority is a key factor in developing his healthy self-image. Obedience helps build a foundation for the development of volition, decisiveness and values. It is encouraging to note that even non-theologians and atheistic psychologists now recognize the value of this principle. I. A. Pechernikova, a Russian child psychiatrist, observed:

> Obedience in young children provides the basis for developing that most precious of qualities — self-discipline. Obedience in adolescents and older school children — this is the effective expression of their love, trust, and respect toward parents and other adult family members, a conscious desire to acknowledge their experience and wisdom. . . .Where there is no obedience, there is no self-discipline, nor can there be normal development of independence. Training in obedience is an essential condition for developing the ability of self-discipline.[5]

Isn't it interesting that psychology is just now becoming aware through general revelation of what God has been saying for millenia through special revelation — "Children, obey your parents."

Authority: Autocratic or Relational?

Notice, however, that the obedience is qualified: "And, fathers, do not provoke your children to anger...." The authority style a parent uses makes a difference. A child can be submitting to an autocratic type of parent, or he can be submitting to a relational type of parent.

Usually, we draw organizational charts in pyramids, putting the leader at the top. This is the person who has authority over other people; he has a position of power. Essentially he says, "I say it; you do it" — communicating to the underling the feeling of "have to, or else." From this power position you may get the desired behavior, but what do you get emotionally? When you are *told* to do something, what happens to you inside? Do you *respond* to that person who is telling you what you *have* to do? Or do you *react* to that person?

I believe that the greatest scripting and conformity that we have to this world is at the emotional level, put there by relationships. "Do not be conformed to this world, but be transformed by the renewing of your mind. . ." (Romans 12:2). Growing up in relational environments that are not conducive to God's will produces the greatest conformity to this world, because it is in opposition to what God would have for us. That is what happens when the ecology of the family falls off.

It's interesting that Jesus never set up a power structure. Philippians 2:5-8 tells us that He emptied Himself of all His power attributes. He could have called on legions of angels, but He didn't. He could have set up a kingdom, but He didn't. Jesus did not get any following from a position of power; He got a following by relating to people. He had such a maturity that people responded to Him and were persuaded by Him.

Notice the difference between an autocratic leader and a relational leader. The autocratic leader is an authority figure; the relational leader is a knowledgeable leader. Autocratic leadership is a power position; relational leadership is an influence position. The difference is pressure versus stimulation; demanding versus winning cooperation; punishment versus logical consequences; reward versus encouragement; imposition versus permitting self-determination; domination versus guidance.

Personality tests show that when a person is extremely domineering, it is usually because of insecurity. People try to control their environment. Do you realize that Jesus never came to His own defense? He defended the innocent, but He didn't come to His own defense. He didn't use any defense mechanisms. He didn't rely on a power structure. He was secure — He knew who He was and what He was doing. He didn't need those mechanisms. And I think the more we become like Christ, the more that spirit will be present in our lives as well.

Form — An Anchor on the Sea of Free Choice

To help our children understand the principle of limits, we must not only help them learn obedience, but we must also provide *form* in their environment. Gwen B. Carr, in her book *Marriage and Family in the Decade of Change*, says:

> To borrow again from Rollo May, man cannot live unbounded in an empty sea of free choice without an increase of inner conflict. To be free, we must commit ourselves to boundaries Traditionally, it is marriage and family and home which has provided the landmarks and boundaries by which we reduce our inner conflict.[6]

We are living in a day and age that does not give us boundaries; traditional values have been rejected. We are adrift in a world of relativism surrounded by an environment of over-choice. Is it any wonder that it is so hard for people to make decisions? They don't even know where to start; they don't have a form or point of reference from which to begin. When we instill biblical principles in our children, those principles will guide their lives and ultimately make their lives easier, not more difficult. Our children will discover freedom in knowing and doing what is right, and they will be equipped with solid reasoning to spurn distracting temptations.

If there is one thing that characterizes the younger generation today, it is the of lack of self-discipline and decisiveness. If a young person is not given standards to which he learns to adhere, he will be confused. He will become uncertain of his goals and ineffective in his decision-making because he has no plumbline on which to base his values. He will be like a person trying to put a jigsaw puzzle together without the box top for a reference.

Remember, however, these limits of obedience and form must be built upon *love*. Discipline should not be seen as punishment for the purpose of inflicting penalty. It is positive training for maturity. When we discipline, we must earn the right to discipline. Paul disciplined the church at Corinth. But first of all he gave his life to them for five years, to the point he was even shipwrecked and flogged during his ministry to them. So it was in a context of encouragement that he disciplined. I do not believe that we have the right to discipline until we have accepted and encouraged our young people. In the technical sense, it is easy to discipline. It takes about one second to say, "Don't do that!" But to become involved in people's lives means sacrifice and work. Young people need the limits of obedience and form, but be sure they are built on a foundation of sacrificial love.

MODELING THE BALANCE OF LOVE AND LIMITS

What is the greatest way to teach people? It is *not* simply through the dissemination of information. The greatest method of instruction is through role modeling. What has made the greatest impact on your life, information or people? The church has existed for all these centuries through relationships within the family and within the body of Christ. We have the information today, and of course it is essential. But Paul tells us in Ephesians 4:15 that the truth has to be balanced with love. Jesus said in John 13:35: "By this all men will know that you are my disciples, if you have love for one another."

Love is not simply the dissemination of information. It is involvement with people. If we are serious about developing people, we will provide them with role models. When objective truth was first given to Israel, Moses constantly referred to transmitting it to the next generation by example, by modeling (cf. Deuteronomy 4:9; 6:4-8; 11:18-21).

In Luke 6:40 Jesus said, "A pupil is not above his teacher, but everyone, after he has been fully trained, will be like his teacher."

Hebrews 13:7 says, "Remember those who led you, who spoke the word of God to you; and considering the outcome of their way of life, imitate their faith." Our young people need more than our advice, they need our example. They need to experience love and limits within the context of a relationship with us.

Rules Without Relationship Lead to Rebellion

Many people today are deficient in their developmental process because they have not had that proper balance between love and limits. What most people need is not more limits but more love. They need somebody who is going to accept them as they are, someone who will get in there with them and encourage them. Generally, when people get out of hand, others tend to come in with limits. I've seen this over and over again in counseling situations. Parents come in feeling desperate and ask, "What are we going to do? I've grounded them, I've tightened up the rules, and it's not working." My response generally is, "Back off on the rules, and work on the relationship."

There is a biblical principle: Rules without relationships lead to rebellion; by the law is the knowledge of sin. The law never made a person righteous. But when you come into a love relationship with the law-giver, then what happens? Love fulfills the law. It's amazing. These same parents will come back in three or four weeks and say, "I can't believe it — the kid is doing what I ask him to do!"

A Call for Para-parents

Young people today need more role models who are willing to demonstrate this balance of love and limits in the context of relationships. Because of the breakup of the family and parents who will not take this responsibility, one of the greatest challenges facing the church today is to find good role models. As youth workers, you cannot do the job alone. There is a warehouse of resources available to you. They are people, not books. Many of them are middle-aged and older.

William Glasser said that at least until age 40, every one of us needs "interfacing" — a close relationship with the generation that precedes us. Ninety percent of the students at our Julian Center between ages 25 and 40 say that they still have the need for a "para-parent" in their lives. I think that one of the greatest resources today in the body of Christ is people who are middle-aged and older working with young people in para-parent roles. They don't have to know theology, they just have to care about people, get involved with people, love people.

We tend to make this whole thing so professional — we hire a "professional" to do the job, and the laity sits back and does nothing. That violates the believer-priest principle of Scripture; older women should be instructing younger women; elders should be in leadership. Are you tapping this resource for your youth ministry? I firmly believe that if you are not, your ministry will not last. It will be the seed that fell on the rocky road.

Approximately 70 percent of evangelical youth who go away to college go "down the tubes" spiritually, not from a lack of information, but from a lack of supportive relationships. Do you know why a young person joins a cult today? It is not because of the cult's theology. It's because there is a support there. God created us as social beings. We need to tap into that. We need to have the body of Christ working together as a support system. Because of what has happened to the family, many young people today need surrogate parents — para-parents who can give them what they have not received in their family of origin. If we do not start to implement that principle soon, 10 or 15 years from now our culture will not be as we know it today. Sociologists say we're already at the "age of alienation."

You can play parent roles with the young people with whom you work. You don't have to be a generation ahead of them. Josh McDowell, the popular author and campus speaker, has been a close friend of mine for 24 years. Recently I found out that Josh considers me a father-figure, although I am only 10 years older. We've lived together, we pray together, we play together, we vacation together, we minister together.

Josh grew up as the son of the town drunk. His dad trusted the Lord one year before he died of cirrhosis of the liver and became a tremendous witness. But there was not enough time for him to compensate for all the years of being a poor father to Josh. I met Josh when he was in seminary, and soon he became almost part of our family. As the head of that family, I became a father-figure to Josh. There are millions of young people who need parent figures, many with the potential of a Josh McDowell or some other unique role within God's plan for mankind.

Do all you can to provide the support system that God intended for the development of mature individuals — the family and the church. Functioning together they can provide for young people, by the grace of God, an environment balanced with love and limits.

PUTTING THIS CHAPTER TO WORK

1. List some creative ways you can communicate acceptance and encouragement to the young people with whom you work.

Try to express appreciation for who they are, as well as for what they do.

2. According to the principle of Proverbs 22:6, list several of the unique characteristics of your youth or other key disciples. How could you stimulate their growth in those areas of strength?

3. There is a great need for role models to demonstrate the balance between love and limits in the context of relationships. Can you think of some adults who could serve as "para-parents" to your young people who lack models?

NOTES

1. Bronfenbrenner, Urie, *Two Worlds of Childhood*, New York: Pocket Books (U.S. and U.S.S.R.), 1973, p. xvii.

2. *Report to the President, White House Conference on Children*, Washington, D.C.: U.S. Government Printing Office, Superintendent of Documents, 1971, p. 252.

3. Ibid., p. 21.

4. Kaluger, George and Meriem F., *Human Development: The Span of Life*, St. Louis: C. V. Mosby Co., 1974, p. 226.

5. Pechernikova, I.A., *The Development of Obedience and Diligence Among Children in the Family*, Moscow: Prosveshchenie, 1967, p. 7.

6. Carr, Gwen B., *Marriage and Family in the Decade of Change*, Reading, MA: Addison-Wesley Publishers, 1972, n.p.

EVANGELISM

7

RELATING CHRIST NATURALLY

by Becky Pippert

Charles Wesley, the famous revivalist and hymn writer, was asked one time, "Why is it that people are so drawn to you — just like a magnet? People seem to always want to be with you. What is it about you that draws people?" And Charles Wesley is reported to have said, "Well, you see, when you set yourself on fire, people just love to come and watch you burn!"

THE FIRE OF EVANGELISM

That is evangelism. Evangelism, first and foremost, is not a program, it is a *fire*. If we know Jesus Christ personally and are hopelessly in love with Him, we will have a fire that burns brightly within us. It is this fire that draws people and warms them in our presence. Our techniques, materials and programs for evangelism may be essential, but they are cold and lifeless unless they come through a life that is aflame with Jesus. As we stoke that fire and are transformed by the presence of Christ within us, others will be drawn to Him. That is what changes the world.

How can we be more effective in sharing our "fire" with others? If Christ's presence in us is so important in evangelism, maybe it would be helpful to examine what Christ's presence was like when He was actually here on earth.

Extravagant Love

When I read the Gospels, what strikes me about Jesus is that He was utterly delightful. Jesus was the kind of man everybody wanted to have over for dinner. He went to weddings. He went to

---

Becky Pippert is an evangelism specialist with Inter-Varsity Christian Fellowship, an inter-denominational ministry to college students. She has ministered for many years on campuses and as a popular conference speaker. Becky received a master's degree from the University of Illinois and has written a book entitled, *Out of the Salt Shaker*. Her husband, Wesley, is a UPI reporter, and they are stationed in Jerusalem. They have one child.

parties. He loved people, and He wanted to be with them.

If I were to tell you that Jesus was going to walk right into the room where you are, sit down across from you, and let you ask Him any question that you want, my guess is that you would be a little tongue-tied. I think this is what we see in the Gospels — at least this is how I picture it. In John 1, Jesus walks by, and John the Baptist says, "You should check this guy out — He is really something." So some of John's disciples toddled along after Jesus, and Jesus turned around and said to them, "Yes?"

The disciples stammered, "Ah-h-h-h, well. . ."

"Yes, what is it?"

And slowly gaining composure, the disciples said, "Well...uh...we've got a...a question here."

"Fine! What's the question?"

"Okay...yes.... We're a little nervous, Jesus. Uh...here's the question."

"Okay."

"Where are you staying?"

Now, have you ever heard a wimpier question? Can you imagine waiting all your life to ask Jesus that? But what did Jesus do? He did not say, "That's probably the dumbest question I have ever heard. Nonetheless, lucky for you, I'm going to deliver a sermon anyway!" Jesus said, "Where am I staying? Why don't you come and see? Why don't you come home with Me? Really, I want you to come home with Me."

What do we see about Jesus? We see a man who is delightful — the kind of man who brought people home. Children adored Him; He affected adults so much that one of them said, "If I only touch His garment, I shall get well" (Matthew 9:21). What would make an adult say that about another adult? I think they correctly perceived the power of Jesus Christ's love. People sensed it, and they wanted to be as close as they possibly could. Jesus loved people extravagantly, boldly. There was nothing cautious or timid in the way that Jesus approached people. His life was a constant demonstration that there are only two things in life that count: God and people, because they are the only things that last forever.

Sensitive to Needs

Jesus was perceptive to need. When the leper came to Him, full of shame and wounds and feeling desperate but timid, he said, "If You want to, You can make me well again" (Mark 1:40, TLB). This is the very first recorded example from the emotional life of Jesus, and it says that Jesus, moved with compassion, turned to that leper and said, "Oh, I *want* to!" And He healed him.

That man was used to walking down a street and seeing people shriek and scatter, yelling "Unclean! Unclean!" If that were you, what would those reactions do to the way you look at yourself? Do you remember how Jesus healed him? He didn't say, "Be healed, but don't get too close. I just hate leprosy." How did He do it? He walked over to that leper, and He *held* him. Do you have any idea what it meant to that leper to be held? Do you realize he probably never had been held by a well person? Jesus held him because He knew the man was suffering from far more than just a diseased body. He was suffering from an equally diseased self-image.

How many of your high school students suffer from a diseased self-image? What they need is people who will be like Jesus — people who will come and put their arms around them and say, "Come home with me. You're special. You count."

When we lived in Rockville, Maryland, one of our next-door neighbors was a darling high school guy who became very open to the gospel. He went to a meeting for Christians at his high school, and he really enjoyed everything about it. But when he went back to school the next day none of the "in crowd" from that group even said "Hello." Nobody spoke to him; they just ignored him. He never went back to the meetings, and he has since rejected the gospel. We have to make an effort to walk alongside as Jesus did, bringing people "home," loving them as they are.

Unconventional When Necessary

Jesus was not only compassionate and perceptive; sometimes He was also exasperating. Here was this man claiming to be God, and He was flinging furniture down the front steps of a temple; He was asking people how they expected to escape the damnation of hell; He was saying things like "I have come to set the earth on fire." He was a man who on one occasion would claim to be holy and sent by God, and on another occasion would mingle with the most unsavory kinds of people. It's one thing to give people evangelistic tracts; but Jesus liked to have dinner with them. And He was accused — the Holy One, the King of kings, the Lord of lords — of being a drunk because He hung around drunks, of being a glutton and, basically, of having poor taste in friends.

People would ask, "What do you do with a man who claims to be holy, and then goes around hugging lepers and talking with prostitutes? This is not the way holiness should be exhibited." But Jesus claimed that He was God's very own audio visual to the world. The chief complaint against the Son of God was that He was not religious enough. Can you see why the Jesus of the Bible shattered people's image of what they expected of the Messiah? But this is what Jesus was like — compassionate, sensitive and unabandoned to His purpose. That is the "fire" that drew so many to Him. And that is the living Christ we must communicate to our students.

A FACE FOR THE GOSPEL

How do we do that? How do we follow Christ's example in a way that can penetrate the youth culture for Him?

Rabbit-hole Christians

First, I think we must start by spending time with non-Christians. That sounds obvious, but it may not be, judging from much of what I see. When I am working with college students, I frequently find what John Stott calls the "Rabbit-hole Christian." The Rabbit-hole Christian is a Christian who leaves his Christian roommate in the morning, pops out of his little hole, and then runs to class and looks around to find a Christian to sit next to. And he continues to go from class to class looking for other Christians to sit next to — which seems a rather odd way to approach a mission field. He then goes back to his dorm where all 60 of the Christians eat together, and they say, "Praise God! What a testimony to all those people out there eating alone, that we're all eating together!" That evening, he goes to a Christian Bible study, followed by a Christian prayer meeting, after which he returns to his Christian roommate. He has somehow avoided all contact with the world except during these brave mad dashes to and from religious activity.

My friends, that is the most insidious reversal of what it means to be salt and light (Matthew 5:13-16). How can we be the "salt of the earth" if we have never gotten out of the salt shaker? We must communicate Christ to the world. But we must demonstrate that evangelism is not a project we do once a week — it's a lifestyle. We don't only give the gospel; we *live* the gospel.

A Life of Love

Whether you like it or not, your life is the first Bible most people ever read. That is why Jesus taught that our lives must be dominated by His love, not by religious activity alone. Our sociology must reflect our theology. How you treat people will be the clearest indication to them of who you really think God is.

In Luke 10, Jesus tells the parable of the Good Samaritan in response to this conversation with the Pharasaic lawyer.

> And behold, a certain lawyer stood up and put Him to the test, saying, "Teacher, what shall I do to inherit eternal life?" And He said to him, "What is written in the Law? How does it read to you?" And he answered and said, "You shall love the Lord your God with all your heart, and with all your soul, and with all your strength, and with all

> your mind; and your neighbor as yourself." And He said to him, "You
> have answered correctly; Do this, and you will live" (Luke 10:25-28).

In other words, Jesus said, "If I were to sum up all of life, the essence of it is not in religious activity alone but in a profound love relationship to God, to your neighbor and to yourself."

One of the problems we see sometimes is when evangelism seems to depend more on technique than on authentic involvement with our neighbor. Nobody wants to be an evangelistic project. People want to be loved; they want to be taken seriously. We must be radically identified with people. Of course, we must also be radically different. That's the tension. But as we achieve the balance, we begin to make a real impact for Christ.

A Glimpse of Grace

We have been examining the nature of evangelism — how it starts from within us and is patterned after Christ's example of loving others and identifying with people. Let me give one example of how it looks in real life. I worked at Reed College in Portland, Oregon, and Reed students are unlike any students I have ever met. They are so intense, so academic and so radical. Portland, by and large, is a pretty conservative town, so the residents are not real crazy about Reed students.

There was a church right across the street from Reed College which was a white, upper middle-class, conservative church — solidly evangelical. The congregation felt guilty because they wanted to reach out to Reed, but they were intimidated. They said, "Hey, God has called us to the mission field, but who needs to go to Bongo Bongo? The natives live right across the street — and they even look like natives!" So they agreed that they were going to reach out to the students.

They started by doing a wonderful thing. They found out that on Sunday evenings the students did not have a meal on campus. So they offered a free meal for anybody who wanted to come, no strings attached. It was about the first or second week after they opened the doors of the church that a student named Bill became involved. Let me describe what Bill looked like. In the three years that I knew him, he always wore the same pair of jeans, and the same T-shirt with holes. His hair was so wild that it looked as though he had stuck his finger in an electric socket and got a charge that never left. He *never* wore a pair of shoes in his four years of college; rain, sleet, or snow, he was barefoot. (Believe it or not, Bill did not stand out as unusual at Reed. You could never have picked him out of the crowd!)

Bill met Jesus. He fell in love with Jesus. He had been a Christian about 48 hours, and he said to himself, "I wonder what

Christians do. I bet they go to church. Far out! I will go to church."
And so he walked across the street and into this very elegant, very
formal, very conservative church. Sporting his well-worn jeans,
holey T-shirt, wild hair and no shoes, he sauntered down the aisle.
"Hey, what's happenin'?" He was one of these love-peace-to-
gether types. To make it worse, he came in late — the service had
already started! As he walked down the aisle, people were not only
asking, "Who is this?" but "What is this?" Some of the members
were saying, "We knew it! We knew if we opened the doors of the
church, things like this would walk in. He doesn't even have shoes
on. It's disgusting!" But many more said, "No, that's why we're
here. We're here to minister to people like this but he intimidates
us. We don't know how."

Bill walked down the aisle, trying to find a place to sit. It was very
crowded, and he kept walking and walking until he finally got right
up to the pulpit. He still couldn't find a place to sit, so he just sat
down right on the carpet — no problem! Everyone collectively
"freaked out." The minister was watching all this, and it was almost
time for him to begin the sermon. He was obviously very uptight;
he went up to the pulpit during a hymn, and he was just not sure
what to do.

About this time, he noticed that way in the back an elderly
deacon was making his way toward Bill. The man was about 85,
had silver gray hair, wore a three-piece suit with a little pocket
watch, and always said "How do you do?" to everybody. He was so
formal and so elegant that, as far as Bill was concerned, he could
have been from another planet. The man walked with a cane, very
slowly. The minister realized there was no way he could start his
sermon until the deacon did what he had to do. Every eye was fas-
tened on this man walking slowly down the aisle — it seemed like
an eternity to everyone! I was told later that people were thinking,
"You can't blame him for what he is going to do. How can he understand? How can he be sensitive to this boy? We don't even like the
fact that he is here. How can someone that old understand?"

Finally, he was right behind Bill, and it was so tense you could
have heard a tissue drop. Bill was obviously the only one who
didn't know what was going on. The man took his cane and, while
everyone watched, he dropped it on the carpet. Then, with great
difficulty, the 85-year-old man lowered himself to the floor, sat
down on the carpet, and worshiped there with that boy for the rest
of the service.

I was told that everyone wept, and when the minister finally
spoke, he said, "What I am about to preach, you will never remember; but what you have just seen, you will never forget. It's always like that when you see Jesus. He is so wonderful; He is so
beautiful that just walking by, getting just a glimpse, changes you

forever." He continued, "And I want to thank God for grace."

Probably the only person who didn't know grace had been be-stowed was Bill. He probably thought, "Hey, have a seat — it's more comfortable down here!" And isn't that the way it is? God is bestowing grace upon grace, and we don't even see it. That man understood what it meant to be a Good Samaritan, because he had been met by the Great Samaritan. He understood that we must walk alongside our brothers and sisters if we are to share the reason for the hope that is within us.

FALSE ASSUMPTIONS AND FEARS

Christ reached out to others in such a natural, loving way. Why, then, do we have so many hang-ups in sharing our faith? Why don't we share our fire?

Complacency

First, we are complacent. A story is told of three devils. They were trying to figure out how to keep Christians from being effec-tive. One devil said, "Let's tell Christians that there is no heaven, no possibility of reward. That will keep them quiet." Another devil said, "No, let's tell them there is no hell, no possibility of punish-ment. That will keep them quiet." Then the third devil said, "No, I've got it. Let's just tell them there is no hurry."

What do you think we have bought into? We are theologically sound, but we are not in a hurry. The Kingdom of God is at hand, and there is a pressing urgency to do the work that we have been called to do while we are on planet Earth. One of the things we can do to jar that complacency is to recognize the historical purposes of God — to seek and to save the lost.

The second reason I think we struggle so much is that we are afraid. One thing I have found very important in evangelism train-ing is to identify fears concretely and label them. There is some-thing therapeutic about being able to identify where you struggle, especially in evangelism.

"I'll Be Like My Worst Dreams!"

All of us have seen poor models of evangelism — people who have blown it in the worst way. And some of us are terrified that if we say anything at all, people are going to think we are just like that terrible model we ourselves saw.

I was at a shopping center a couple of years ago, and somebody came up to me and said, "I am going to give you the gospel."

I thought, "Okay. I am not going to tell him that I'm a Christian, that I 'do it for a living,' that I wrote a book on the subject. I'll just see how he does, then give him a little grade when he is through!"

So he began giving me the gospel, and the more he talked, the angrier I got. I could just feel my blood level start to rise, because he never asked my name; he didn't ask one thing about me. If he had asked any personal questions, he would have realized we could have had fellowship.

Finally, I interrupted him, "Listen, I should have said this from the beginning. I am a Christian. I mean, I really am a Christian. So you can stop now."

He said, "Don't interrupt me, I haven't finished my second point."

What had happened here? This person had become a victim of what I think has happened to too many of us in America. Evangelism, for some, has fallen into the category of "sales." I was really rather irrelevant to him in comparison to the content he was determined to get through.

That is an extreme example, in fact, the only time that it ever happened to me. But it says something about why we get paralyzed. Some of us are afraid that if we say anything about Christ, the person we are sharing with will think we are just like that guy at the shopping center. And Satan has been very, very effective in making us think of the worst possible examples every time we try to say something about Jesus. Too many times people will excuse themselves from witnessing, saying, "Hey, I would witness, but I just can't. You seek, I love people." There is something wrong with that view of evangelism! Love and evangelism are not mutually exclusive!

"They'll Think I'm a Fanatic"

A second problem is that we are afraid of being identified as religious fanatics. And I have to say that this is very true of me. What I began to see was that the way people saw me mattered more to me than how God saw me. That is part of what I had to die to. Ironically, I have found that people respect and respond to you much more when you have definite ideas and communicate them clearly, than when you are wishy-washy and apologetic.

I think I got the best perspective on this problem when I did undergraduate work in Spain. All these Marxists would come down in the student cafeteria to pass out pamphlets, and they were so bold and evangelistic. I, on the other hand, was embarrassed; I didn't want anybody to know I was a Christian, and I thought it was because I didn't want to offend. Actually, it was because I didn't want to be rejected.

At the time, I had a roommate who was very cynical about spiritual things. I had been a Christian only about a year, and one day while I was having my quiet time, she walked in unexpectedly.

She asked, "What are you reading?"

I quickly slammed my Bible shut, put it under a bunch of books and answered, "Nothing."

Again she asked, "What are you reading?"

I said, "Nothing."

"Becky, tell me, what are you reading?"

"All right...the Bible." Now, I behaved this way so she wouldn't think I was strange!

It hit me as I contrasted that rather neurotic behavior with the Marxists' boldness and excitement. I learned the difference between exposing a value and imposing a value. What frees us from the fear of being religious fanatics is realizing that we are not called to impose our faith. We really can't impose it on anybody. All we are called to do is just *expose* it — "This is who I am! Come and see! Be a part! It's really an adventure!" Expose people to what really means so much to you.

"I Can't Change My Personality!"

Another fear that I have had is that if I shared my faith, I'd have to develop a different kind of personality. I thought of people who witnessed as those who were pushy, a little obnoxious and weren't afraid to "mow them down for Jesus." But that wasn't me. And it took me a long time before I began to see that God is glorified in the context of my personality. I had to learn how to develop a style of witnessing that truly reflected Becky, not someone else, no matter how effective he was. God has given each of us unique gifts and personalities.

One of the things that stymied me, however, was waiting for someone to come along with "the new jelled approach" that would work on one and all or your money back! You know what I finally realized? Even if I found such an approach, it still wouldn't work, because the problem in evangelism is not that we don't have enough information; the problem in evangelism is that we don't know how to be ourselves. We haven't grasped that it is okay to be who we are. When we are asked about cults, and we haven't got a clue to the answer, we can say so. We can say to someone, "Boy, am I glad God has brought you into my life. You're going to sharpen me intellectually." We don't have to be intimidated. God can use us in our weakness as we trust the Holy Spirit's control.

Have you ever really wanted to share the gospel with a friend and then hesitated because you were afraid you would turn that friend off? Most of us have had that experience. In light of that, have you said to that friend, "You know, I really would love to tell you about my faith in Christ, but I am so afraid I will turn you off that I just hesitate saying anything at all." Most people I've talked with haven't thought to do that, but I think they'd be amazed at the response.

One time I was talking to a friend of mine, and I admitted how afraid I was. "You know," I told her, "I don't like Bible-bangers; I don't like people who are shoving something down someone's throat. If I'm coming on too strong, please let me know."

My friend said, "I never knew that Christians were aware that we hate being the recipients of nonstop, running monologs," which was a commentary on my style in that situation!

I said, "Listen, the main reason Christians don't share their faith is that they are afraid of turning people off."

She responded, "Well, then, why don't they say so? As long as you say so, we suddenly realize you are just like us." The irony is that then she said, "Okay, Becky, tell me more about your faith — I have become interested." And the bond whereby I shared my faith in Christ was when we both agreed that we didn't like the wrong kind of evangelism, which we both agreed I had just been doing. She saw that I was normal after all, and then she became interested in how God made a difference in this normal person's life. Therefore, don't sacrifice one of your most important tools of evangelism by not being yourself.

"I'm Not 'Together' Enough"

I think we are sometimes paralyzed because we think we have to be perfect before we can say anything. High school kids especially struggle with this feeling, though we all do to some extent. How can I share Christ when I don't have my life "together" as I would like it to be?

Stephanie was the second person I ever saw come to Christ. One day she said, "Becky, I want you to know what it is about you that moved me to faith. I want you to know specifically what you did." I told her that I would love to know! She continued, "First, I got to know you and really liked you. I found out that you were religious and I thought it was okay as long as you kept it to yourself. Then you invited me over for a meal and asked me if it was okay if you prayed for the food. I thought, 'Oh, isn't that a cute medieval custom that she has kept.' Only you didn't just thank God for the food, you thanked Him for me! I had never heard anyone pray, much less say my name out loud. That touched me. I thought, 'This is ridiculous — thanking Somebody who doesn't exist for me.' But it touched me, though I didn't know why. I almost felt like crying.

"A little bit later you invited me to a movie and mentioned afterward that you studied that very thing that day in the Bible. I remember making fun of you for reading your Bible, because I really thought at the time, 'What's in that Book that has anything in common with modern cinema?' You kept taking me along in parts of your life, and somehow the gospel kept applying.

"Then you asked me to a no-strings-attached study of the person of Jesus, where people who did not believe explored the Bible and learned about who Jesus was. I thought, 'Fine, I'll go. What do I have to lose? It will be fun.' The problem was, I started to like Jesus. My thoughts kept turning to God every time I was by myself — and for an atheist, that can be rather unsettling!

"All my life, I used to think, 'How could anybody say, "I'm a Christian," as if he were saying, "I'm so together; I'm so perfect" ?'And then I got to know you! The first shock was that you really blew it sometimes, just like I did. The second shock was that you could admit it, and I couldn't. I used to think that being a Christian meant that you never failed — that you swung from one victory to the next. You showed me that being a Christian means you know where to go with your brokenness; you know where to go with your failure; you have the courage to face your failure. So, Becky, even your confession of weakness drove me to Jesus."

One of the most powerful tools in evangelism is how we deal with our failure, how we deal with our brokenness, and knowing that there is a God who forgives.

But I have to tell you that when I first heard this, I thought to myself, "I knew I should never have let her get to know me, because she is seeing all my flaws." It's a struggle because, especially in America, you always have to be on top. But I realized that although Jesus is not glorified by sin, He is glorified by weakness — and there is a difference. I began to see that when I let her inside my life, when I let her see me as I really was — the flaws and the successes — she saw God through it all.

Ironically, at the times when I tried to appear together, in charge and in control, never acknowledging a fear or problem, I'm afraid she could see only Becky. I had to learn from experience what 1 Thessalonians 2:8 tells us: "We . . . impart to you not only the gospel of God but also our own lives. . . ." We have got to allow people into our lives to see how Jesus is our Lord both when we fail and when we succeed. If you have not grasped that you are free to be authentic, I am afraid you are going to see evangelism as a project and not as a lifestyle. I am afraid you are going to see evangelism as a category that you "go and do" and then return to normal living. Evangelism occurs when you let people in to where you live — allowing them to see Jesus as Lord in your life.

FREEDOM TO SHARE CHRIST NATURALLY

What can we do that will free us from our fears? How can we develop a style of evangelism that is natural for each of us as individuals, yet effective? Let's look at several communication models that I think can help.

Investigate, Stimulate, Relate

First, we must *investigate* — find out about the person to whom we are speaking. We need to row around people as if they are an island and we are in a rowboat seeking an approximate point to land. Find out how God has made you alike. Don't begin by finding out how you are different. Ask questions, get inside their lives. In so doing, you develop empathy. Don't be so eager to get your message across that you fail to find out about the person to whom you are speaking.

Next, after we investigate, then we *stimulate*. We need to learn how to arouse curiosity about the gospel. Paul said in Acts 26:18 that he was called to the Gentiles "to open their eyes so that they may turn from darkness to light . . . in order that they may receive forgiveness of sins. . . ." Paul implied that he was first called to arouse curiosity — to open their eyes, to make them want to hear. How do you arouse curiosity? Jesus and Paul did it in very different ways. Paul was very "cerebral"; to the Thessalonian Jews, he said, "I argued, I persuaded, I proved, I reasoned." Jesus aroused curiosity by throwing out very provocative statements. To the woman at the well in John 4, He talked about living water.

"But you don't have a bucket," she said.

"Oh, I don't need a bucket. It boils up to eternal life — you never have to come here to draw."

"What?"

So what is He doing? He isn't hunting; He's fishing — just reeling her in. She gets more and more fascinated by this water.

In John 3, Jesus talks with Nicodemus, the prominent ruler and Pharisee.

"Nicodemus, you must be born again."

"I don't get it."

"I know, that's why I said it."

We tend to overkill with words. We need to be more provocative. Throw out something tantalizing. Fish! See how they respond. And the reason it is so important is that if they get curious, they are going to want to hear.

One of the best ways to stimulate curiosity is through the witness of community. If the kids in your youth group love each other, and if you teach them how to love the people that they bring into their meetings, it is the foundation of evangelism. You can break every rule in communication, but if you love, you are home free. Believe me, the non-believer will be stimulated when he comes to your meeting and observes, "Look how they love one another —

and how they love me."

After you investigate and stimulate, then you *relate*. Once you know who you are speaking to, once you have aroused their curiosity, you can share the reason for the hope that is within you, and they will want to hear.

Let me give you one example of how investigating, stimulating and relating work in actuality. See if you can observe the distinctions in the flow of this situation.

When I first started working as a staff worker with Inter-Varsity, I flew from Portland, where I was assigned, to Chicago. I sat down in the plane by an intellectual-looking man in a tweed jacket and glasses. It turned out that he was a professor at a very good university. We were talking about all kinds of things when he said, "By the way, Becky, what do you do for a living?"

I said, "Ah, well, I'm in Christian work" — in a way that sounded apologetic. I could see the look on his face: "Funny — she looked reasonably intelligent. Who would have thought it?"

"Well, what's the name of your little organization?"

So I said very proudly, "Inter-Varsity Christian Fellowship." He had a strange expression, and I asked, "What is it?"

"No, never mind."

I prodded, "No, really, go ahead. What is it?"

"Becky, I hope you don't mind my saying this, but you just don't look like a Christian athlete."

I really thought he was kidding. So I said, "Yes, well, I play basketball for Jesus. You know, it's a living!"

"Well, I'm sure it must be very rewarding."

He believed me! You don't know how tempted I was to play along with what he was expecting. However, with uncommon restraint, I said, "No, actually playing basketball for Jesus — that was a joke. Sometimes we make jokes." But I picked it up and continued. "You asked me if it is rewarding. Actually, that isn't the first word that comes to my mind. It is terribly *intriguing*."

"Intriguing? Why is it intriguing?"

His curiosity had been aroused through the use of provocative words. This man, who did not intend to have a spiritual discussion with me, found he couldn't help it. His curiosity had been aroused, and he wanted to know why it was so intriguing.

Another way to arouse curiosity is to ask yourself when you are speaking to someone, "What is his greatest point of resistance to the Christian faith?" Then you mention it before he does. In this case, I thought he would probably have questions about the intellectual basis for faith. So that is what went through my mind when he asked, "Why is it so intriguing?"

"I'll tell you why it is so intriguing to me. I work with very bright students, I work at Reed College; it's one of those academic private colleges where every day we have to deal with the question, 'How do we know Christianity is true? How do we know that we are not taking our own little world and labeling it reality? How do we know we're not worshiping some glorified version of our father figure?'"

"Becky, you are not going to believe this! Those questions were going through my mind!"

"Oh, for heaven's sake!"

"All right, how do you know it's true?"

This man was an historian and a scholar. So we began discussing the historical evidence for the faith — why the New Testament documents were historically reliable, why Jesus and not Buddha, and on and on. Then he said, "Becky, I want to say something to you. I am committed to scholarship, but in the conversation we have been having, I realize that as a child I blindly accepted Christ's Christianity. As an adult, I blindly rejected it. For the sake of intellectual integrity, I need to know what I have rejected, and I want you to know that I am going to investigate the credentials of Christianity with an adult critical mind. But I want you to know what it is about you that really strikes me. You seem to be a woman of hope and not despair, and I would like to know why."

"Well, you see, sir, the reason I am a woman of hope and not despair is that I am a woman who has fallen hopelessly in love with Jesus. I am not the same; I am new." I had spent much time *investigating* and *stimulating;* now was my opportunity for *relating* the reason for the hope that is within me. If I had not done the first two, I do not think I would have had the audience to share that message of hope.

Relationship, Belief, Knowledge

There is another model I would like to suggest, and that model is relationship, belief and knowledge. *Relationship* means that you are just asking basic questions that pertain to a person's life. You are building an acquaintance. In the process, a person's system of *beliefs* emerges. It is possible that the conversation can degenerate into argument, if you both have beliefs that are diametrically opposed. For example, somebody says, "I think that born-again movement is ridiculous." Instead of jumping to the defense, I find it best to ask merely, "Why?" That way, I move from the area of beliefs into the area of *knowledge*, identifying sources of authority. "Why is it that you think the born-again movement is so ridiculous? I am really fascinated. Tell me about it." If you ask him to reveal his source of authority, then he is probably going to ask you the same question. That is one way to keep the conversation from degenerating into argument and to provide you opportunity to present the gospel in a situation that otherwise could become a "lost cause."

General to Specific

The final model for communicating the gospel has four levels. Picture four concentric circles. The outer circle is *general interest questions*. Moving in, the next circles are *specific interest questions, abstract or philosophical questions*, and finally, in the center is *theological questions*. Here is an example of how I get from the general interest questions to theological issues, moving from a natural conversation to a spiritual one.

I was talking with a student. I said, "Hi, what is your major? [General interest question.]

"Art."

"Oh, I love art. Tell me more. What is your area of interest; what do you like?" [Specific interest questions.]

She began telling me about it.

Then I said, "Tell me something. Why is it that you major in art?" [Specific interest question.]

"Because I love beauty."

"Yes! I do too. Let me ask you something. I had a professor who began every biology class by saying, 'Man is nothing more than a meaningless piece of protoplasm — a fortuitous concourse of atoms.' Do you think a fortuitous concourse of atoms could appreciate beauty?" [Philosophical question.]

"That's very interesting. Where do I get my ability to appreciate beauty? I know I'm more than a machine. I don't think a machine could appreciate beauty, but I never asked myself that question before."

"You know something I think is interesting? What do you think is the source of beauty? What is the source from whence all beauty comes?" [Theological question.]

"You mean like God?" she questioned.

"Oh, that's interesting!" Rather than just announcing my opinions, through the use of focused questions I wanted to try to help her recognize, on her own, that she was able to appreciate beauty because she was made in the image of God. These questions can be effective in helping a person turn a surface-level conversation into a conversation about Christ.

GOD CAN USE *YOU*

To summarize these principles about sharing Christ, I will conclude by describing the thing that changed me the most — finally seeing someone come to Christ. It was one of the most terrifying experiences of my life. I was a student in Spain, had been a

Christian about two years, and had never seen anyone come to Christ. One day my roommate, who was a very mature Christian, said, "Becky, why don't you ever lead people you talk to about Christ across the goal line? You need to being them to Christ."

"Ruth, I don't know how. I'm not very good at it."

"Becky," she said, "you need to do it."

Just to show Ruth that my friends were too difficult to ever lead to Christ, I decided that I would ask the one person of all my friends who I thought was the most unlikely to ever become a Christian. I had been leading an evangelistic Bible study class all year, and one of the guys who came was named Martin. He was a friend, but he was also the most obnoxious human being I had ever met. He would come every week just to tantalize me and put me down. Martin would certainly prove my point.

One day after an exam, we were sitting in a restaurant, and I said, "Martin, let me say something. You have received a lot of information about Christianity. Some day, some year, way down the pike, God is going to speak to you and ask you what you are going to do about it." (Pressure tactics? Who, me?) I continued, "Now when that time comes, I hope you say yes to God."

And he said, "Becky, I could never become a Christian. I'm not good enough."

That response amazed me, coming from Martin. "Martin, of course you're not good enough. We just studied the crucifixion — He died because we are not good enough."

"Oh, yeah, I forgot. Well, how about 'I'm so young. I've got so many good years left. Think of all the fun I'd miss.'"

So we discussed whether or not this lifestyle of his really brought him joy. All this time, even though I was terrified of the responsibility of leading someone to Christ, I was confident that Martin was a long way off, at best. So I said again, "Some year, some time, God is going to speak to you, and when He does, I hope you say yes."

"Becky, He just did, and I decided yes."

"That's what I mean, Martin. And some year, some time, some day — I beg your pardon? What did you say?"

"Becky, as you were speaking, it was clear as a bell. God said, 'Martin, NOW.' And I decided yes."

"Oh, no, you haven't. No, no, no. That isn't possible!"

"Why?"

"Well, Martin, I don't think you have thought this through enough!" And I went on and on about all the things I thought he needed to reconsider.

Finally, he said, "Becky, I want to become a Christian now!"

"Well, I'm sorry, I can't help you."

"Why not?"

"Martin, I've never done anything like this before."

"Well, Becky, don't worry — I haven't either!"

"But I don't know what to do!"

"All right, here's what you do," Martin instructed. "You kind of kick it open with a prayer, and then I'll pray, and you wrap it up. It will be over before you know it."

"Okay, but I'm so embarrassed," I confessed.

"Just do it fast."

So I prayed, and he prayed, and I have to confess to you I really thought nothing had happened. "Now Martin, it doesn't matter that you don't feel any different, because it is a decision of the will, not of the emotions. But I am just wondering . . . do you feel any different?"

"Oh, Becky, yes!"

"Oh, Martin! Oh, my goodness! It works!"

So we went racing home to "show" Ruth! But I have to confess in shame that I still didn't think it was a real conversion.

The phone rang, and it was my best friend, Stephanie. Martin said, "Let's all go out together, but don't tell her what has happened."

So we got together at a restaurant again, and Stephanie, who was also in the Bible study, said (if you can believe this!), "You know, Martin, I am just sitting here looking at you, and you have really changed. I don't know what it is — you just seem happier, more at ease. I think Spain must really agree with you."

I remember Martin saying, "It's not Spain, Love, it's Jesus!"

"Oh, that is *not* funny! Don't joke like that in front of Becky. That is so rude!"

"I'm not kidding; I'm a Christian."

"Right. I'm Santa Claus! Give me a break!"

"I'm not kidding! Becky and I are brother and sister in the Lord." He put his arm around me.

"Wait a minute. Are you serious? Did you do this?"

"Yes!"

"That is the most depressing bit of information I have ever had in my life. Martin, if you can become a Christian, anyone can become a Christian."

Well, Martin started really speaking to her with great force, and he said, "You know it's true, and I know it's true — I just had the character to do something about it." Martin's great gift was never humility.

So we left, and she was shell-shocked! She went back to my apartment to spend the night with me. And before bed, Stephanie said, "Becky, I want to ask you something. If somebody wanted to become a Christian, what would he do?" And I thought, "I'm too young for this." I panicked inside. Then, I'll never, never forget this.

She looked at me and said, "Becky, all my life I have been running *away from* God. Would you help me run *to* Him, please?" And in a way I never knew with Martin, we prayed. I knew my very best friend had just been converted before my eyes.

It was a life-changing experience. Five people in our Bible study became Christians, and they, in turn, led others to the Lord. When I said good-bye to Stephanie six weeks later, there was still a lot of baggage. She smoked and drank, but she loved Jesus! Five years later, I went back to England where she lived. Stephanie met me. She still had that same fun and spunk, but she had become a godly woman. I couldn't get over it; and she had married a wonderful godly man. Two years later, they gave birth to my godchild — Dominique!

When Dominique was four, I had the privilege of returning to England. It was Easter Sunday, and I had little Dominique on my lap. I said, "Dominique, someday I am going to tell you about the bond your mother and I have and how much we love Jesus."

And she said, "You don't have to tell me that. I know Jesus — I love Him! Mother introduced me to Him."

And I just held her and wept and said, "Jesus, I can't believe this is true — that I would share my faith and someday inherit a grand-daughter."

There are Stephanies and Martins out there. Your high schools are full of them — people who hunger for Jesus, people who seem unreachable waiting to be reached. My prayer for you is that God will use you to help change the world and to communicate the message that while Jesus radically transforms us, He leaves us more ourselves than we ever dreamed possible.

PUTTING THIS CHAPTER TO WORK

1. How's your fire? Becky says that evangelism starts with a vi-brant relationship to Christ which is like a fire within us. What can you do to "fan the flame," making His warmth more notice-able to others?

2. Are you a "Rabbit-hole Christian"? List the names of the non-Christians you see regularly. Does your list include young people?

3. Specify some ways that you can let people "into your life" or that you can be more a part of theirs. There are probably some leadership students that would be influenced if they saw you up close. Are there some "lepers" you need to hug, as Jesus did, or some people like Bill who need a "glimpse of grace"? How could you do that?

4. List some people with whom you want to share Christ, but with whom you are hesitant or even afraid. If honesty can be as effective as Becky says, write down what you might say to one of these people.

5. Do you know any Martins or Stephanies? Who is the most unlikely person to receive Christ that you know? Should you think about talking to that person? How could you begin?

8

HELPING STUDENTS SHARE CHRIST

by Chris Renzelman

When I was in college, I had no desire to go into full-time Christian work. In fact, that was the last thing I wanted to do. But through an experience in which my life was on the line, the Lord caused me to think about my priorities. I was stranded in a snowstorm for nine and a half hours, and I really didn't know if I'd make it out alive. With the chill factor at 35° below zero and no vehicles around, I could not help but do a little serious thinking. One of the thoughts I had was, "If I should check out of life tonight, of all the things I had, what would make a difference — what would really matter to me?"

As I boiled my life down, I eliminated my Irish Setter, my girlfriend, my '64 Chevy, my college education, my parents, my family — if I died, all these things would matter no longer. The only thing left at the bottom of the barrel was what I had in my personal relationship with Jesus Christ. And I thought, "If I can boil life down to that level and that's the only thing that's going to make a difference, then in reality, that's the only thing worth living for. And if that is true for me, then it is also true for other people."

That experience was a turning point in my life that eventually drove me into involvement in full-time vocational ministry. I look forward to being in heaven someday, but it has occurred to me that, in the meantime, there is one thing I can do here that I won't be able to do there — share the good news of Jesus Christ with those who don't know Him. And for the past fourteen years I have been trying to do that by ministering to young people, the most responsive group to the gospel. Seven of those years have been with Campus Crusade for Christ, and the remaining seven have

Chris Renzelman is the director of student ministries for Highlands Community Church in Renton, Washington. He served with the high school ministry of Campus Crusade for Christ for seven years. Chris received a Bachelor of Arts in secondary education from the University of Northern Colorado. He is the vice president of Student Impact International and is also northwest regional coordinator of the National Network of Youth Ministries. He and his wife, Rebecca, have one daughter.

been at Highlands Community Church in Renton, Washington.

I have noticed some differences in working with those two different types of youth ministries. In working with an interdenominational group like Campus Crusade, we could say to the students, "All right everybody, here's who we are; here's where we're headed. Those of you who are committed to that same intent and purpose, follow us!" But when I came to the church, I found that it was the students who were saying, "All right, here we are. Now do something with us." There was quite an assortment of individuals. Some were there because their partents had made them come; some had always come; and some had the mentality, "I dare you to teach me anything that I don't already know — just try." So that was a rather radical shift for me. Yet I have found that in both ministries the challenge is still basically the same, "equipping the saints for the work of service..." (Ephesians 4:12).

FISHING — A BY-PRODUCT OF FOLLOWING

If our lives are going to make the kind of difference we pray they will make, then we must invest our lives in equipping others. We must help them develop what I discovered in the snowstorm to be the most valuable of all of life's possessions — their personal relationship with Jesus Christ. This is the ministry of evangelism and discipleship. It is so important that we commonly call it the Great Commission. Notice how Jesus begins the command. In Matthew 28:19, Jesus says, "Go ye"; but the phrase would be better translated, "as you are going." Our evangelism and discipleship are a product of a lifestyle. As we are going about our lives, we set the example of reaching out, winning others, discipling and building. That is why Jesus said in Mark 1:17, "Follow Me, and I will make you become fishers of men." Jesus wants us involved in evangelism, but notice He does not say, "Become a fisher of men and then follow Me." He is saying, "Follow Me. And the by-product of following Me is that I will make you become fishers of men."

Maybe it's difficult for you to picture your students as fishers of men — or even yourself, for that matter. Notice Acts 4:13. "Now as they observed the confidence of Peter and John, and understood that they were uneducated and untrained men, they were marvelling, and began to recognize them as having been with Jesus." So often we say, "Well, I'm not educated, I'm not trained." But what gave the disciples their boldness and confidence was their association with Jesus. We see this again in the Gospel of Mark:

> Jesus went up into the hills and called to Him those He wanted, and
> they came to Him. He appointed twelve — designating them apos-
> tles — that they might be with Him and that He might send them out
> to preach and to have authority to drive out demons
> (Mark 3:13-15, NIV).

His intent in calling them together was, first of all, that they might be *with* Him.

DEEPENING THEIR RELATIONSHIP WITH CHRIST

As we work with young people, one of our first objectives should be to get them into a *relationship* with the Lord, that they might get to know Him. It is this association, this relationship, that gives birth to ministry. After the disciples had been with Jesus, His intent was to "send them out to preach." And this He did. He trained them and sent them out in pairs (Mark 6:7).

The Cycle of Relationships

Notice the cycle of relationships. When we are secure in our relationship with Jesus, we have freedom to be accountable in a relationship with Christians. We also have a desire to build relationships with non-Christians, which, in turn, helps them come into a relationship with Christ! So it should be clear that if we want to start "the cycle," our students must first have a fresh relationship with Him. This comes, in part, by helping them get into the Word of God and apply it to life.

Front-line Thirstiness

Please note, as well, that this relationship is progressive. Developing a fresh relationship with Christ does not take place in a vacuum. You cannot hold students in reserve for fifteen years until they get the Bible memorized and then tell them, "Now you can begin to share your faith." I have found that there is a correlation between the intensity with which I study the Word and my being on the front lines.

I think one of the problems that we have in many churches is that we do not have people on the front lines. As a result, they have a tendency to develop a mentality that essentially says, "I've never had to use what I know, so why do I need to learn more? Maybe I know it all." But I find that once you get people on the front lines, all of a sudden they begin to realize they don't have the answers they thought they had. Then they come back with an added thirst to get into the Word, to do some research.

A book that is well worth your reading is Douglas Hyde's *Dedication and Leadership* (Notre Dame Press). Howard Hendricks, a noted Christian educator, says that every Christian worker should read this book every six months. The book describes methods that the Communists have used in building and training people. One of their basic principles is to get people on the front lines right away — discussing their beliefs with others and identifying them-selves with the cause. This is an excellent method to make them hungry to know more, because they graphically see their need.

As we get our young people on the front lines, they will begin to feel some of the burden that Jesus felt in Matthew 9. He traveled throughout the villages and cities, mixing with the people, "and seeing the multitudes, He felt *compassion* for them..." (Matthew 9:36). Howard Hendricks shares that one of the most helpful things to him has been his ministry with the Dallas Cowboys. He says he needs to get into a locker room every once in a while; he needs to hear some "hell's" and "damn's" to remind him why he is here. I think we all have a tendency to get wrapped up in our "holy huddles," and we forget some of the need that is there. One of the ways to gain a greater burden is to be out there among people.

Loving His Sheep

I used to walk up on the hillside when I lived in Bellevue, Washington, and say, "Lord, I love You. Give me a burden for people." And I would look out at the many houses and the glittering city lights at night and pray fervently about this. I struggled and tried to get a burden. Nothing really happened. Then one day I was reading in John 21, which records Jesus talking to Simon Peter. The conversation went something like this.

Jesus said, "Simon, do you love Me?"

"Lord, You know that I love You."

"Feed my lambs." Then He asked again, "Simon, do you love Me?"

"Well, I answered that once; Yes, Lord."

"Then take care of My sheep." He asked him a third time, "Simon, do you love Me?"

And in frustration, I think Simon Peter responded, "You know all things — *Yes*, Lord!"

"Then feed My sheep."

Never once in that passage did Jesus ask Peter if He loved sheep. He asked, "Do you love Me? Then, if you love Me, you will take care of the sheep." Again, that comes back to our relationship with Him. If we have fallen in love with the Lord, our hearts become His. And if our hearts are truly His, we will spend time with the sheep. Spending time with the sheep increases our burden for them and motivates us to a deeper walk with Christ as well.

DEVELOPING A VISION FOR OUTREACH

The second way we must help our students achieve long-range effectiveness in sharing Christ is to help them develop a clear vi-sion for how God can use them. Basically, vision is seeing what needs to be done. People need to get a picture of what needs to be accomplished.

Preparing the Way Through Prayer

A beautiful illustration of that is in Nehemiah 1. Nehemiah heard the report of the people, it struck his heart, and he went to the Lord in prayer. That time of fasting and praying kindled his vision for what he could do, and he became personally available. I believe that much of evangelism takes place in prayer. What we often label as evangelism is merely picking up the spoils of a battle that has already been won. I believe this is one of the reasons that people like Bill Bright, President of Campus Crusade for Christ, can walk up to someone and say, "Are you a Christian?"

"No."

"Would you like to become a Christian?"

"Yes."

I don't have that happen often, but I've heard that from him many times. Prayer prepares the way for the gospel (Colossians 4:2-6), and it also makes our hearts sensitive to those people with whom God would have us share. That gives us confidence that God is going to lead us to the right people and enable us to say the right things.

A youth pastor friend of mine recently shared how prayer is helping him overcome his fear of evangelism. He has sought out a number of senior citizens who have committed themselves to be his prayer warriors. In fact, as a single man, he is now sharing a house with a 79-year-old lady who is a prayer warrior of his. He told me, "It's refreshing to wake up in the morning and see her in the living room on her knees, just pouring her heart out before the Lord." I think that when we get to heaven, we are going to be a little shocked at some of those to whom God gives acknowledgement. We never will have heard of them, but they will have done some mighty battle in prayer.

Knowing Where to Start

Vision has to have ownership. Students may run on your vision initially, but you need to help them develop their own vision. That will come about progressively as they spend time doing the work of the ministry, internalizing Scripture and developing convictions within their own hearts. One of the things I do is to study Acts 1:8 with my students: "But you shall receive power when the Holy Spirit has come upon you; and you shall be My witnesses both in Jerusalem, and in all Judea, and Samaria, and even to the remotest part of the earth." We try to approach this verse in such a way that students can begin to envision it in terms of their world.

When we talk about reaching their high school campus, that's the "remotest part of the earth" to them. It's unheard of; there is no way they could do that.

We try to determine what is the "remotest part of the earth" for them, what is their "Samaria," their "Judea," their "Jerusalem." We try to help them narrow their Jerusalem down to a sphere of influence of about three or four people. One student's "Jerusalem" might be a fellow junior, and the "remotest part of the earth" for him might be the junior class. He may have a chemistry class, which might be his Samaria. In the chemistry class may be fifteen students from the junior class. And out of those fifteen students, three of them are his lab partners.

So I try to help my students begin to get a picture of what needs to be done. That is the definition of vision. You can use this process with athletic teams and any other natural grouping. Narrow their scope; get them to begin praying specifically for one, two, or three people. Who is their Peter, James, and John whom God would raise up for them to begin pouring their lives into? Students need to have their visions stretched, but they don't need to be blown away. Give them a picture of what needs to be done, but help them know where to begin.

Stepping Outside the Comfort Zone

Oftentimes, the things that God calls us to do are the things that we write off because we think they are impossible. Yet those are the very things that God wants to do through us for that very reason — we cannot do them in our own strength. We have to trust Him entirely. Consider how God deals with Moses in this same kind of situation described in Exodus 3. God says to Moses, "I want you to lead the children of Israel out of Egypt." Moses responds, "No way!" We may criticize him for his response, but think about it. Population-wise it would be like taking the city of Denver and moving it to Nebraska! "And by the way," God said, "you'll all have to walk — there are no cars or planes yet." That's quite a vision God tried to impart to Moses. I bet you also would have said, "No way!"

But God didn't give up on Moses. Note how He brought the vision down to earth for Moses. He started with what was familiar and comfortable to him.

> And the Lord said to him, "What is that in your hand?" And he said, "A staff." Then He said, "Throw it on the ground." So he threw it on the ground, and it became a serpent; and Moses fled from it. But the Lord said to Moses, "Stretch out your hand and grasp it by its tail..." (Exodus 4:2-4a).

Moses, I think, went through a process of logical thinking here. "All right, it was a staff, and I saw God change it in front of my eyes. He told me to throw it down, now He tells me to pick it up — it's a little risky, but I think I can do it." Then, I believe he very cautiously reached down and picked it up.

What God did at that point was to move Moses out of his "comfort zone." Likewise, growth will take place in our lives and in the lives of students when we have to venture beyond our comfort zones. It's interesting that as God prepared Moses to leave, He said, "Now, Moses, don't forget your staff." God allowed him to keep that as a reminder of what God had already done. That gave Moses confidence to step out into hard areas and to do the things he had not done before. But later in Scripture, God tells Moses to use his hand — not his staff. It's as if God is saying, "Now, Moses, I want to wean you off of that staff. It is not a magic wand; it is I who is doing these things."

We see in the life of Moses that as he allowed God to stretch him, that which seemed impossible became something that was accomplished. As you work with students, help them to bring that vision down to something that becomes tangible — something specific to pray about, something to trust God for. That way vision becomes something that they can picture, something that is approachable. Likewise, in our own lives I think we need to be asking ourselves the question, "What can I be doing now that is tough, something I haven't done before, to nudge myself just outside my comfort zone?" That is the way growth will take place.

Multiplication Adds Up!

When it comes to evangelism, one thing we need to give our students a vision for is how to use their time to produce the greatest possible result. We need to teach them the difference between multiplication and addition. Let's imagine you have a very mature student named Steve who likes to speak. He hears one of your talks on the need for evangelism and wants to start sharing the Lord. So he goes downtown, stands on a street corner, and begins proclaiming the gospel. To his surprise, a crowd gathers, God moves, and more than 1,000 people say yes to the Lord. Significant!

Now Steve is pumped up. He says, "Wow! The Lord used me today; I'm going to do that tomorrow." The next day he gets the same response. He continues, and every day he sees 1,000 people trust Christ. Considering his newly discovered gift, he sets up an organizational structure and travels around the country putting on crusades. Let's assume he could continue winning an average of 1,000 people to Christ every day — that's pretty preposterous, but who knows how God may use the influence of your ministry!

Now let's say that Dave, a friend of Steve's, also makes a commitment to share his faith. But in the first year he sees only three people come to know the Lord. He is a little intimidated by Steve, but he sticks with his three friends, helps them get grounded in their faith, and helps them learn how to share Christ, also. They each win three people to Christ, so that in the second year there are 16 of them altogether. Steve has seen 730,000 come to Christ in that same two years. But Dave remains faithful and in five years, due to the multiplication chain he initiated, more than 1,000 have come to Christ. Steve, on the other hand, has won almost two million in five years!

At this rate, it may seem that it would take a long time for multiplication to catch up with addition. But if both Steve and Dave remained faithful to their methods and the statistics remained consistent, how long do you think it would take each one to reach the present world population of 4.5 billion? Dave's chain of multipliers would reach it in a little over 16 years. Steve, however, even at the rate of 1,000 per day would need over *12,000 years* to reach the same number! Obviously, we don't have that kind of time! Though we praise God for those who come to Christ through addition, it is obvious that addition alone will not reach the world. That is why Jesus equipped His men with a mindset toward multiplication as the means of fulfilling His Great Commission.

As you illustrate the difference between addition and multiplication for your young people, they will begin to get a vision for how an enormous goal like the Great Commission can be brought into perspective. When you begin to talk about faithfully pouring your life into two or three people and teaching them to do the same, you begin to make the vision tangible for them. Suddenly, it becomes approachable — though still on the edge of their comfort zone!

COMMUNICATING THEIR TESTIMONY

A Consistent Christian Life

A third ingredient which will help to produce an evangelistic lifestyle in our students is a personal testimony. We think of a testimony as a form of verbal communication, and it is; but words are meaningless if they are not accompanied by a consistent Christian life. Educators tell us that as much as 85 percent of communication is nonverbal. That is why people say, "What you are speaks so loudly, I can't hear a word that you say." Jesus said it in Matthew 7:15-17, "You will know them [people] by their fruits....every good tree bears good fruit; but the rotten tree bears bad fruit."

In John 15, Jesus said that we will bear fruit if we abide in Him.

I'm sure you have never seen a fruit tree that had to strain to produce fruit. The tree merely does what it was meant to do. As the roots continue to receive nourishment, fruit is produced as a natural by-product. Likewise, as we abide in Christ, the fruit in our lives that naturally results will be an attractive, essential backdrop for the gospel.

I had three young men in my office recently. One of them was a non-believer, the other two were Christians. In the course of the conversation, I did something rather radical. I asked the non-Christian, "What have you seen in the lives of these two other men that would cause you to want to become a Christian?"

He said, "Well, nothing against them, but I haven't seen anything."

We talked about it, but it was very sobering.

How about you? Ask yourself the question, "If you were on trial today for being a Christian, would there be enough evidence to convict you?" Our answer matters a great deal, because it affects the lives of all the young people with whom we have contact.

I cannot overemphasize the importance of modeling. Paul said in 1 Corinthians 11:1, "Be imitators of Me just as I also am of Christ." Frankly, I don't always like what I see in some of the students with whom I work; I have a tendency to be critical until I observe that the things I am critical of are often the very things that I do myself. As I have learned with my own child, kids model what they see. That's why a fresh relationship with Christ is so important. It is the only way they will ever see Jesus in us. I know I've got a way to go.

Caring Enough to Verbalize

But we need to do more than nonverbal modeling. There needs to be the verbal — a good witness is willing to talk. 1 Peter 3:15 says, "But sanctify Christ as Lord in your hearts, always being ready...to give an account for the hope that is in you...." I translate that to mean, "Know your personal testimony."

Can you imagine Jesus coming down to the earth, spending three years with people, and never sharing with them why He came? Can you picture Jesus allowing people to follow Him and observe what He did, yet never verbalizing to them His purpose? Suppose that at the end of His life, His men had come up to Him and said, "Jesus, tell us, why did You come?" What if He would have said, "Men, I'm sorry, I can't tell you. It's personal." Things would be a lot different today! Sometimes I think we have that mentality. People may observe a difference, but they cannot always put the picture together. However, as we begin to verbalize it, the reason for the difference begins to come into focus.

A major emphasis for us in training our students is helping them develop the presentation of their personal testimony. I have each of my students take a blank sheet of paper, sit down with one other person, and casually share how he came to know the Lord. What was his life like? The person who is listening takes notes and gives them to the person who shared; then the process is reversed. Next, he takes his notes and rewrites them in a structure that deals primarily with three areas: (1) What was his life like *before* he had a relationship with Christ? (2) *How* did he come to know Christ? and (3) What has his life been like *since* he came to know Christ?

I assist the students in working through the structure, helping them to be as specific and clear as possible. When they are through writing their testimony, I have them edit it down to about three minutes and memorize it. After they get comfortable with it, we film their presentations on a video camera so that they can observe how they come across. Then, as time goes along, I try to give them an opportunity to share their testimonies with the entire church congregation. Be sure to give your own students opportunities like that to use what they have developed.

One of the best testimony presentations that we have had in a church service was by one of our high school gals. I asked her to share, and later she said, "I've got to review that tape!" She went through the video tape for three hours, and when she was through, she went into the empty sanctuary and even practiced speaking from the pulpit. When her turn came on Sunday morning, she did a super job. It is worth the effort to help train them, because as they gain confidence in this one area, it helps them in other areas as well, including their confidence in witnessing. It gives them something they can always use, either in an abbreviated or expanded form.

OBSERVING YOUR WITNESS

Another important ingredient that I'm sure you will agree is essential for witnessing is non-Christian friends! We must get our believers out of the "holy huddle" and we need to set the example. Outside of casual acquaintances, how many non-Christian *friends* do you have? List them in your mind. The general pattern among many Christian workers is to be so caught up in their own world of Christian ministry that they do not have many non-Christian friends. I recently talked to a youth pastor who admitted that he didn't have any. If our students are going to learn about evangelism, we must be demonstrating to them that we are meeting and spending time with non-believers. Even if your students don't always see you with them, ask them to pray for specific friends for whom you are burdened.

I have a non-Christian friend who is a band teacher in one of the high schools. I have gone on his band tour for three years. At first, he was a little leery of me, but now, we have a good friendship. We have talked about spiritual things, but he hasn't come to know the Lord yet. When his name comes up, I tell the kids, "Keep praying for him; he is one of my friends."

It is much easier to *talk* the work of the evangelist than to *do* the work of an evangelist. Yet nothing will train our students better in the area of evangelism than getting out there and doing it. Share "war stories" of what you have been through. Take them with you when you witness. Recently God has convicted me that I need to do this more often.

When new believers come into your group, rather than yanking them out of their friendships with non-Christians, help them reach out to them. Help them learn to talk about their changed lives with these friends, because this is probably one of the most prime times for Christians to influence their peers.

TRANSITIONING INTO THE GOSPEL

To this point, we have talked a lot about preparing to witness — the students' relationship with Christ, their vision, their personal testimony and their observation of you as a model. But now, let's focus on how we can help them learn to move into the presentation of the gospel.

Using Questions

One of the best tools for evangelism is to learn the art of asking questions. Go through Scripture and observe how Jesus used questions. G. Campbell Morgan's book, *The Great Physician*, gives some guidance here. It gives vignettes of Jesus' contact with several different people and shows how Jesus dealt with them as individuals.

There is one good exercise I like to do that gives insight into how to use questions. Split your group in half. Have one half leave the room. Tell the other half:

> I want you to engage in casual conversation with one person from the other group when they come back in. In the course of the conversation, I want you to find out some things: his middle name, whether his father is bald or not, whether the baldness is in the front or the back, what kind of toothpaste he uses, his brand of deodorant, etc. However, I don't want the other person to know what you're after. You have to engage in conversation and guide it to the point where you can find the information as naturally as possible.

It is fun to do, and it is a challenge. Through it, you begin to realize that by asking questions, you can guide conversations.

Guiding Conversations

One of the main things that we must begin to do is take leadership in conversations. That doesn't necessarily mean that you're talking all the time; in fact, you are asking questions to lead the *other* person to talk in different areas. Sometimes we are fearful about how awkward this would be. We may be thinking, "Okay, here I come." And we anticipate that the other person is thinking, "Yep, here comes a Christian, and I know what he's going to do — he's starting to make conversation, he's going to make transitions, and then comes the big question...." They're not thinking anything like that at all! They are just casually relating to you. Spiritual issues are very much a part of conversation in today's society. Don't be afraid of it. Make those transitions. Get into the gospel.

When I go on campus, or when I am otherwise in contact with secular kids, if someone asks me what I do, I don't say I'm a youth pastor right at first. I tell him I am a resource person. I find that if kids introduce me as their youth pastor, a lot of times a wall builds up that I have to work through. So I encourage them to introduce me as a friend of theirs.

"Well, what do you do?"

"Well, I'm a resource person."

"Oh. What's that?"

"Well, I work with people in developing their total lifestyle."

"Okay. What do you mean, exactly?"

"Well, I work with people in developing the mental dimension in their lives." I then talk about the mental — how we help people develop that important side of their lives. Then I say, "We also concentrate on the physical area. We believe that people need to be in good physical shape." I tell them about some of the things that we do here, including our wilderness camp. The third area I talk about is the social area; we talk about some things that we do socially to help build people.

Turning Conversations to Christ

Then I usually make a transition at this point. I say, "There is a fourth area a lot of people don't think about that is very vital to building the total person. It is the spiritual dimension in one's life. Now a lot of people write that off, yet I find that what happens in the spiritual area influences what happens in all three of the other areas. So rather than writing it off, I find it is a very crucial hinge for building a whole person. When you think about spiritual things, what do you think of?" And then you can begin to move into the gospel.

Utilizing Tools

There are a lot of tools you can use to present the gospel: the *Four Spiritual Laws,* the Navigator's *Bridge,* the *Roman Road, Steps to Peace With God,* and others. I would encourage you to train your students extensively in one of these tools. They can always expand from there. But at least they will know how to use something as a starting point. After they learn the tool, have them role-play it with another person, then share it with someone they don't know or someone they know is not a Christian. Get them out evangelizing, one way or another.

Special surveys are also helpful. We designed surveys for Easter and for Christmas that we tabulate and use. We surveyed all of the freshmen at one of the high schools one year.

Newspapers, like *Live Option, Issues and Answers* and *Olive Branch*, are helpful tools in introducing the gospel. Give an article to a person and ask him to read it. When you get back with him say, "What did you think of the article? Did it make sense to you? Have you experienced what the article presented in regard to a personal relationship with Christ? May I take a few minutes to share with you what would be involved in that?"

CREATING AN ENVIRONMENT FOR EVANGELISM

The environment you create for evangelism incorporates all of what you are trying to do in helping students share Christ. Different environments are created for different purposes. You need to have environments within your ministry that are specifically, regularly geared for evangelism. We have started something that is called Sunday Night Live — an environment in which students feel comfortable bringing their non-Christian friends because they know it is going to be geared for them, with a presentation of the gospel and an opportunity for them to receive Christ. We also have some retreats that are geared specifically for evangelism. I use the Sunday morning hours to train people in effective ministry. So use an environment that you already have, and modify it to do some of these things that need to be done.

We also have a wilderness camp that we use to get students out of the environment they are used to and into what we call the "classroom of creation." We specifically invite street kids from Seattle who are non-believers. During the camp, our Christian kids have a chance to relate to them, share Christ and have fun together. We also go to Mexico and Alaska to give them an environment that yields experience and vision.

DEVELOPING A SENSE OF URGENCY

We are reminded in 2 Peter 3 that the second coming of Jesus will be like a "thief in the night." Ephesians 6 reminds us that we are in a war. Both passages exhort us to action. We dare not be about business as usual. We need to analyze everything we are doing in light of what is urgent, what is priority and what yields a "payoff" spiritually. Without question, leading our students in evangelism ranks at the top of every one of those categories. The fruit of this labor is being able to say with John, "I have no greater joy than this, to hear of my children walking in the truth" (3 John 4).

For most of us, however, despite the urgency, the priority and the payoff, this area does not come easily. We find within ourselves a tremendous inadequacy, but 2 Corinthians 3:5 reminds us that we are not to look for adequacy within ourselves; "our adequacy is from God." He can enable us to model the lifestyle that will multiply the message of the gospel through our students to reach the world for Him.

PUTTING THIS CHAPTER TO WORK

1. If "fishing" is a byproduct of "following" (Mark 1:17), how would you evaluate your group as a whole in terms of the depth of their personal relationships with Christ?

2. Chris says that growth takes place when we are just outside of our "comfort zone." Where would that be for your students in the area of evangelism? Specify activities, etc., which would put them on the "front lines" in a way that would make them thirsty for growth.

3. Think through all of the ministry activities you are involved with. In the columns below, divide the activities between those that contribute toward addition to the body of Christ and those that contribute toward multiplication. If you see that you need a greater emphasis on multiplication, how should you begin?

Addition Activities	Multiplication Activities

4. Summarize briefly what you are currently doing to help students share their faith. Review the main points presented regarding vision, testimony, modeling, transitions, etc., and consider any changes you may want to make in the future.

9

STIMULATING SPIRITUAL INTEREST THROUGH CLASSROOM SPEAKING

by Bill Reif

Studies show that 95 percent of all who receive Christ do so by age 21. The potential for reaching today's young person is exciting — and yet it can also be overwhelming when we realize that the vast majority of American youth do not go to church, much less understand how to receive Christ.

How can we take advantage of this tremendous openness to the gospel? As outstanding as our church programs may be, only a few courageous non-Christians will come to an evangelistic event held at church. If we ever expect to make an impact on the youth culture, if we envision reaching many students for Christ, then we must orient our ministry to their world. We must go where non-Christian students are, we must try to understand them, and we must relate Christianity to their needs.

PAUL'S MINISTRY EXAMPLE

The apostle Paul is a good example of what I am talking about. Let's look in on his ministry at Athens.

> Now while Paul was waiting for them [Silas and Timothy] at Athens, his spirit was being provoked within him as he was beholding the city full of idols. So he was reasoning in the synagogue with the Jews and the God-fearing Gentiles, and in the marketplace every day with those who happened to be present. And also some of the Epicurean and Stoic philosophers were conversing with him. And some were saying, "What would this idle babbler wish to say?" Others, "He seems to be a proclaimer of strange deities" — because he was preaching Jesus and the resurrection. And they took him and brought him to the Areopagus, saying, "May we know what this new teaching is which you are proclaiming? For you are bringing some

---

Bill Reif has spoken to thousands of young people across America each year as a part of his speaking ministry. He served on the staff of Campus Crusade for Christ for ten years, speaking extensively as a traveling representative. Bill received a bachelors degree in history from Dennison University in Ohio. He has produced several audio and video tapes. Most recently, he was Minister to Youth at the First Presbyterian Church in Dothan, Alabama, where he currently resides with his wife, Linda.

strange things to our ears; we want to know therefore what these things mean." (Now all the Athenians and the strangers visiting there used to spend their time in nothing other than telling or hearing something new.) (Acts 17:16-21)

I think we can get some real insight as we look at Paul's approach to influencing his culture for Christ. First, notice that Paul was greatly distressed because the city was full of idols. He had a burden due to the state of the culture around him. We, too, must be burdened to reach the masses of young people around us with the good news of Jesus. We have every reason to be as distressed as Paul was because of the idols young people are choosing to pour their lives into today.

Next, notice that Paul reasoned in the synagogue with the Jews and the God-fearing Gentiles. These were the people who were somewhat religious, though they did not necessarily know God personally. I see a similarity here with those who come to my office at church and those who come to our youth group on Sunday mornings, Sunday evenings and Wednesday nights. These are my "God-fearing kids," and I spend a lot of time reasoning and talking with them. At our church, Sunday school is the hour that consistently brings out the most kids. So I hardly ever attempt to do any teaching per se because Sunday school is almost like an evangelistic meeting. I've got kids there who aren't believers, so that's when we get together and reason about the good news of Jesus and the impact that God can have in our lives.

A MODERN MARKETPLACE FOR YOUTH

Finally, we notice in verse 17 that Paul not only reasoned with those who called themselves "religious," but he also reasoned "in the marketplace every day with those who happened to be present." The high school campus is the marketplace of ideas in our youth culture today. And the main place on a campus where the ideas are kicked around is the classroom — just as in Acts 17:21, a place where people "spend their time doing nothing but talking about and listening to the latest ideas" (NIV).

There are a number of ways we can mix with young people in their environment, but I am convinced that one of the best ways today is to utilize the opportunities we have in the public classroom. Paul had an advantage. He didn't live in a so-called Christian nation as we do where we can't talk about Jesus! He had a lot of freedom to preach, as in Athens, and he spoke out boldly about the good news of Jesus. We're not going to have that kind of freedom in the classroom, but when handled properly, this forum can be used in a way that is completely legal, desirable and effective. It can be a means of getting inside the culture, gaining exposure, building credibility and introducing a Christian perspective.

THE BENEFITS OF CLASSROOM SPEAKING

Specifically, why is it so beneficial to utilize classroom speaking?

Countering the Philosophy of the World

First of all, it gives us an opportunity to meet the world's philosophy head-on in a way that can influence young people. Classroom speaking can be one of the most enjoyable things that you can ever do. It can also be as close to crucifixion as you may ever come! I began speaking in classrooms in 1973 in the San Francisco Bay area. My first classroom talk was in a two-hour sociology class that I shared with Pat Hurley, who is a real master in the classroom. We were asked to give the Christian perspective on sex and dating. One of the students, whose name was Ron, was *very* antagonistic. He had spent two days priming his fellow students on how to handle these two preachers.

After our talk, which lasted 30-40 minutes, we opened it up for questions. The students had obviously ignored everything we had said and basically were saying, "You guys are narrow-minded." It went on this way for about 15 minutes, and we were trying to answer questions, stay "mellow" and figure out what was going on. Then Ron raised his hand and, by his comments, revealed that he was an atheist. A little later, he raised his hand again and admitted that he was a homosexual. By this time, I was feeling pretty intimidated — and to top it off, the whole discussion was being video taped. I'm sure the camera caught my sweat! But somehow the Lord helped us to stay calm, and we just continued to answer questions as best as we could.

Pretty soon, instead of being antagonistic, the kids began to show a real interest in what we were saying. The change made Ron even more antagonistic, however, and he began to ask more questions. At one point, he went off on a long tirade about how Christians and their hang-ups were responsible for all the sexual problems that people have, for racial prejudice, and on and on and on! Finally, one of the kids stood up and said, "Ron, shut up," and sat down again.

I was supposed to return the next day to answer more questions. Ron met me at the door and said, "I don't know how you guys did it. I've watched the video tape three times, and I can't figure it out yet; I don't know how you guys did it." We really didn't do anything clever. All we did was try to be as honest and real with the kids as we could so that we could get into the marketplace of ideas and show how Christianity relates. Without being intimidated, without feeling that we had to preach, without feeling that we were there to proselytize, we just shared our ideas in the marketplace, and students began to respond.

When you go into a classroom, you're not really there to convince or to be a crusader against humanism. But Christianity will stand out when compared to the world's philosophy, and it is such a different perspective than what the kids are getting today that many non-Christians will sit up and take note. So will your Christian students.

Stirring Up Interest

Second, as we have just seen, being in a classroom stirs a great deal of interest. One of Francis Schaeffer's books stimulated me with the thought of attempting to lead people to a point of personal despair in their own philosophy; I'm sure that's a great deal of the reason that I came to Christ. But how can you lead a 16-year-old student to the point of despair in his personal philosophy? You probably won't do it through a philosophical conversation — that's pretty difficult to do with today's high school student. But you can walk into a classroom, dig down beneath the surface and, by using real-life situations, begin to relate to students the absurdity of their own life philosophy.

Sex and dating is a great subject to start with. I begin relating to the students by saying, "Here's what people are saying to you — do this, this, this and this. Everybody's doing it, but here's how it makes you feel. It makes you feel this way, this way and this way." And they sit there looking at each other saying, "This guy is uncool," but inside they're saying, "The guy's right." I can't evangelize in a classroom, but I *can* stir up a great deal of interest. I can't make someone drink; but I can make him thirsty. And if I make him thirsty enough, he'll go find water himself.

At the end of a classroom talk, if acceptable to the teacher, I usually use "comment cards," asking students to give me feedback on how they felt about the talk and giving them an opportunity to ask for a related article or personal appointment. Comment cards help me to find out who was really interested and to follow up with those students at their own invitation. For those of us who have found it challenging just to find non-Christian kids to meet, this is an excellent solution. Even if students don't fill out cards, when they see you around campus in the future, there may be opportunities to talk since they now recognize you and have a point of contact.

As I begin ministries in two new high schools, I am going to use classroom speaking to stimulate lots of interest, momentum and contacts. I am going to get into every classroom that I possibly can.

I'm going to use Christian doctors, lawyers and others in my community. I'm going to give them some simple training, help them put some talks together, and then shove them into classrooms! This will expose the campus to these Christians, stir up interest and, through feedback from the comment cards, we will have many opportunities to share Christ and get kids involved.

Filtering Out Quality Contacts

Another reason to use classroom speaking is that it will save you tons of time. You may say, "Well, I don't have time to make the contacts, write the talk and all the rest." But think about it. It may take you two to three hours to make the contacts, three to four hours to put the talk together, and an hour or two in the classroom. You may have made a ten hour investment, but ten good contacts may result. How many lunch appointments, evangelistic meetings, etc., do you have to have before you get to talk to ten kids who are really spiritually interested? Classroom speaking can serve as that kind of "filter" to enable you to make your time count most effectively.

Building Credibility

Another benefit of classroom speaking is that it attracts attention to you in a positive manner and builds your credibility. Sometimes you may feel that when you walk on campus or get together with high school students, attention is attracted to you in a negative manner. You know, "Who's the old guy that dresses weird?" Or people may wonder, "Why are you 30 and still hanging around with high school kids?" Classroom speaking can identify you in a very positive manner. Sometimes it can even make you a hero on your campus — not that you need to be a hero. It helps you to be seen as a resource, a contributor, an authority figure on your campus — someone who understands kids and cares about them.

Some of us are worried too much about being a friend of kids and not worried enough about being an authority figure for them. Most kids have many "friends," but their friends aren't doing anything for them. On the other hand, many don't have fathers and mothers who really care. They don't have authority figures who are sitting down with them saying, "Look, I know you hurt; I hurt with you and I understand; let me help you find some solutions." Speaking in classrooms can give you that opportunity to establish yourself as somebody who cares about students and is available. If you do a good job, classroom speaking will establish your credibility quickly. Before long, they'll be asking you to speak and counsel — really!

Strengthening Your Faith

A final benefit is that it builds your faith and the faith of any of your Christian students who are in the class. They are encouraged to become more verbal about their faith because you have given them a platform to start talking. God can do so much through you as you step out in faith. The following incident is an example of that, though you may not believe it — I barely believed it myself.

I was in California speaking at San Bernardino High School. It was a civics class held at 8:00 on Monday morning — I couldn't imagine a worse time. I came rushing in a little late, and the Christian student who had set it up met me at the door. "Oh, Bill, I know this is going to be great!" He was so excited; I'm sure he pictured the whole class on their faces praying at the end. I went through my presentation, but the class was dead — I mean, they were *dead*. It was one of those times when you say, "Okay, shout some things out, and I'll write them on the board." Silence. We just suffered through this class.

Now this was several years ago when you could still talk about the Christian perspective in explicit terms. I was using a concentric circle diagram to show that actions affect society, then attitudes affect the actions. The center circle that affects the attitude is labeled sin. At that time, I talked a little bit about the impact that Jesus had in my life. I related about 30-seconds' worth of "That's why Jesus Christ came — to take care of sin," and wrapped up my talk.

When I asked for questions, the teacher asked, "Now I've heard this stuff before about how Jesus deals with sin, but could you explain that a little bit more?" And I'm thinking, "Uh-oh, this is a setup by a Christian teacher." I didn't want to go for it, so I gave him a vague answer. He said, "Yeah, I've heard that part before; but I've heard other people talk about a personal relationship with Jesus. What does that mean?"

So, hesitantly, I drew the two circles out of the Four Spiritual Laws on the board, describing the left circle (the person without Christ) and the right circle (the person with Christ). Then he asked, "Say you're in the circle on the left, how would you get into the circle on the right?" I'm beginning to realize that this guy is not a setup; he really wants to know. So I went through a prayer response in front of the whole class — a highly unusual occurrence in a classroom talk, I might add!

After class, the teacher said to me, "This makes so much sense. I've always heard people talk about it, but I never knew how to make the decision before." And within a month, this teacher had a prayer and Bible study group of thirty to forty students meeting on his campus.

Now I'm not predicting that this will happen to you, but I am saying that God can do supernatural things through your classroom speaking. He will honor your courage and faith. And if you've never stood before a class of thirty kids when you didn't know if they were pagan, if they were hostile, if they were armed — try it sometime! See if it doesn't build your faith!

CLASSROOM SPEAKING DEFINED

In defining what classroom speaking is, let's clarify a couple of things that it is *not*. It is not using the teacher's desk as a *pulpit*. I will guarantee that if you go into the classroom with the idea that you're going to proselytize, your classroom speaking will be a disaster. You may have one successful experience, but it will be your last in that school, and you will close that school down for others in the near future. Even if a student asks a very specific question, resist the temptation to go into a full gospel presentation. You are limited by law, and you are limited by principle. You are there to communicate some academics and to stimulate interest, so don't overstep your limits.

Nor is classroom speaking presenting Jesus as *an alternative*. Jesus is not an alternative, unless you want to say that heaven is an alternative to hell. Jesus is the solution. And whether or not you ever get to mention the name of Jesus Christ in the classroom (and many won't), don't go in with the idea, "I'm here to give you an alternative." You are giving them a different perspective, but it's not an alternative. It's the truth!

What, then, is classroom speaking? In a school setting, it is presenting biblical truths in a culturally relevant manner with academic credibility.

Biblical Truths

When I go into a classroom, I purposely do not quote much Scripture. What would I gain? However, if you were to ask me to speak in a classroom on self-image, my self-image talk is based on John 15 — the vine and the branches. If you were to ask me to speak on sex and dating, my sex and dating talk is largely a study of Philippians 2 — considering the needs of others more important than ourselves. Almost all of the talks I have put together for classrooms are applications of biblical truth put into secular language. Biblical truth must always be the basis of everything you share — unconditional love, freedom from guilt, the impact of sin. Now, you may never use those words. For instance, I wouldn't say, "We're going to talk about the impact of sin today." But what is another word you could use to communicate sin that secular students might identify with? How about "selfishness" or "self-centeredness"?

Culturally Relevant

Communicating in a culturally relevant manner merely means that we're going to speak in a way that kids can understand. Now that means, first of all, that you need to know something about the kids to whom you will be speaking. When you line up a classroom, find out if it is a special class such as an accelerated or remedial class. What is the age of the kids? If the teacher is open to it, one of the best things you can do to prepare for a classroom is to sit in on the class one day. Find out if these kids are used to discussion — it sure can be a disaster if you find out too late that this class never discusses anything. Find out if the teacher uses humor, if he or she is casual or formal. Determine what type of atmosphere is usually prevalent in that classroom. What is the school like? What are the kids like?

Second, tailor your communication to the students, not to yourself or to the teacher. Don't put together a classroom talk that has 53 interesting facts in it. They get facts all the time; they don't want facts from you. They want something that relates, something with illustrations. They have a very limited attention span. Don't walk in and try to lecture for 40 minutes. Make sure that your language communicates — you may have an unbelievable vocabulary; they don't. And please be careful to remove the Christian jargon.

Think about what their interests are. Remember, if they're fifteen years old, they are interested in the things that fifteen-year-old students are interested in. You may not be interested in those things at all — in fact, some of the things might even be distasteful to you. But that really is not important. You are there to speak to them, and you must make sure that you are relating on their level. That's what I mean by being culturally relevant.

Academic Credibility

Sometimes you go into a classroom, especially after you've done it a few times, and you think, "Hey, I can handle this. I don't need to prepare that much!" Famous last words! A youth pastor friend of mine recently stated:

> I had an opportunity to do a classroom in Canada. The teacher allowed us to come in, but she really wasn't in favor of what we were talking about. It was an uncomfortable situation and we could sense the tension, yet we did have the opportunity to present Christ to the class. It was a little hard, though, because it was a subject in biology that I didn't know much about. It would have been good to have studied my biology a little bit first!

You need to know what you're talking about!

I was in Indianapolis a few years ago to speak in classrooms. It happened to be the same week as my wedding anniversary, and my wife was with me. The night before our anniversary, the person who invited me to speak told me that the next day he had three classes lined up for me in History. They were studying the Great Depression, and the teacher wanted me to talk about it. I said, "Well, I'll have my wife come in, because she'll certainly be depressed by then!" I had to spend the evening in the library! Even though I was a history major, which gave me a little bit of an overview, I didn't know much about the Great Depression that I could talk about. I had to think, "How can I relate the impact of sin to the Great Depression?" Well, I had to do some studying, because I wanted to go into the classroom with the credibility that I knew what I was talking about.

I didn't feel that I had to know everything about the Great Depression, because I wasn't there as an expert on the Great Depression; I was there as an expert on high school students and the impact of sin in their lives. But if I were going to relate from the area of my expertise, I needed to know enough to be credible on the subject that they had asked me to speak on. You don't have to be an expert; you just have to be credible. It's not a question of your qualifications or training; it's just a question of whether you are willing to sweat a little bit. You need to have some background.

You may be invited to science classes to talk about evolution versus creation. Let me give you a word of warning: Don't just bone up on all the arguments against evolution without having gained at least a working knowledge of what evolution teaches. Otherwise somebody is going to ask you a question, and you're going to say, "Well, it violates the second law of thermodynamics, etc."

They will say, "Well, yeah, but let's take the fourth law of thermodynamics and apply it to the situation."

You can really look like a "yo-yo" when someone asks a basic question and you don't have the foggiest idea of an answer. However, if someone asks a good question that you are not sure about, then you can simple answer, "I don't claim to be an expert on the subject, but I'd be glad to do some more study and get back with you later." Whatever you do, don't tey to bluff. Relate biblical truths in a culturally relevant manner with academic credibility.

SETTING UP A CLASSROOM SPEAKING OPPORTUNITY

How do you get into a classroom? How do you get your foot in the door? The major problem is coming up with contacts.

Choosing Potential Classes

I discover classroom speaking possibilities through my

students. I ask my leadership students to fill out 3" x 5" cards listing their entire academic schedules. I ask them to mark the classes whose teachers they think might be open to having an outside speaker. Surprisingly, they will probably mark classes that you will question — geometry, P.E., English. Don't give up yet.

Brainstorming for Topics

Once I have a list of classes, I ask myself, "In which of these classes could I possibly offer something unique to the teacher?" So I just sit for awhile and brainstorm. There are a lot of unique things you can do in the classroom, but they may not all occur to you at once! I'll give you an illustration.

When I was in the San Francisco Bay area one time, I told some high school students that while I was there I would be glad to speak in some of their classrooms. A kid called me and said, "Hey, I just talked to my geometry teacher; he'll let you come in." And I thought to myself, "What do you do in a geometry class?" So my wife and I went to work, poring over geometry books, learning about postulates and theorems and all this stuff. Finally, we just stopped and said, "Wait a minute. What do they teach in geometry? *Logic.* Maybe we could relate to logic in general." Now we started thinking of an approach to take.

Most kids I know hate geometry. It's almost as though if they died without Jesus, they'd go to a geometry class! What's the biggest job of the teacher? Trying to get kids motivated. So I went to the teacher and said, "Look, here's what I can do. I can explain to students how geometry and the study of it can help them in their logical thinking by giving them some very real situations to which we can apply both inductive and deductive logic."

The teacher said, "That would be great!"

So during the talk, I said, "This is why you're studying geometry." I threw out a couple of real-life situations and, because this was a few years ago, I felt free to be very direct. "Let me give you a problem that you are going to have to use logic for — the same kind of logic you are learning in geometry that could effect your life in a very real way." I wrote on the board, "JESUS: LORD, LIAR, LUNATIC." Then we used the logic of geometry to discuss how a person could decide who Jesus really was. There is no limit to what you can do in any classroom. Even if it seems unlikely, don't throw it out. Think about it, and brainstorm with others, if possible.

When you are brainstorming ideas, I would like to recommend a very helpful resourse — the *Classroom Speaking Notebook*, published by Student Venture of Campus Crusade for Christ. It is an excellent manual, packed full of more than 100 outlines and back ground material already prepared for you. I have found the outlines to be very helpful time-savers as I research and write my talks.

Meeting the Teacher

Once I've selected a class and have two or three topic ideas, I need to meet the teacher and try to set it up. First, let me point out that this is a tremendous opportunity to relate with faculty and administration. We can make the mistake of seeing these people as our adversaries — barriers that we must get through to reach our harvest field. This attitude often can come through in our conversations. Classroom speaking is one of the greatest ways to begin building relationships with teachers, because you must talk to the teacher! There is no way to get into classrooms without relating personally to teachers, so see them as part of your mission field and relate to them as peers.

I arrange a time with the student when he can introduce me to the teacher. I ask him *not* to introduce me as his youth pastor. If the teacher asks me what I do, I'm not going to lie to him. I tell him that I work with kids through one of the churches in the community and that I work with people of several denominations. It helps if the student can give me a positive endorsement identifying me as someone who works with him, who has been a great help to him, etc.

Proposing to Speak

After the introduction, I might say something like, "It's good to meet you. Joe has mentioned to me that there are times when you are open to having outside speakers, and I wanted to let you know that I work with students here in the community. While I am not an expert on your subject, I do spend a lot of my time relating to a students, and I would be happy to make myself available to you as a resource. In fact, I brought along two or three topics I could speak on that I think might relate to your class." At that point, I give him a list of several potential topics, preferably typed. The talks aren't written yet, as I don't want to waste my time writing two or three talks that I might never use. All I have are topics. I might give the teacher a title and a short synopsis, but all I need is something I can put in his hands to let him see where I am headed.

I try to be very honest in explaining my approach. I don't want to give teachers a line or be defensive. If he asks me why I am interested, I will tell him that I am there because I want to influence students' lives in a positive manner. I want to do anything I can to show that I care and to be available as part of that student community. If I am going to pass out comment cards, I do not go into detail, but I let the teacher know right off the top that I'd like to get some feedback from the students when I'm in his classroom. Being aboveboard helps teachers have confidence in you right from the start, and it helps them to know what to expect.

If a teacher asks me if I intend to share the gospel, I tell him I won't. I view classroom speaking as pre-evangelism. I seldom talk about Jesus in a classroom. The geometry story I related earlier took place nine years ago. The mood of our country and the classroom has changed a great deal since then. I live in the heart of the Bible Belt, and I find it acceptable to talk about Jesus a little in some classrooms, but even then, I do so in generalities. I find it a little unsettling to share only part of the gospel. In addition, I find it wiser to share too little than too much — I want to be invited back. I am there primarily to stimulate interest and thinking in what is a whole new area for most kids, and that's the way I explain it to the teachers.

Confirming the Details

Most teachers won't fall all over themselves to sign you up. If they are good teachers, they will probably say, "Let me think about this." Give them your topics, and then ask, "Can I check back in a couple of days and talk with you again?" If they are reluctant, then I offer to bring in an outline of one of the talks. A couple of days later I go back to the teacher and attempt to confirm everything. I am hoping to discuss my talk and then set an actual date and time.

Sometimes a teacher will say, "Well, this should be really good; how about tomorrow?" I used to think, "Boy, I can get in! I can get in! Yeah, I'll do it tomorrow!" But I knew I didn't have a chance of getting prepared in time, so I'd be up all night long, trying to cram and get ready. Now I say, "Well, my schedule is pretty full, and I really want to do a good job. I think I could be much better prepared if we could wait a few more days." Most of them, being teachers, will understand the need for good preparation!

PREPARING TO SPEAK

Let's assume that you have selected a class in which you want to speak. You have made contact with the teacher and have agreed upon a topic. You have confirmed a date and time. Now it's time to prepare your talk.

Creativity

First of all, let me encourage you to be creative. You can speak on anything. Believe me, there is not a class in your school in which you can't speak, if you will exercise your creativity. Get with some other people and brainstorm your approach. Do all you can to get through to kids. Use illustrations, stories, life-simulations. Paul tells us in 1 Corinthians 2:16 that we have "the mind of Christ." The mind of Christ can certainly communicate truth creatively in many situations. You have God-given creativity. Exercise it!

Outlining Your Talk

Be sure to select a topic you are motivated to speak on. If, by chance, you have very little background on the subject, find someone with expertise and ask him to give you a general overview. Based on Student Venture's *Classroom Speaking Notebook*, I would suggest dividing your outline into the following categories:

General Analysis of the Topic. Acquaint the students with your topic and your personality. Try to develop a casual atmosphere and a rapport. Get to know them a little.

Definition and Role of Topic in Society. Start narrowing your perspective to lead you where you want to go.

Major Problem of Your Topic. Keep this simple, focusing on two to four major problems. Limit yourself to general areas, if possible. (Example: A problem in family life is poor parental leadership.) Focus more on solutions than problems.

Individual Responsibility. Emphasize that the individual bears responsibility for the problem and that each of us has a role to play in the solution.

The Source of the Problem. Draw three concentric circles. Draw a line to the area inside the outer circle and call it Actions (outward behavior). Then discuss and write in some of the actions that characterize the problems of your topic. Mark the next circle Attitudes (motivations). Discuss and note the attitudes that underlie the actions — actions find their source in attitudes. The center circle is marked Source (attitude toward God or sin). Define sin ("missing the mark" in one's relationship with God). Show how the circles interrelate.

Conclusion. Point out that changed individuals bring about a changed society. Illustrate with an actual appropriate example. Pass out comment cards, if approved, and open up the time for questions.

"AND NOW. . .RIGHT HERE ON OUR STAGE!"

When the time comes to deliver your talk, let me encourage you to keep several things in mind.

Be Yourself

First of all, *be yourself.* If you're not humorous, don't try to be funny. There's nothing worse than someone who is "unfunny" trying to be funny. If you are funny, let the humor flow. If you're a casual person, be casual. If you're not, then be whatever you are. Kids can see through hypocrisy, and you are a positive model to them when you are comfortable with yourself.

One of the greatest classroom presentations I ever witnessed was given by a girl in southern California. She was a sweet Louisiana girl, much like my wife, but she was doing a terrible job. She was trying to be authoritative and lecture the kids, and her efforts were bombing. I was in the classroom supposedly critiquing her, but I didn't have the guts to do it — she was obviously suffering enough. After about twenty minutes, she shoved her notes aside, walked around to the front of her lectern and said, "Look, I'm doing awful. I just came here to let you guys know one thing. I'm here because I love you and I want to do anything I can to help you." The class was stunned — and from that point on, she was communicating. Be yourself.

If you do bomb, don't be too hard on yourself. Learn from the situation and prepare better next time. Don't be too quick to assume this, but it is possible that God has not gifted you to speak in classrooms. That doesn't mean you're a lousy person with youth. We are all gifted in different ways, and we should not elevate the value of one particular skill over another. But if God has not gifted you in the area of communication, and classroom speaking is not the thing for you, I am sure there are people in your community who can do it. So put them up in front, but make sure that you introduce them. That will give you some "face time" in front of the class and may work just as well in establishing yourself as a resource who is available to the students in an ongoing way.

Be Courageous

Second, as you prepare your mind to lead the class session, ask God to make you courageous. Ask for the courage to speak forthrightly when you're in the classrom talking about the self-centered lifestyle or other things that make students uncomfortable. Sometimes we're gripped by the fear, "I came in so they'll like me, and now they don't like me." You're not necessarily in there to be liked; you're in there to stimulate them. But I think kids want to have their minds and hearts stimulated. Chances are, the long-range by-product is that they will like you for it, but it's a risk.

Ask God to help you not run away from controversial subjects when they come up. You're there to show students that you can relate to them and their needs and questions. So when it gets thick, don't run. Fight the tendency just to be likeable. You need the courage to demonstrate your own character while you're in there.

In our area, abortion is a very hot issue right now. We have a very tasteful and excellent film that relates to abortion, and we are going to use it to get into a lot of classrooms. I know that it's going to be quite controversial, but we plan to focus the presentations not so much on the abortion issue as on the underlying influence of humanism in our culture today. We want to stimulate the thinking of those who *claim* that absolutes and moral principles mean something. God has given us courage — and I think we're going to need it!

Use Comment Cards

Before you begin, clarify how you plan to use comment cards. Check in ahead of time with the teacher. Tell him that you find it helpful to get some feedback from the students. Use 3" X 5" cards, or simply have them write on sheets of paper. At the end of the talk, I tell them I want three things: (1) I ask for any specific comments or questions. (2) I ask for their names. I tell them the reason I want their names is that comments without a name are cheap; that's why people always put their names on letters to the editor in a newspaper. (3) I say, "If this has stimulated you at all and you would like to talk about it further, just put your phone number down there." If you have an article related to your subject, which could include a gospel presentation, let them know it is available for the asking. Make the presentation low key and simple, but make sure you clear it with the teacher first.

FOLLOW-UP — THE FRUIT OF YOUR LABOR

After you have received the completed comment cards, you have the important task of following through with any who are interested. Do this as soon as possible. This is the primary fruit of your labor, but Satan will resist you here for that very reason. Pray that God will give you the discipline you need. Frankly, I struggle here. I *love* to communicate to kids. If I could be in classrooms every day, I'd do it. But when I get out of the classroom, I really struggle with the courage to pick up the phone and call the kids that said they want to talk further.

Sometimes I find myself afraid that they're going to say, "Well, I *did* want to talk to you, but now I've thought about it, and I think you're a jerk!" No one has ever said that exactly, but it still takes courage to pick up the phone! The first couple of calls are the hardest, especially if you have a card that says, "Please call me tonight, I really need to know more" — so you call and find out someone gave you the phone number of one of his friends! But persevere, and keep on calling! If you get only one contact from the talk, it will have been worth your effort.

Also, don't neglect the opportunity to let your students help you in following up the contacts. Go through the cards with the student who helped you line up the classroom, and ask him if there are any kids he would like to contact himself. It can be a great way to get your students involved in pre-evangelism and evangelism.

STRATEGIC OPPORTUNITY

The Roosevelts, the Churchills, and the DeGaulles all sat in the classroom once. So did Adolph Hitler and Josef Stalin. We cannot predict who our world leaders will be tomorrow, but we can be sure they will be educated. Abraham Lincoln once said that if we want to influence the world tomorrow, we must influence the generation in the classrooms today. That statement still stands, and with a little creativity and courage, we can help to give exposure to the Christian perspective by our lives and by our words.

PUTTING THIS CHAPTER TO WORK

1. In Acts 17, Paul speaks of a twofold ministry context — in the synagogue and in the marketplace. What percentage of your youth ministry time is spent in their "marketplace"? Should you adjust your percentage?

2. Review the "Benefits of Classroom Speaking." Should you consider making that a more integral part of your plan to spend quality time in their "marketplace"? If so, sketch some plans for when and where you could speak in classrooms this year.

3. List the names of some leadership students you could talk to about gathering a list of potential classes.

4. In relation to speaking, what does "Be yourself" mean for you? Are you funny, casual, serious? How would you characterize yourself? Have someone evaluate you in a speaking situation (pro and con), and draw some conclusions about how you can

communicate best to a classroom of secular students.

5. Build your faith and demonstrate your courage by scheduling one classroom speaking engagement in the near future! To start the ball rolling, write down the first step you need to take, and then put it into your schedule.

DISCIPLESHIP

10

DISCIPLESHIP — STEPS TO BECOMING LIKE CHRIST

by Barry St. Clair

Discipleship is such an important subject that I find myself very concerned about presenting it in just the right way. I feel very much like the youth minister who, for the very first time, was left totally in charge one Sunday when his pastor was gone. He was feeling the pressure of the responsibility. His first duty that morning was the pastor's Sunday school class — and it was a disaster. Then he went into the worship service and became completely confused about the order of worship. When he got up to preach his message, the breeze from a window caught his notes and blew them off the platform. The pressure was building! The morning concluded with a baptismal service, at which time the pressure peaked. He was doing fine at first — he walked into the baptismal pool, made his opening remarks and brought in the first candidate. Buoyed by his momentum, he put the man under the water and said, "Drink ye all of it!"

I'm sensing a little of that pressure because I truly desire to encourage you and help you to be all that God really wants you to be in this area of making disciples. You are the ones who are fighting on the front lines of battle every day. Quality discipleship will not be achieved if everyone is a traveling speaker, if everyone is a general. The job is going to get done by those who are out there in the trenches, in the local ministry where you are. You are there, and that is the most important place you can be. I want to encourage you to move toward a plan for discipling students.

Barry St. Clair is the founder and director of Reach Out Ministries in Atlanta, Georgia, an organization which trains students and youth pastors in evangelism and discipleship. He is also pastor of Christ Community Church and is chairman of the board for the National Network of Youth Ministries. Barry has written several books and has earned a doctorate of ministries from Southwestern Theological Seminary (Fort Worth, Texas). He has worked with young people as a pastor, youth pastor, and as a representative of both denominational and interdenominational organizations. He and his wife, Carol, have three children.

143

THE ESSENCE OF DISCIPLESHIP

Let's look at that familiar passage in Matthew 28. Maybe it is too familiar; maybe it has become stale for you because you have heard it so many times. Let's ask God to give us a fresh look at what He is trying to say to us about the tremendous opportunity and responsibility we have in discipling the students whom He has put under our care.

> And Jesus came up and spoke to them, saying, "All authority has been given to Me in heaven and on earth. Go therefore and make disciples of all the nations, baptizing them in the name of the Father and the Son and the Holy Spirit, teaching them to observe all that I commanded you; and lo, I am with you always, even to the end of the age."

As you look at that passage, circle the words "make disciples." That is the primary verb in this passage. Everything else hinges on it. In the same sense, everything in your ministry hinges on making disciples.

Perspective From Pancakes

I remember the first time that I became conscious of the significance of that concept. It was my first year as director of youth evangelism for my denomination. I wasn't quite sure what I was supposed to be doing, so I decided to take a "vision trip" to California. It seemed that everybody I talked to told me to go see a man by the name of Chuck Miller. I had never heard of Chuck Miller. But after being told "go see Chuck Miller" time after time, I finally decided to follow the advice. I found out that Chuck was minister to youth at Lake Avenue Congregational Church in Pasadena, California. I called him, and Chuck said, "Barry, I would love for you to come. Be here at 6:00 on Tuesday morning."

I got up on Tuesday morning at 5:00. As I was driving through the Los Angeles traffic before it was even light, I remember thinking, "Why am I doing this? I know what is going to happen. There will be two wimpy kids sitting there reading Dawson McAllister's Manual and saying, 'Isn't this incredible? Isn't this incredible?' I know, I've seen it before. I'm not really up for this at all. . . ." But to my surprise, as I walked into the building, instead of two kids there were *300* kids sitting there eating pancakes off of paper plates. Have you ever seen kids do that? It only takes one slice of that plastic knife, and there is syrup running all over. So here are 300 sticky kids sitting there eating pancakes off of paper plates at 6:00 on a Tuesday morning. I was thinking, "What's going on here? Is Billy Graham coming? Is a music group going to be here? *Somebody* special is going to be here."

They had a very simple presentation of the gospel, a few songs and skits, and then these kids left. I said, "Hey, there has got to be more to it than this, something that I am not seeing." I sat down with Chuck afterward, and he explained to me what he was doing. He had a group of leaders who were meeting together each week to be trained by him. Those leaders were each working with six or eight high school students, and the students in those groups were bringing their friends to the breakfasts. So every Tuesday morning at 6:00 there were about 300 kids coming to hear the good news of Jesus Christ. When I saw the quality of the life of those leaders and the quantity of students who were there, it completely changed my whole concept of ministry. I began to realize that the greatest way to fulfill the Great Commission is through making disciples.

Discipling a Computer

Tragically, however, we have bludgeoned the word *discipleship* to death. We have taken this great concept like a beautiful new sports car and run it at top speed over a road that is full of potholes and ruts. We have reduced it to the point where it is nothing more than going to a Bible study and memorizing a few Scripture verses. Maybe we have even included teaching our kids how to have a quiet time and how to witness. But basically we have beaten the idea to death.

Bible study, Scripture memory, witnessing — all of us would say those are very important. But a computer can do those things. Can a computer do Bible study? You bet. Can a computer memorize verses? You bet. Can a computer share the gospel? You bet. So what's so unique about disciple making? A computer cannot be transformed into the image of Christ. That is what disciple making is all about — transforming individuals into the very image of Jesus Christ (Romans 8:29). It is then, and only then, that the students you are responsible for will begin to transmit the aliveness and vitality of what He is doing in their lives to their friends at school. Thus, the heart of disciple making is a life transformed.

THE FOUNDATION OF AUTHORITY

Matthew 28:18 gives the foundation for disciple making: "All authority has been given to Me in heaven and on earth." Jesus has the authority. This authority literally means Christ's "absolute right to exercise power" over all the resources of heaven and earth.

Here is an illustration that helps clarify the picture. Light travels 186,000 miles per second, about 6 trillion miles per light year. The North Star, one of our closest stars, is 400 light years away. Can you imagine how far that is? It is incomprehensible, but the Scripture tells us that all the authority of heaven and earth belongs to

Jesus Christ. Hebrews 1:3 tells us that He is upholding the whole universe "by the word of His power."

Jesus not only *has* authority; Jesus *gives* authority. Jesus says it again in Luke 10:19: "Behold, I have given you authority to tread upon serpents and scorpions and over all the power of the enemy, and nothing shall injure you." The power that Jesus has — the power that enables Him to uphold the whole universe — *lives in me!* Isn't that something? Jesus Christ lives in us; we have all authority. Do you believe that? Let that truth sink into your mind and burn into your heart.

I'm sure that you believe that Christ and His authority live in you. But have you ever wondered why you have not experienced His authority when you have needed it personally and in your ministry? I have struggled with that. Then one day it dawned on me. It was as if God was saying, "The reason, Barry, is that I am not sure that I can trust you yet with all the authority that I have and that lives in you. But as you mature, I am going to let it loose."

I have come to believe that God will unleash His authority through your life and the lives of your kids, only in direct proportion to your maturity level. How do you become mature? You become mature through the discipling process. As we continue going through the discipling process, being conformed to the image of Jesus Christ, He will progressively release His authority and power as we need it in our lives. So, then, Christ's authority is the foundation for making disciples, but it can be fully experienced only as each of us submits to the discipling process.

What is the discipleship process? And how do we go about putting it into action in a way that will bring about that kind of maturity in us and our students?

Let's get practical — like my son Jonathan. I took him along with me one Saturday afternoon as I ran some errands. He was 4 years old at the time. I said, "Jonathan, how about letting me give you my sermon for tomorrow?"

He said, "Okay, Dad."

So I started running through my outline. After about five or six minutes, I was really getting into it, and all of a sudden he interrupted me and said, "Okay, Dad, what do you want me to do about it?" Pretty profound for a 4-year-old! But we do need to bring discipleship out of the clouds and into specific action. What do we do? What does God desire in terms of this disciple-making process?

We have built the foundation on the authority of Jesus Christ. Now we are ready to build four stair steps that will lead young people to spiritual maturity We see these stair steps again and again — not only in Jesus' ministry, but throughout the Book of Acts. The process of walking up those stairs will transform us more and more into the very image of Jesus Christ Himself.

EVANGELIZE — GOSSIPING THE GOSPEL

In Matthew 28:19, Jesus' command begins, "Go therefore and make disciples . . . ." As we look at the book of Acts, we see that Jesus' disciples were continually gossiping the gospel. Everywhere they went, wherever they were, any place they could talk, in any conversation — their top priority was gossiping about the good news of Jesus Christ.

We have been trying to gossip about the gospel in our church. For several months we worked with one young lady who needs Christ. She had a 4-year-old, has never been married and has had some real struggles. Her sister belongs to our church, and she has shared Christ with her; other people in our church also witnessed to her. Finally one Thursday she asked Jesus to come into her life.

The following Sunday morning after the service, she came up to me and said, "Barry, I have one real big question I want to ask you. A long time ago I bought a wedding dress — a white one. My boyfriend and I are talking about being married; he is getting his life straightened out with the Lord, and now I have Jesus in my life. Do you think it would be okay, now that Jesus has cleansed me from my sin, if I wore that white wedding dress?" Man, I get fired up about stuff like that! Changed lives result from gossiping the gospel! The whole disciple-making process starts with telling others about Jesus Christ.

Setting the Pace

For most of us who work in youth ministry and are trying to get on the campus, it seems to be getting harder and harder to get out there where students are and to share the gospel with them unhindered by the powers and the authorities around us. If you have been a fun-and-games youth minister and have dawdled in this area of evangelism, let me challenge you. If you are going to evangelize, gossip the gospel, get your kids doing it and set the pace for them, then it is going to cost you.

Last year, for the very first time in my life I was removed from a campus. And that campus probably has more needs than any other school in our county — drugs, parent problems, all kinds of problems. Being barred from campus was disappointing, but it has not stopped us from reaching out to kids. We just have to be a little more creative.

There is a community college across the street from us, and over the months, God has been impressing upon my heart to start an open-air Bible study on that college campus. Quite frankly, it scares me to death, and it's probably going to cost me, but I'm fired up about getting out there and doing that. It is going to cost us to evangelize. But evangelism is the seedbed of discipleship. You will not effectively disciple until you evangelize. So whatever it takes to get you setting the pace and involving your kids in the process, do it!

ESTABLISH — MASTERING THE BASICS

The second stair step in discipleship is to establish and ground our young people. Matthew 28:19 says, "Make disciples . . . *baptizing.* . . ." We see in Acts 2:41-42 how the disciples carried out that command of Jesus.

> So then, those who had received his Word were baptized; and there were added that day about 3,000 souls. And they were continually devoting themselves to the aspostles' teaching and to fellowship, to the breaking of bread and to prayer.

Identified as Christ's Property

The initial step in following Christ was to be baptized, to be identified with Jesus Christ. In fact, in New Testament times the idea was that a person became the property of another person when he was baptized. A person who was baptized as a follower of Christ was so totally immersed in Him that he became the property of Jesus Christ, who was now his Lord and Master. As one pastor joked, "When I baptize them, I hold them down until all the bubbles are gone, and then I know the old man is dead!" That's one way to do it! However, the point is that baptism is the first step in establishing a believer because it is an outward, open step of obedience. It says, "I am identifying myself as the property of Jesus Christ."

Learning the Fundamentals

Acts 2:42 goes on to say that the new Christians devoted themselves to the apostles' teaching, fellowship, the breaking of bread and prayer. In other words, they began to grow. It is exciting to watch somebody grow and learn to do something that he has never done before, isn't it? When my daughter, Katie, was 7, I taught her how to ride her bike. It was a whole new experience for me and for her. Before we started, I gave her a few instructions — basic things like, "If you keep it going forward, it won't fall on the ground!"

And so we started. I held onto the bike and ran along sideways. At first that bike wobbled all over the street, and I became soaked with sweat as I tried to keep up with her. Then when she began to get up a little confidence, I said, "Okay, honey, see that truck 15 yards ahead? I want you to go to the truck by yourself. I'll be right beside you."

"Okay, Dad."

She started out, wobbled a little bit and then took off! She went all the way down the street by herself. It was exciting to watch that take place! We did it two or three more times with me running alongside.

Then Katie said, "Oh, Dad, I can do it myself."

"Okay. . . ."

Bam! Right into the side of a car — we left a little piece of her skin right there to mark the spot! But soon, she began to get the hang of it, as we worked together establishing her ability to ride that bike. Before it was over, all the kids in the neighborhood were out, riding their bikes up and down the street! Do you see the parallels for establishing someone in his faith?

Growth comes gradually, starting with making an initial commitment, mastering the basics and then going on from there. The process may take time, but it is exciting. And it is the only way to make disciples who are conformed to the image of Christ.

Make It or Break It

Several years ago, I worked with a group of high school guys — Rusty, Mike and Clayton. We met at 6:00 one morning a week. Our agreement was, "If you are going to be 15 minutes late, we'll give you that. After 15 minutes, we will call your house." At that time of the morning, a boy's Dad needed to answer only *one* time — after that, we found he was never late again!

We started by focusing on how to spend time alone with the Lord. We wanted to get that discipline established first. I said, "Okay, guys, the challenge is for every single one of us to do this for seven straight days in the coming week. Will you take the challenge?"

"Yeah, man, we'll take it!"

The next week only half of us had done it. I said, "Okay, we are not going on. We are going to do the same thing again. Can I issue the same challenge?

"Yeah, we'll do it."

Only about two-thirds of the group did it, about half the time. And this went on for 10 straight weeks. Some of you may ask, "Barry, why didn't you just go on and do something else?" Because these guys needed to be *established* in their faith. I knew that if they did this one thing right, they could handle the rest of it down the road.

We struggled and talked, and finally I told them, "The issue for your whole life is right here. You are going to make or break it right here on what you learn from this. So let's go for it." And do you know what? After 10 weeks, everybody spent time with God every single day! Everybody was so excited that we skipped the next meeting and went out for breakfast. We had a great time, just being together and celebrating.

What has happened to those guys as a result of getting them established in just one little area of their lives? One of them just graduated from seminary. I preached the ordination sermon for the second one not too long ago. The third one has graduated from the University of Tennessee Law School and has committed his life to sharing Christ through the profession of law.

I believe the turning point was when I said to them, "Guys, we are going to be established in our faith if it kills us all!" I loved them, and they loved me, and we hung in there together. I guarantee that if you will give kids the basics, their lives will be transformed and they will begin to be conformed to the image of Christ.

EQUIP — TEACHING THAT TRANSFORMS

The third step on the staircase of discipleship is to equip our students for ministry. Matthew 28:20 says, "Make disciples . . . *teaching*. . . ." Because discipleship is a chain reaction, it requires more than rote knowledge. It requires a change of life.

Transferable?

On the first day of class, a seminary professor I know gave his students these instructions: "This is what we are going to do this semester. I am going to teach the course; you are going to take the notes. Then you are going to go out and teach five laymen in your church exactly what I am teaching you. At the end of the semester, I am going to give you the test, and you are going to give the test to your laymen. The grade they make on the test is going to be your grade in the course." Pretty tough! But do you think the students saw the need for mastering the subject so that they could effectively transfer it to others?

Cabinets and Disciples — One Thing in Common

That is what our ministry is all about. Establishing young people in their faith is more than just stuffing their heads full of knowledge. It is helping them incorporate Christian principles into their lives and then equipping them to communicate those to others. We need to be raising up people who are disciple makers — just as there are cabinetmakers. Cabinetmakers make cabinets. If there are no cabinetmakers, there are no cabinets. If there are cabinetmakers, there *are* cabinets. It is the same in making disciples. Disciples are made because there are disciple makers; if there are no disciple makers, there are no disciples. If there are disciple makers, there *are* disciples. Do you get the idea? Somebody has to be a disciple maker if we want disciples. And that is what God has called us to do — to make disciples who will reproduce themselves. The essence of God's call for those of us in ministry is "the equipping of the saints for the work of service" (Ephesians 4:12).

Give the Process Time

From the first day that Ken walked into my office, I knew that the potential was there. He was established in the faith. He really desired to know God. So we brought him on our youth staff as a summer intern in our church. Ken did have at least one flaw in his personality — he worried about everything. He would get so excited one minute and so worried the next. He was going to get married in three months, and he was always worrying. "Are we going to have enough money? Man, I don't know. I wonder if we can get everything ready. I'm not so sure."

I remember how excited I was the morning I walked in and handed him a check for $400 that someone had sent him anonymously. I said, "Ken, does this help you trust God?" And that was the beginning of his learning how to do that. Over the months taht followed, I gave him specific, individual attention, helped him examine the areas of his life and spent time with him one-to-one every week. As a result he has begun to mature, especially in the area of trusting God. Because he wants to know God, he realizes that he has to know God's Word. Although he never studied much in school, he now spends two hours every morning studying the Scriptures.

Just recently, Ken's wife decided to quit her job. They are raising financial support so that she can be involved in the ministry with him. They are not sure that the money is going to be there, but they know that God is going to take care of them. Theya re trusting Christ and standing on His promises. Ken is growing up into the image of Jesus Christ and is going to be one of God's great disciple makers in the years ahead, but we must give the process time.

The Apostle Paul's Approach

How do we go about developing an atmosphere for making disciples? 1 Thessalonians 2:4-10 gives us a specific picture of how Paul discipled others. First of all, in verse 4 it tells us that we need to have *God's approval* to be able to make disciples. If He hasn't called you to do it, don't do it. Don't jump into it without conviction from Him. Verse 4 says, ". . .just as we have been approved by God to be entrusted with the gospel, so we speak, not as pleasing men but God who examines our hearts." Has God given you His full approval?

Second, verse 7 calls our attention to the need for a spirit of *gentle acceptance* when it comes to working with our disciples. "But we proved to be gentle among you as a nursing mother tenderly cares for her own children."

Third, verse 8 speaks of a *deep affection*. "Having thus a fond affection for you, we were well-pleased to impart to you not only the gospel but also our own lives because you had become very dear to us." It is the gentle acceptance and deep affection for the people around you which creates the atmosphere to help disciples overcome some of the difficulties in their lives.

Fourth, *diligent action* is needed. Verse 9 says, "For you recall, brethren, our labor and hardship; how working night and day. . . ." Disciple making is hard work. You may think evangelism is hard work, but disciple making is doubly hard.

Finally, *consistent accountability* is essential. It has to be there if you expect to make disciples. Look at verses 10 and 11: "You are witnesses, and so is God, how devoutly and uprightly and blamelessly we behaved toward you believers; just as you know how we were exhorting and encouraging and imploring each one of you as a father would his own children." When there is an atmosphere of gentle acceptance and deep affection, then you can exhort and charge and encourage in the weak areas of a person's life, so that he might be transformed by the Holy Spirit into the very likeness of Jesus Christ Himself.

Crowns in Heaven

Look at verse 19: "For who is our hope or joy or crown of exultation? Is it not even you in the presence of our Lord Jesus at His coming? For you are our glory and joy." When you stand before Jesus Christ at His coming, what is going to be your hope? What is going to be your glory? What is going to be your joy? It is going to be those people into whom you have poured your life and have equipped to be disciple makers so that they, in turn, make other disciples. You will then be able to stand before God and know that your life has counted for eternity.

There is no greater satisfaction than being a follower of Jesus Christ and making disciples for Him.

EXTEND — MULTIPLYING TO THE WORLD

When you come to the top of a staircase, you have reached the level where you want to be. All of the steps along the way are meant to get you to that point. The step of evangelism gets you started. Establishing and equipping keep you going strong. But the purpose of it all is the fourth and final step in discipleship — to *extend*, as spoken of in Matthew 28:19: "Make disciples of all the nations. . . ."

Generation to Generation

The first five chapters of the book of Acts report that the church added and added and added in the area of evangelism. But when you get to Acts 6:7 (KJV), ". . .the number of the disciples multiplied. . . ." They continued to multiply throughout the rest of the book of Acts, to the point that in Acts 17:6 their enemies claimed that they "turned the world upside down. . . ." They did that through the process of evangelism, establishing and then equipping until they extended themselves to the ends of the earth. "How do I do that?" you ask. "How can my ministry help reach the world when I am in this little town, or lost in this big city?" One good word of advice: Bloom where you are planted! God will multiply you beginning right where you are. Bloom where you are planted!

Let me illustrate. I discipled my friend, Bill Jones, when he was in college. He began to disciple another fellow named Bill who was a high school student. That Bill began to share his faith, and when he went on to the University of Georgia, he met a fellow named Jock and began discipling him. Jock was in a fraternity, and he began to give his life away by sharing Christ with some fraternity brothers. After three or four years, 22 people accepted Christ in that fraternity; seven guys were in a discipleship group. That's at least five generations of disciples — and I have never even been to the University of Georgia!

To Russia — With God's Love

Trace it down another way through Bill Jones. I gave my life to him, establishing him and equipping him to be the kind of young man he needs to be in the image of Jesus Christ. During that time, Bill met John and helped lead him to Christ. In the process of establishing and equipping him, Bill and John went on an exchange program to the Soviet Union.

One day while traveling on a train, John sat beside a Russian man named Eugene who spoke English. John shared the gospel with him. The man was an athiest, but he had been going to Moscow Baptist Church and was interested in what John was telling him. He did not respond to Christ that day, but several months later, John and Bill got a letter from Eugene saying that he had accepted Jesus Christ into his life. Several months later, they got another letter from him saying that he had come to the United States, studied communications and had just recently returned to Eastern Europe where he produces a radio program that beams the good news of Jesus Christ to approximately 15 million people in the Soviet Union each day!

In my wildest, wildest dreams I never, never would have imagined that that could have happened, starting in my little community of Avondale Estates, Georgia. And the discipling process goes on. Bill Jones is now a team member with me on the staff at our church. What an exciting privilege to be linked up with a guy that I poured my life into. There is no greater satisfaction.

SIGNIFICANT LAST WORDS

Are you taking this process of making disciples seriously? Are you believing God for the Bills, Jocks, Johns and Eugenes around you who could be multiplying their influence around the world for Christ? Are you really investing your life in others who will also multiply? Is there anything more important?

When I was in high school, the person who was the very closest to me of all the people in my life was my grandmother. She was about 80 years old. I loved my grandmother, and she loved me. On August 27, 1963, she wrote this letter:

> Dearest Barry and my lifelong pal,
> You are leaving many memories for me. As you take this big step in your life [college], let me say I know you will do will. You have what it takes — good character, a loving disposition, and ambition to do your best. Your sound Christian belief will continue to grow, and God will go with you. I am praying for you, as I know you are praying for me. May God bless you always. We have loved you dearly since you first came to our house when you were 6 weeks old. I know the Lord will be with you every step of the way.
>
> > Love always,
> > Grandmother

That is a special letter. On August 28 it was lying beside her bed, and she was gone. Those were the last words she ever wrote or spoke to anyone, and those words have been a source of anchor and encouragement and strength to me for all these years. She discipled me through her love and belief, and those last words of hers made a real impact on me. If those last words of my grandmother were so significant in my life, how much more should we take seriously the last significant words of our Lord and Savior, Jesus Christ:

> Go therefore and make disciples of all the nations, baptizing them in the name of the Father and the Son and the Holy Spirit, teaching them to observe all that I commanded you; and lo, I am with you always, even to the end of the age.

God's desire for you and me, as we slug it out in the trenches every day, is to make disciples. He wants us to lead young people up the steps to spiritual maturity — to the point of transforming them into the very image of Jesus Christ. I challenge you to give your life to the task. Ask God to give you the courage to invest your life even more strategically in evangelizing and establishing and equipping and extending your ministry for His glory around the world. Give your desire to Him, trust Him for it, and expect Him to bless you with a legacy of disciples who will multiply beyond your wildest dreams.

PUTTING THIS CHAPTER TO WORK

1. We all must shudder a little at the illustration of the seminarians being evaluated according to the grades their students received on their final exam! But what if the Lord evaluated the worth of our ministries based upon what was evident spiritually in our students' lives? What characteristics of your youth would stand out as definite signs of Christlikeness? Which characteristics would need the most work?

2. List some people to whom you have ministered who are now discipling others. List any who are currently serving the Lord in a Christian ministry. List those who are preparing for full-time Christian work. Praise Him! These are our "crown . . . our glory and joy" (1 Thessalonians 2:19,20)!

3. In light of the model of Barry's 6 a.m. discipleship group, what basics could you teach your leadership students which would "make or break" them?

4. If the long-range purpose of discipleship is multiplying believers to reach the world, what kind of objectives and programs should you be building your ministry around? List a few that would help you "bloom where you are planted," yet set the stage for multiplication to the world.

11

CREATING A WILLINGNESS WITHIN STUDENTS FOR SPIRITUAL MATURITY

by David Busby

Growing up, I was burned out by the whole church scene. My dad weighed 220 pounds, and we didn't take a vote at my house on whether or not we were going to church. He just said, "Get up. Be happy. Enjoy it. Here we go." When I was 9 years old, I prayed a prayer and was baptized. I actually remember thinking how cool it would be to go swimming in church.

At six months of age I contracted polio, and it wiped out my right thigh and lower left calf. As a result, I was a kid that really hated myself — I was extremely insecure and easily intimidated. As a young teenager, I set out on a journey to find acceptance and worth — something of meaning and value in my life. In junior high, I focused on academics, and though I won some honors, I was still very empty. In high school, I sought popularity. I was elected president of the student body, owned a Corvette, and had some girlfriends, but I was still empty on the inside and lacked meaning and purpose in my life. I couldn't seem to put a finger on it.

AUTHENTIC CHRISTIANITY

Even as a university student, I still hated myself, was easily intimidated, and was just scared to death of rejection. Then in my junior year at the university, I met a young man at a Christian meeting who had an exciting, genuine, radical commitment to the person of Jesus Christ. I had never met anybody like that in my whole life. He shared about his relationship with Jesus Christ, and that night I got down on my knees and asked Jesus Christ to be my Lord and Master. Basically I said, "All of me I give to all of You,

---

David Busby is the director of student ministries for Grace Church of Edina, Minnesota. He also serves as the executive director of the Student Ministry Training Center in Minneapolis, which trains youth workers in ministry skills and philosophy. He is on the board of the National Network of Youth Ministries and has had 15 years of youth ministry experience. He received his B.A. from Tennessee Temple University, where he graduated summa cum laude. He and his wife, Lawanna, have one daughter.

Jesus. Make me a new person."

Immediately God began to put within my heart a deep desire to minister to students who somehow, like me, had missed authentic Christianity along the way. I even dropped out of the university and began to travel with this young man who led me to Jesus Christ. For the next 18 months, we travelled all over the United States and saw about 6,000 people come to know Christ. Despite my spiritual infancy, I was excited about having an authentic relationship with Jesus. After that, I decided I wanted to stay in one place and minister to students on a long-term basis.

Several years later, doctors discovered that I have cystic fibrosis, an hereditary disease of the lungs and pancreas. At that time, I thought about my life as never before. I desired that my life would make an impact for the Kingdom of God. Since then, I've had this tremendous urgency to make my life count in the student community — to help young people find the "authentic Christianity" that seemed so illusive to me for so many years. God has also given me a new intensity to see kids grow to maturity as disciples whose lives can have impact and can reproduce themselves in the lives of others.

THE DOOR TO SPIRITUAL GROWTH

In the process of seeking to be faithful to these desires, I have discovered some barriers. In fact, most of the youth workers I know have faced one barrier in particular. At one time or another, we have experienced very deep frustration because we have wanted to disciple people who were not willing to be disciples. We all have kids in our youth groups who simply do not have a willingness to grow.

However, in recent years, I have seen a deeper level of willingness developing in our kids than I have ever seen before. We have had less attrition with new Christians than we have ever had. God has been teaching us some principles that are really working. I am convinced that by incorporating these principles we can see a level of willingness develop in the lives of our students that will open the door to their spiritual maturity.

David's Downward Spiral of Unwillingness

One principle began to surface in my thinking as I was studying the life of King David in 2 Samuel 11 and 12. It was the time of the year "when kings go out to battle" (11:1), but David decided that instead of going out to war, he would stay home in Jerusalem. This was the first symptom of David's problem. He should have accompanied his armies into battle, but a spirit of *unwillingness* to respond to God had started to form in his heart, so he stayed home.

The plot thickens. David saw a beautiful woman bathing on the top of a roof. He could have dealt with his glands and his desires, but he continued to allow that unwillingness to develop in his life. Consequently David called for Bathsheba to come to the palace, and because he did not quench the growing unwillingness developing in his life, he committed adultery.

He had the opportunity to repent and deal with his sin, but by then his unwillingness had bloomed into a hardness against God. Not only would he not deal with the sin God was showing him, but he also compounded the problem through greater unwillingness. He plotted and indirectly caused the death of Uriah, Bathsheba's husband.

As the story continues, the Lord sent Nathan the prophet to David to tell a little story (12:1-4) that finally got through to the King. David was greatly moved by the story, but Nathan actually had to say, "You are the man!" (12:7) — in other words, "This story is about you" — before David finally woke up to what was happening. It was at that point that he finally admitted, "I have sinned against the Lord" (12:13). His pride, which had led him down that long road of unwillingness, was crushed.

Sustained With a Willing Spirit

The willing heart surfaces again in Psalm 51. Here we see a brokenhearted David reviewing his sin and confessing it to the Lord. He says, "Be gracious to me . . . I know my transgressions, and my sin is ever before me. Against Thee, Thee only, I have sinned. . ." (verses 1-4). He finishes his confession in verse 11, and then in verse 12 he begins to ask for healing and restoration: "Restore to me the joy of Thy salvation. . . ." And then in 12b, he says a very interesting thing: ". . . and sustain me with a *willing spirit.*" Do you see what David has learned from his past? He was saying, "Give me a willing spirit — that was the obstacle that derailed me in my Christian life. Grant me a willing spirit again that I might be sustained, that I might never again move away from being a 'man after God's own heart.'"

Foundation of Discipleship

Notice what Jesus had to say about the willing heart in Matthew 16:24. It is the basis of His appeal for us to follow Him. "If anyone wishes to come after Me, let him deny himself, and take up his cross, and follow Me." He appealed to their will.

We see it again in John 6. Jesus had just said some profound things about eating His flesh and drinking His blood (6:52-59). His disciples' response was, "This is a difficult statement; who can listen to it?" (6:60). As a result, many of His disciples left Him; Jesus then challenged the willingness of the twelve, "You do not want to go away also, do you?" (6:67). Essentially, Jesus was saying, "How's your willingness? Are you still willing to follow Me?" Jesus saw the issue of willingness as foundational in making disciples. If this principle is so important, what can we do to stimulate a young person's willingness? There are three things that we are doing that God seems to be using to create a willingness for spiritual growth within our students.

CREATING A WILLINGNESS THROUGH "SALTY" CHALLENGES

The way in which you challenge your students to involvement is crucial. Whether you are challenging them to come to know Christ, join a discipleship group, or apply a Bible study truth, it is important that you bring to the surface their desire, their need for what you are introducing. Introduce them to a little salt — it will make them thirsty!

Drink This — You're Thirsty!

If someone offered you a glass of water when you were not thirsty, you would say, "No, thank you."

But suppose the person is very insistent. "Listen, this is the greatest spring water in the world; I'd really like to bring you a glass of water."

"No, no thank you. I'm really not thirsty."

"Hey, listen, Jack. I want you to drink this water."

"No, I really don't want the water."

"Drink it!"

So to end the hassle, you finally drink it down, but it is an unpleasant experience. I'm afraid this little scenario resembles a lot of our teaching in student ministries today. We say, "Take this, kid; you won't grow without it!" But there is no willingness on his part. We must spend time making people thirsty, but how are we to do this? There are several ways that have worked well in my experience.

Making the Most of Life Experiences

I was in California conducting a high school summer camp, and the theme of the week was "A Willing Heart." Some of the kids had the attitude, "Well, you know, Dave, I'll get around to this commitment stuff someday; just give me a break, I'm only 16. When I'm 85 or so, I'll give it a real serious shot." We were trying to think of some way to illustrate the need so that we could communicate: "Hey, listen, crew. If God's Spirit is dealing with you, you need to respond. It's a big deal to say no to God."

About halfway through the week, one of the young men climbed up on a big tower, fell off and broke both of his wrists. At first the paramedics thought he had broken his neck. He was lying there crying and screaming and moaning. You can imagine the change of environment that took place at that camp. A soberness flooded the entire place. There was no flippancy in anyone anymore.

We could have just moved right on in our program: "Boy, that was really bad, wasn't it? Okay, now, let's go to session number two." Or, we could utilize that life experience — which we did. We brought all the kids together and said, "Hey, let's talk about this. What are you thinking? What are you feeling?" The reality had hit them that "hey, my life is just a vapor!" They were salted! They were now ready to talk a little more about radical commitment to Jesus Christ.

A life experience is a real event that takes place which you utilize for a teaching purpose. A young man in our area took his life a few months ago, and all of our high school students knew him because he graduated from the key school that we were working in. This guy was Mr. Athletic; he seemed to have it all together. But tragically, he jumped off a bridge and killed himself.

At the time, we were doing a series on body building — building up the Body of Christ, loving each other, developing intimate relationships. The next morning's newspaper included an interview with the boy's best friend. The reporter said, "No one seems to have any idea why he would take his life — not even his parents. You are his very best friend. Why do you think he took his life?" And his best friend said, "I don't know. We were just too macho to talk about things like that." So we used that life experience to salt them for the Bible study instead of beginning with, "Okay, now, our Bible study is going to be 'Getting Intimate With One Another.'" Life experiences salt the thirst of students for the truth you know they need.

Skits With a Purpose

You may already use skits in your youth ministry, but I challenge you to use them with a real purpose in mind. When I was a youth pastor in Nashville, some of the students in our group seemed like evangelism maniacs — they would assault anything that moved within a 10-foot radius. We had an abundance of spiritual babies. It was incredible! We had a lot of kids receiving Christ, but only a few were taking care of the babies. The kids needed a session on spiritual parenting, but up to that point, they had not seen the need. We came up with a simple skit to try to bring the message to life. Two guys came on stage and one said, "Hey, how's it going?"

"Everything's great!"

"Hey, listen man, school's going to start in a few minutes. I'm just believing God for 10 new babies today — ten new babies every day!"

So they walked off the stage, and sure enough, you could hear them coming back from school, rejoicing, "bringing their sheaves with them" — and they had all these baby dolls. They were so excited, and they were shaking those dolls all around in the process. We repeated the sequence to correspond to eight or ten days, and we had babies all over the stage. Stacks of babies. And these guys continued to walk in, and because the dolls were everywhere, they would step on the babies and the doll's heads popped off, the arms popped off — it was quite a sight! About the time all the kids were getting grossed out, one guy stood up and said, "I wonder if we're not doing the same thing to some of the spiritual babies that we are giving birth to in our own ministry." Then he sat down. The kids had gotten the point; now they were thirsty, and we had a great talk about spiritual parenting.

Life Simulations — When It's Okay to Lie In Church!

A life simulation is a pre-arranged experience that teaches truth in a true-to-life fashion. Recently we simulated a life experience with our college kids. We flew in a guy by the name of Alan to do our college retreat. We wanted to focus on the character quality of developing a heart of compassion. I think our college students are just like most college students, and they were saying sarcastically, "Oh, boy! A heart of compassion — lay it on me." They just weren't very thirsty for that, so we prepared to salt them a bit.

We flew Alan in early and had somebody plant him out on the highway that led to the camp so that he could appear to be hitch-hiking. He hadn't shaved for a while, and he looked like a real bum. Some of the students we work with are considered the "upper crust," coming from very wealthy families. So we were cruising by in these nice buses, and all of a sudden, the bus driver and a couple of guys who were clued in to the scheme spotted Alan. The driver pulled the bus over, and opened the doors, and the guys said, "Hey, come on in!"

About that time, everybody in the bus was saying, "Hey, man, haven't you heard of the hitchhiker massacres? What are you doing? He's probably a drug addict. You're going to kill us all!" They had zero-level compassion. They were scared to death. Before long, the "plants" in the group had issued Alan an invitation, "Why don't you come with us to our retreat this weekend?" By this time, the kids were thinking, "What? *What*? Oh, no!" You can imagine what happened when this "hitchhikin' bum" turned out to be the camp speaker! The simulation gave them a little glimpse of themselves, and they were "salted."

Questions That Stimulate Interest

As you study the Gospels, you will notice that Jesus asked twice as many questions as He gave answers. He was incredibly skilled at asking questions. We have purposely tried to follow His example in our follow-up of new Christians. We are seeing that it really works, and it's exciting! In the past, when we led young people to the Lord, we got frustrated trying to follow them up. We would meet with a new convert and say, "Hey, you're not going to grow, man, if you don't meet with me! When will we meet?"

The new Christian would mumble, "Oh, I don't know, I'm not really interested. I really don't want to; I don't think I'm into that after all." So we began to ask the Lord how we could salt these new Christians to begin to have a desire to meet with us for follow-up. The Lord gave us the idea of asking several key questions shortly after leading someone to Christ. We would sit down with him and say, "Hey, do you mind if I ask your opinion about some things? I'd like to get to know you a little better. Last night we went through the gospel again, and you invited Christ into your life, right?"

"Yeah."

"Are you sure Jesus Christ came into your life?"

"Yeah, yeah, I'm sure."

"Let's suppose that tomorrow you are eating lunch at school and one of your friends who's a little skeptical about Christ comes up to you and says, 'Robert, what's the big deal about a man who died 2,000 years ago? I mean, Robert, what's the big deal? What's so special about Jesus?' Robert, would you know what to tell him?"

"Uh, uh. . . ."

"Well, Robert, let me ask you a second question [I'm really trying not to embarrass him, I'm trying to salt him]. What if you wake up in the morning and you have the flu and you don't feel that Jesus is in you anymore. Robert, how would you handle that situation?"

"Well, I'm really not sure."

"Let me ask you a third question. Let's say you really blow it big time — I mean, you blow it bigger than you ever thought you would. Would you have to carry all that guilt around, Robert, or would you know how to get things straight between you and God again?"

"Well, uh . . . ."

"Let me ask you another question, Robert . . . ." And we go through about five questions relating to the initial felt needs of a new Christian. Questions like "What happens if your friends at school start noticing the difference in your life and they begin to react to you negatively. Would you know how to handle that?" Or, "Maybe they begin to respond to you in a positive way — would you know how to communicate to them what has happened to you?" We use questions to begin to create a willingness and a desire to be followed up. And it's been great. We've noticed a dramatic increase in the effectiveness of our entire follow-up approach.

Challenges, in Summary

So these are a few methods that we have found effective in salting young people — methods which increase their thirst for greater spiritual growth in their lives. But, let me say this: These examples of salting take work, sweat, creativity and prayer. It's a whole lot easier to come in, spit out a Bible study and then leave. The problem with that is that kids do not really take in what you are saying. Consequently, they are not willing to learn and they don't grow.

Salting is only part of challenging, but since it is so neglected, I have emphasized it. You also must give them *information*. What is it you are specifically challenging them to? Four follow-up appointments? A six-week Bible study? A discipleship group? And what expectations do you have of them? "Homework" every week? Scripture memory? Mandatory attendance?

Third, you must *penetrate their willingness*. Have you ever tried to disciple somebody who doesn't want to be discipled? That's a contradiction of terms! So after you give them specific information about what is involved, lay out the challenge — "Are you willing?" And then wait for a thoughtful response.

Finally, it is not a good challenge if you leave out *accountability*. Unless you make the person accountable, then all you can do is assume that people are growing, assume that their lives are changing. Most people who make assumptions like that are in for a rude awakening! So, then, creating a willingness for growth within students starts with giving a proper challenge.

CREATING A WILLINGNESS THROUGH PRAYER

The second way I know to create a willingness for spiritual growth is through praying for students. In Philippians 2:13, we see the crucial jugular vein of willingness. The Scripture says, "For it is *God* [catch the emphasis] who is at work in you both to *will* and to work for His good pleasure." It is God who puts the willingness in any of us! He is the God of the willing heart. I have been going through our rolls — name after name after name — praying for God to give each of our kids a willing heart. I try to pray for some everyday — name by name and need by need. I know you are probably very busy, even as I am. I know what it's like when you feel like saying to God, "But Lord, I have these staff people who report to me, there is training to do, we have interns coming in, we have kids coming out our ears. Oh, Lord, listen, I'm just too busy to spend much time praying! I'll catch You at the next conference, and we'll talk about some of these things then, Lord!"

Name By Name

Isn't it ironic that we can be so busy serving the Lord that we never take time to talk to Him about what we want to see Him accomplish? The tragedy is that if we are too busy to pray specifically, then we are not going to see students develop the willing hearts that we long to see. I challenge you to cut out anything you need to cut out in order to have time to pray. And then spend the time bringing students before God name by name. One person I know defines intercession as "love on its knees." That is what we are doing when we pray like that for our kids.

Lately, I have seen some guys whom I considered hard as nails begin to develop willing hearts. I have nine guys in a little shepherding group who are so flakey. I've been praying for these guys, "Jesus, they don't really give a flip about You, and I'd really like for You to give them willing hearts. I don't know what it's going to take." Day by day I have been bringing these guys before the Lord.

Sometimes when I am up in front of a room teaching or leading, I see them in in the back, disinterested and out of it. Most of them come from wealthy families, but none of them is willing. In my mind I am saying, "God, what is it going to take to reach these guys?" I love them; I can't help myself, I love them. So day by day and week by week I have been bringing these guys before the Lord.

One night two of the guys were driving their cars around the church parking lot during one of our youth meetings. One guy was driving very slowly, and the other guy intended to put his foot on the front bumper and lie down on the hood. However, when he stepped up on the front bumper, his foot slipped, the tire caught him, and he was pulled right under the tire of the car. When he fell back, he cracked his skull hard on the pavement. One of the kids I had been praying for ran into the back of church during the meeting, grabbed me and said, "John's been run over — we've got to pray!" I had the opportunity to spend three hours with those guys as they cried over their friend in the emergency room. After that, we began to see some light dawn in the area of their willingness.

Praying to the God of the willing heart. That is the only way you can be sure of getting through to your kids.

CREATING A WILLINGNESS THROUGH
SPIRITUAL MODELING

Finally, we can see God develop a willingness for spiritual maturity within our students through modeling. This has been a much-talked-about concept in recent years, but let me touch on one facet of it — *reality modeling*. Normally modeling focuses on positive areas — and obviously it is essential that we demonstrate an exemplary Christian life. But part of the modeling process must include how we deal with difficulty and failure.

The Phantom

How many of your students have ever seen you work through a sin area in your life? I know that may sound a bit threatening, but to most of our kids, we are phantoms. We come in, "Well, praise the Lord! Praise Jesus! I just read 40 chapters in the Old Testament today and led 30 people to Christ at lunch! I can't wait until supper!" We may think we are really encouraging our kids because we are such "godly models." But those kids are saying to themselves, "I'll never be like that guy — always praising the Lord and witnessing." The fact is that just 15 minutes before the Wednesday night meeting, you and your wife had a knock-down, drag-out!

"What? You're going out again? You haven't spent any time at home for a month!"

"Boy, Lady, do you need to get your priorities straight! Seek ye *first* the Kingdom of God!"

And you walk into that Wednesday night meeting and someone says, "How is your wife doing?" And you say, "She's the *loveliest* thing! She's the light of my life!" That's not modeling — that's hypocrisy! Be real with kids. Nothing motivates them more than a *real* model.

A "Regular Person" — Submitting to Christ

True, it jacks the jaws of our kids when I share with them about a sin area in my life. I have had kids come to me and say, "You're not supposed to do that." You know why it rattles their cages? Because I can't be on the pedestal anymore — I'm down there walking with them, doing my best to live in the Spirit, but failing sometimes. Then they have to deal with the fact that, "Hey, he's a regular person and he needs to submit to the lordship of Jesus; I am a regular person, and I need to, too." It brings personal responsibility zooming right in the front door of their lives.

We do need to exercise some caution, asking God to give us wisdom about what not to share. But that shouldn't stop us from being real with kids. It is extremely therapeutic, but sometimes it is so hard. One day a girl came into my office, weeping bitterly. She was burdened about something, and she asked me things about an area that was cold as dry ice in my heart. I could have given her some glib advice or some pat answers, but instead I found myself saying, "You know, you have more compassion in this area than I do. I am not even sure I can help you, because my heart is cold in this area. Instead of counseling you, why don't I just let you pray for me for a while?" Reality modeling. It encourages their willingness to grow — not alone, but along with you!

WILLING HEARTS, WINNING THE WORLD

A willing heart — responsive to God, open to His leading, thirsty for spiritual growth and maturity. There is probably nothing more foundational and central in the entire Christian life. By and large, we do what we really want to do. If we really want to pray, we pray. If we really want to share our faith, we share our faith. We will overcome any barrier in the power of the Holy Spirit if we really want to do it. Almost every day of my life I pray, "God, I love You. Give me a willing heart today." If I don't receive that willing heart everyday, I could derail as easily as King David did.

It's so easy for that spirit of unwillingness to begin to creep in gradually, almost unnoticed. Often this happens in the area of pride. I was in a meeting one day, sitting in the back of the large room talking with a good friend of mine. Some beautiful music was being presented up front, and a young guy whom I didn't know came up to us and said, "Sh-h-h. I think you guys should be quiet." Well, immediately my pride surfaced, and I felt like saying, "Hey, turkey, who do you think you are?" But the Holy Spirit said, "You know he's right; you need to be quiet and listen. I might have something I want to say to you through this music." This is just one little scenario of the kinds of things that constantly present themselves to us. We must conscientiously deal with each of these to keep that spirit of unwillingness from developing in our lives.

God is the Source of the willing heart. As we secure His power through a willingness in our own lives, and then in the lives of our students, we will see some phenomenal results. Kids who are unwilling, apathetic, and even hardened will be transformed into disciples and disciple makers. Then the authentic Christianity that people like me almost missed will begin to become a reality for growing numbers around the world.

PUTTING THIS CHAPTER TO WORK

1. A "willing heart" must start with those of us who are in leadership. Even King David may have felt he had a willing heart at first, but the unwilling spirit crept in gradually, starting with his

refusal to go to battle and ending in adultery and murder. If this could happen to a "man after God's own heart," it could happen to us. What *specific area* of your life do you need to guard so that unwillingness to respond to God will not hinder your ministry? What areas of your students' lives? What can you do to guard your heart?

2. As you think about the character qualities that you are trying to build into your disciples, what are some of the key *current issues* that they must face or be equipped with if they hope to become more spiritually mature? (For example, the character quality of "faithfulness" might bring to the surface a need to learn the meaning of "commitment.")

3. As you reflect on the above issues, what are some *life experiences* you know about that could help to bring out their desire or need for the truth? What *life simulations* could you arrange? What *skits*? How could you use *questions*?

4. Dave challenged us to bring the names and needs of our students before the Lord regularly, as a key strategy in helping them to develop willing hearts. Will you accept the challenge? How will you get your list together? When will you start?

12

EQUIPPING DISCIPLES WHO MULTIPLY

by Daryl Nuss

What is it that brings tears to your eyes when you think about it? What motivates you to the extent that you feel like pounding the table when you talk about it? These two questions were posed by consultant Bobb Biehl during recent national planning meetings for Student Venture. What brings tears to my eyes? Whenever I see a high school student and start thinking about what is happening to him in the context of the student culture today, I feel like weeping. About 50 percent of today's high school students are living in broken homes. At least one out of every 10 teenage girls will have to deal with an unwanted pregnancy during her teenage years.

What causes me to pound the table? In 1981, George Gallup conducted a poll revealing that approximately 50 million people in the United States claim to be born-again Christians. In 1982, Campus Crusade for Christ did a survey of all the incoming freshmen at UCLA. Twenty-six percent claimed to have had a born-again experience. There is something kind of exciting about these statistics, but on the other hand, there is something equally depressing about them — something that makes me want to pound the table. All around us we see our national values going downhill; this is reflected in our moral lives, in the media, in politics, everywhere. For instance, did you know that for every four babies born, three more have been aborted? These things certainly don't reflect a culture influenced by the salt and light that should result if one-fourth of our population actually is born-again. I ask myself, what's the missing link? I believe that it is discipleship. Discipleship is the key

---

Daryl Nuss is the San Diego city director for Student Venture, the high school ministry of Campus Crusade for Christ. He has served with Campus Crusade for 14 years and has been a national traveling representative for Student Venture since 1978. Daryl graduated with honors from Sterling College in Sterling, Kansas. He and his wife, Donna, live with their two sons in Poway, California.

in developing Christians who are salt and light in their culture.

Maybe you have experienced some of the frustration and bitterness that can come when you have a group of kids into whom you really want to pour your life, but they apparently are not interested. Or you have a meeting that you spent hours preparing for, and only half of the kids show up. All kinds of emotions can arise and you say, "I wonder if this discipleship isn't just another word that we've run into the ground, another program that I've tried but should forget. There has got to be something better."

In the past I have felt like a cowboy in a closed corral full of cattle. He begins to whip the cattle until they start running in a circle, kicking dirt and manure in the air, and working up a real sweat. He quits whipping them, and after a while they calm down. Realistically, they have not moved an inch, but they sure are tired. When it comes to discipleship, there are probably a lot of us who feel like the cowboy — we are pouring all of our effort into "whipping" these kids. They go around and around. But when all is said and done, they haven't moved an inch. They haven't grown a bit.

I think the problem is related to a lack of understanding about the nature of discipleship. If we are properly selecting students, challenging them and leading them into discipleship, we will have more born-again Christians who are truly acting like salt and light in their culture. That is what this chapter is all about. Though not all-inclusive by any means, these principles may help us to open that corral gate and get moving in the right direction.

DISCIPLESHIP IN PERSPECTIVE

Discipleship begins between our ears. Whether we like it or not, what is happening in the lives of our youth group or our disciples is a direct reflection of our perspective of discipleship. If we are not clear about what discipleship really is, then as I've heard it said, "A mist in the pulpit is a fog in the pew."

What Discipleship Is Not

What do you understand discipleship to be? One way to find an answer is to clarify what discipleship is *not*. First of all, discipleship is not just another *Bible study*. Studying the Bible is certainly a part of discipleship, but that is not all it is. A couple of years ago I was on the phone with a friend of mine from college, and he said, "Daryl, I'm so excited. I am in a group of men who are being discipled!"

I said, "Great! What are you doing?"

"Well, this assistant pastor is really into the Greek. We are going through the book of Ephesians phrase by phrase in the Greek, and we are memorizing the key verses. It's just so exciting to be discipled!"

I hung up the phone and thought, "Well, it's exciting that they are going through the Greek, and that may be a *part* of discipleship, but that's not all there is to it."

Second, discipleship is not going through a set *curriculum*. Personally, I encourage my staff to use a curriculum or a manual or whatever, but discipleship is *not* merely going through that curriculum. We can run our kids through a course and when they get done, their lives may not have changed a bit, except to be inoculated against ever trying something like that again!

Finally, discipleship is not merely a group of *warm relationships*. True, relationships are vital to discipleship, but they are not the end result and do not necessarily generate disciples. I saw this fact illustrated several years ago with a new girl on our staff team. She had been in our city about two weeks when she announced at staff meeting, "I now have my discipleship group!"

I thought, "Well, that's neat, but in two weeks?" I said, "Tell me about it."

She said, "Well, I was over at McDonald's with one of the Christian girls I met, and we ran into two of her friends who happened to be Christians. I asked them if they wanted to be in a group, they said they did, and now I've got my discipleship group!"

As far as she was concerned, her year was a success — she now had a group of three girls who wanted to get together. That was good, but she had missed a lot of the important components of discipleship. To her, discipleship was having a group of kids who liked her and would get together with her on a regular basis. That is what discipleship is *not*.

What Discipleship Is

What, then, *is* discipleship? Mark 3:13-15 shows how Jesus looked at it. "And He went up into the mountain and summoned those whom He Himself wanted, and they came to Him. And He appointed twelve, that they might be with Him, and that He might send them out to preach and to have authority to cast out demons." Let's take a closer look at the passage. Verse 13 says that He went to the mountain and "summoned those whom He Himself wanted." Jesus selected His disciples. To do what? Verse 14 points out two objectives: ". . . that they might be with Him, and that He might send them out to preach. . . ." That is discipleship — the twofold process of falling more and more in love with Christ based on an intimate knowledge of Him and becoming increasingly available and effective in ministry.

Another excellent verse on discipleship is 2 Timothy 2:2. Paul is speaking to Timothy, helping to clarify for him what is really important in ministry. Paul says: "And the things which you have heard from me in the presence of many witnesses, these entrust to faithful men, who will be able to teach others also." Paul is saying that discipleship means multiplication. It is seeing the life of one maturing believer implanted in the life of another maturing believer. That is what discipleship *is*.

SELECTING THE RIGHT STUDENTS

I think the reason that we do not see more multiplication among high school students is *not* that high school students can't multiply or that we as leaders can't disciple. Rather, the main hindrance to multiplication is that we select the *wrong people* to disciple. How did Jesus select the right people to be His disciples? Luke 6:12,13 reports that His decision was based upon spending "the whole night in prayer." But He spent the night in prayer after doing what? After spending weeks and months observing His disciples in various situations. Of course, He had more than 12 men who followed Him; but after observation and prayer, He initially selected only 12. Later on, there were 70, and finally there were 120 in the Upper Room. But the initial selection was 12 men. How would one go about making a selection like that? I believe there are some biblical guidelines that help us in forming criteria for selecting disciples.

Faithful

2 Timothy 2 instructs that we should "entrust to faithful men." What does "faithful" mean here? Obviously, it means full of faith; it can mean dependable. But to me, it means more. First of all, I look for people who have a *heart for God*. As you observe your group, you will find that typically there are students who come up after the sessions and say, "What did you mean by that?" Or, "I was reading the Bible the other day, and I noticed this statement; could you explain what it means?" Or they are the ones who say, "You know, God has just pointed out some sin in my life." You begin to observe their heart for God.

The second thing I look for are students with *teachable attitudes*. Again, you will begin to observe that there are some kids to whom you can say, "This is what the Word says; what is your response?" — and they will respond. With other kids, it's like water off a duck's back. It doesn't mean that they are any less valuable to the Lord, but it might indicate that they have a way to go before they are ready to become disciples. As far as I'm concerned, faithfulness is the primary ingredient, and faithfulness is evidenced by a heart for God and a teachable attitude.

Able to Multiply

Notice that 2 Timothy 2:2 qualifies the kind of faithful men we are to select: ". . . faithful men who will be able to teach others also." This raises the standard of discipleship to a point that will ensure multiplication. Though we need to be nurturing all of our young people, I believe this passage is speaking about the people who will become our leadership core — the people we select to pour our lives into. These people must have a basic emotional security, the beginnings of an ability to teach, lead and model to other people. These abilities can grow and develop from a formative stage, but if they are not there, multiplication will not occur.

Committed to Evangelism

Jesus involved His disciples in evangelism right from the outset (Mark 2:14-15). Likewise, we need to be looking for the kind of disciples who are open to involvement in this area. Which kids in your group often bring their friends? Or when you ask for prayer requests, who would respond, "Pray for my lab partner — he really needs to know the Lord; and pray for me, to know what I can do"? Who is always there when you are doing something related to evangelism? Those kinds of kids always stick out. They show their concern for what is happening with their friends. These kids probably have a heart for evangelism. They will likely be excellent candidates for your discipleship group.

Available

Sometimes you can find students who may meet all the other criteria, but they still do not qualify for your discipleship group. They may seem to be quite interested, but when you try to get them involved, they are always too busy. They are just not available. I remember some of our staff girls telling stories similar to the following.

The staff member attempting to involve a key student in discipleship says, "I want to pull together a discipleship group; I've prayed about this, and you exhibit to me the qualities I'm looking for. Would you be interested?"

"Oh, yeah, I'm really interested!"

"Well, I've been talking with some of the other girls, and we would like to meet on Wednesday after school."

"Oh, I can't do that; I've got pompon practice Wednesday after school."

"Well, we could probably flex with that. What about Thursday?"

"Oh, Thursday. I'm the president of French Club, and that's when we have our French Club meeting."

"Well, what about Saturday?"

"No, I can't. I'm working over at the Yogurt Shop every Saturday, and Saturday is just out."

"Well, what about Monday morning, early. I'm willing to get together at 6:30. . . ."

"You are not going to believe this, but Monday morning just happens to be the morning that the pompon girls go out with the band to get our routine together."

Finally, the staff member is thinking, "What about 3:00 in the morning?" That doesn't mean we throw people like this on the rubbish heap and consider them unspiritual. But at least we need to have enough savvy to realize that right now, until they change their priorities, they don't qualify for our discipleship group. No matter how many other qualities they have and how much you may want them involved, if they don't have the time, they're not going to pan out.

However, God may want to use you to help this type of person sort out her direction. You might take this approach: "Well, I sense that you have no time available for the discipleship group. How important is this to you?" Then begin to help her clarify her objectives. You may want to give her some time to consider writing down those priorities. If she really does meet the other criteria, she may decide to alter her other commitments. Many times, however, we are attempting to adjust our primary discipleship to accommodate kids who really don't have the time. And if they are not willing to make some adjustments, then we need to face the fact that they are not the leaders the Lord gave us for this time. That will be one of the ways the Lord will help us select the right people to disciple.

CHALLENGING STUDENTS TO DISCIPLESHIP

Once you have carefully selected the kids whom you consider to be qualified for a discipleship group, it is very important *how* you go about challenging them. There are several principles to keep in mind that will make a big difference.

Focus on People, Not on Programs

A couple of years ago, I traveled into a city that I was responsible to supervise for Student Venture. One afternoon I was going to accompany a staff member on his lunch appointment with a student named Bob. When I asked for a little background on Bob, the staff member related a very interesting story. Bob had come to Christ the spring before and had grown a little. Over the summer, the staff person was gone a lot, and they had lost some contact. Also in the summer, Bob got involved in a weightlifting program for football. By the fall, he was so immersed in football that he wasn't available to meet with the staff or do anything in the ministry. As a result, he was going nowhere in his spiritual growth. That spring he was involved in an end-over-end car accident, and he found himself lying at the side of the road with the car resting up against a tree. He was aware that his life was spared, and within a couple of days he called the staff member and said, "I'd really like to get together!

This appointment was in response to that call. The staff member told me he planned to share about the ministry of the Holy Spirit. That sounded good to me. We met at a hamburger place, and after a little bit of conversation, the staff member led into discussing a booklet we use about the Spirit-filled life. He was really on the money — it was exactly what the student needed. Bob said, "You know, I've had self in control, and I really want to have Christ in control." When they came to the point in the booklet offering a suggested prayer, Bob prayed, "Lord, I really want you to take control of my life." It was great.

Then a most interesting thing happened. I couldn't believe it — the staff member just went into orbit! He said, "Well, this is so good; I'm so glad you have reached this point! Now here is what you need to do. You need to start having a quiet time. A quiet time is where you get up early every morning, and you start working yourself through a book of the Bible or a meaningful passage. A quiet time is essential. The second thing you need to do is start sharing your faith. Disciples grow when they share their faith. So share your faith. And I'll tell you what. We have just decided we're going to start a discipleship group — we're going through this manual, and I have a copy in the car I'll give you. We meet on Tuesday nights at 7:30, and you need to be there. Can you make it on Tuesday nights?"

The kid was stunned! He said, "Well, yeah, I probably really need to be there."

I could see that this kid was totally confused. At that point, I couldn't help myself. I just had to jump in! So I said, "Bob, let's back up just a second. Obviously, from your physique, you're interested in football, right? You have also mentioned that you are interested in weightlifting. Do you enjoy weightlifting? I mean, do you really enjoy having your muscles hurt and all the aggravation that you go through three days a week in that weight room? Do you *enjoy* that?"

"Not particularly."

"Well, why do you do it?"

"Well, as you notice, I'm a little bit shorter than some of the other guys whom I'm up against, and I've just got to be 'overwhelming' in terms of strength."

"That's why you lift weights — so you can be on the team and excel?"

"Well, yeah, that's right."

"Would you lift weights like that if you weren't trying to make the team?"

"Probably not."

"Can you see how the same principles stack up in the Christian life? If we really want to see God work in our lives, there are certain things that are helpful for us to do. Just as we need to eat and exercise to be good athletes, we need to eat and exercise to grow in our Christian lives. What are some of the things you would like to see God do in your life?"

"Well, I really would like to learn how to get things out of the Bible."

"Anything else?"

"Well, I'm not there yet, but someday I would like to be able to tell others about why Christ is so important."

From that point, we were now ready to talk about how the Tuesday night discipleship group would be an excellent way to meet his needs — and he was open to it.

The above experience is an illustration of the difference between a challenge which is content-centered and one that is student-centered. It is easy to challenge people to a program, to content. "I have this Bible study; would you like to come?" "I have this manual; do you want to go through it?" Rather, we need to be challenging a student in light of his felt-need. Building on our relationship, we need to determine where he is coming from and how to communicate our challenge to discipleship in a way he can visualize as helping to meet his need. It makes a big difference in his long-range motivation, ownership and commitment.

Notice in Matthew 4:19 that when Jesus challenged some of His early disiples, He said, *"Follow Me, and I will make you fishers of men."* He did not say, "Men, I am going to give you a theological course that you won't believe." So then, our challenges need to be student-centered and person-oriented, not content-centered.

Challenge to Action

The second thing to consider in challenging students is the need to challenge them to action. I don't know about you, but I am not motivated to be involved in know-nothing, do-nothing groups, and I don't think our young people are much different. Don't be afraid to challenge your people to *action*.

Jesus is our prime example. He did not say to His disciples, "Follow Me, and I will make you men of God." He said, "Follow Me, and I will make you fishers of men" (Matthew 4:19). He was action-oriented. He took them with Him everywhere He went. And when the disciples got to the point where they began to grow, what did

He do? He sent them out to preach and heal (Luke 9:1-6). After they reported back (Luke 9:10), they traveled with Him for a while. Then Jesus sent 70 of them out again, two by two (Luke 10:1). When they came back, they were just "buzzin'" about all the things they had seen (Luke 10:17). Jesus rejoiced with them, and then He moved into another time of teaching. Jesus was a man of action, and He challenged his disciples to action. Likewise, we need to be challenging our disciples to action in a way that will motivate and challenge them.

I have confirmed this principle in my own personal experience. My mom was a very diligent, godly woman. She helped me establish the habit of reading a verse of Scripture every morning and every night, beginning the day I could read. But do you know when I started to really learn spiritual concepts? It was when I was a junior in college, because I began to be aware that I needed to be sharing my faith. I was very jumbled-mouthed, but somehow a guy across the hall came to Christ; later, he came to me and said, "Now what do I do?"

My first reaction was, "I don't know; go see the Chaplain!" But I hung in there with him, and even though I was just one step ahead of the hounds, it was amazing how Scripture came alive, because I had been moved into action. I think we are all the same way. We don't learn much until we are out in the action, and then we learn all kinds of things.

Communicate Vision

I also believe that we need to challenge our young people with a vision. God is working in your life, and you are in the process of developing and carrying out some kind of vision that God has given you. What is it that motivates you to be involved in youth ministry? You may not have thought about it enough to aritculate it immediately, but if you are working with youth, there is something that motivates you to do so. That motivation has given you some dreams and desires that are affecting what you are doing with kids.

Maybe you are thinking, "I would really like to see every student at this high school have a chance to be exposed to the claims of Christ. How are we going to do that?" For starters, one of the things that might come to mind is to have a weekly meeting that is sharp and attractive to non-Christians. So you have a vision and you've thought of a program to accomplish it. Now you pull together some of your leadership kids and say, "You know what we're going to do? We are going to start a Friday night After-Game Bonanza! A lot of people are going to come, and some of them are going to come to Christ."

You announce that idea with your vision clearly in mind, but your kids see only the program. They are with you for about two weeks. Then two or three of them come to you and say, "We can't come this Friday night — the drama teacher needs some stagehands. It really would be fun to be a part of the play, so on Friday nights for the next three weeks we need to be there to build the props." And in your mind you are saying, "I'm talking about reaching kids, and they're building props!"

This kind of scenario repeats itself with youth workers across the country. What is their typical solution? They go back to the drawing board and come up with another program, only this time, bigger and better. Students may be excited initially, but eventually their interest wanes. Why? Because the student was committed only to the program itself, not to the vision that prompted the program. That is why it is so important that those we challenge to our discipleship groups have a clear understanding of our vision — at least the broad strokes of it. So think it through and seek to become proficient in articulating it. That vision will motivate them long after the programs are history.

Clarify the Cost

In challenging our young people to discipleship, it is also extremely important that we clarify the cost factor. Sometimes we water down the challenge because we don't want the people to reject us. As a result, we are not very clear about what it is going to cost to be involved in the discipleship group. We want to be cool, so we say, "Let's get together every so often, and we'll probably go through this manual — or whatever — and it should be fun." So the kid responds, "Well, okay." But it is a ho-hum response, which will produce ho-hum results because we never gave a clear explanation of what it was going to take to be in the discipleship core.

Several years ago I selected five guys to be in a discipleship group. In this particular situation, I had typed out the expectations, and we went over them at my apartment. I presented the challenge as clearly as I could:

> Men, as we have talked about this, you know that I have prayed about whether I should ask you to be involved in this discipleship group. If I didn't want you to be involved, I would not have asked you. Now you need to decide whether you want to do it. But before you make a decision, I want you to know clearly what is involved.
>
> First, I want you to be able to commit to being together an hour and a half each week — maybe two hours, realistically. We will spend that time together in the Word, in prayer and in planning strategy. You choose the night, but it is going to be two hours in the evening.
>
> Second, at our Monday night Student Venture meeting, I want you guys to provide the leadership, so you will need to come every Monday night.

Also, I want you to have at least one appointment with me each week. Most of the time we will go out witnessing, so I want you to be available to go witnessing with me once a week. And, as we see people come to Christ and opportunities come up, I would want you to be available to begin to disciple other kids.

That is what's involved.

All five of them said, "Great! We're with you."

About six weeks later, we got together for our regular evening, and one of the guys, Dave, wasn't there. I thought he might be sick or something, so I called his house and his mom said, "Dave is at work." I thought, "Work? What is this?" Throughout that next week, I could never reach him. Our regular evening came along, and he missed again. I finally reached him on the phone, and we set up a time to talk in the school library. I thought quite a bit about what I would say to Dave. We sat down at a table and talked a little bit. Then Dave looked me straight in the eye and said, "Daryl, I've got to tell you this. I can no longer be in your discipleship group."

I asked, "Why?"

He explained, "This is going to sound immature, and I know I'm growing, but I saw a car down at the car lot that I've got to have. For me to fulfill some of the needs I have, I really need to have a car. Furthermore, if I had a car, I could bring kids to the Monday night meeting. It's a yellow Camaro, and since I really want it, I've made the decision that I'm going to get a job and buy the car. Because I have made that decision, I just know I can't be in your group anymore. I just want you to know."

I said, "Well, that's your decision. Maybe you have some things to learn here about priorities; you may even find out that there is more to life than that yellow car! But that is where you're at, and that's fine. You are always welcome at our meetings; and if you ever want to get together, that's great. In fact, I'm going to call you every so often, because you are still my friend!" That's where we left it. I didn't have to say a word about his qualifying for our group; he told me because he understood the expectations.

About three months later, Dave gave me a call and said, "You know, this working to pay for this car is a real bummer. I've sold the car, and I'm wondering if I can be back in your group. I think I have learned my lesson about that, and I really want to come back on board." Exciting!

Later that spring, we needed to appoint somebody to lead our movement through the summer while we were gone. Guess who volunteered and whom we selected? Dave. But if I hadn't been clear on what I expected in the discipleship group, I would have been frustrated, he would have felt guilty, and eventually there could have been a rupturing in the relationship that might have led to his dropping out spiritually. So it's important — and exciting —

to clarify the cost factor.

LEADING A DISCIPLESHIP GROUP

So far, we've given the bulk of our emphasis to determining who should be in our discipleship groups and how we should get them involved. If we do those things right, we are well on our way! But now that you have your group, how should you proceed?

Clarify Your Goals

Don't be too anxious to pull your group together. Take some time to plan and think through these questions: "What are my goals? What do I really want to accomplish?" If you are going to help develop disciples who will be salt and light in their culture — disciples who can help to multiply the faith throughout the world — what specific goals should you try to accomplish in your limited time together? If you had to boil down what you are doing with these students to three goals, what would they be? I'll tell you what they are for me. I want to help students walk by faith, share their faith and help others grow. Most of what I do I can hang on those three goals. Whatever your goals, I would encourage you to boil them down; consider where you are going and how you are going to get there.

Personalize Your Goals

After you have established your general goals, then you need to personalize them to your group, your situation. You need to ask yourself, "How am I going to get these goals into the lives of my students?" Your answers will guide you in putting together your approach to discipling your unique group of students. For example, take the goal of "walking by faith," and ask yourself four questions:

1. What are the specific *needs* of the members of my discipleship group in the area of their spiritual walk? Identify where they are right now.
2. What *truth* (biblical concept or training) could I communicate to help meet those needs?
3. How can I *demonstrate* the application of the concept or truth?
4. How can I *delegate* action which will help the students take a step of application?

What kinds of things can I give them to do that the Lord will use to build them in those areas of need? Think through each of your goals and answer these questions on paper. It is a way of objectifying what you sense God wants to do in their lives and focusing your time and energies to the point where you can see it practically lived out.

Another aid in personalizing the goals of your group is simply asking the students what their goals are. Most of them probably have not thought about goals, but the process of asking will not only give you perspective but could also help give them some real direction. Your conversation might go something like this:

"Well, Joe, I have really observed the Lord doing some good things in your life. Tell me, what would you like to see God do in your life this coming year?

"Well, I'd like to glorify God."

"Oh, that's *good* . . . but in your heart, what would it mean for you to glorify God? How would you know if you were ever glorifying God?"

"Well, if I could just have a decent relationship with my parents, that would be one way I could glorify God." On a sheet of paper I write down "Relate better to parents."

Then I ask, "What else would you like to see God do?"

"I'd like to be man of the Word."

"Well, what does 'being in the Word' mean to you? I mean, it could be a theological degree or lots of things. What does it mean to you?"

"Well, if I could just spend five minutes every morning in the Word, I would feel like that was significant. You know what I mean?" So I write down, "Five minutes in the Word."

"What else?"

"I'd like to share my faith."

"Well, what would be sharing your faith?"

"Boy, if I could just share with one friend a week, that would be significant to me!"

"Great!" I write down "Share with one friend a week."

Going through this process with your students helps them objectify their feelings and clarifies what is important to them. It gives them a vision for their lives and a motivation for being involved in discipleship. It also gives you tremendous insight as to how to personalize your overall discipleship goals in a way that will make an impact on the lives with which you have been entrusted.

UTILIZE DISCIPLESHIP GROUPS

Finally, we need to pursue our goals. Selecting, challenging and planning are crucial, but they are only preparatory to the main event — day-by-day discipleship. There are a variety of means by which we can pursue our goals. One very effective way is through discipleship group meetings. Typically I try to include a number of very basic things in my meetings. There is a time of *sharing* what God is teaching the kids and what important things are taking place in their lives. We *pray* together about our requests and praises. We spend some time in *the Word* —not just content for content's sake, but content that we try to apply practically to their lives in meeting the goals we have previously laid down. We try to focus some time on *training* in ministry skills or problem areas. We use role-play, discussion and question/answer format to help them understand and desire to use what we are covering.

As our disciples mature and God begins to place in their hearts a burden to reach out, we include the area of *strategy* in our meetings. Here we focus the students on their campuses, their spheres of influence and the gifts God has given them. We talk about how we can combine those elements to reach others and get them discipled as well. These kinds of meetings can be a dynamic tool for building disciples.

BUILD PERSONAL RELATIONSHIPS

Another crucial element of the discipling process is relationships. It has been a popular topic lately, but one cannot overemphasize the vast importance of modeling in discipleship. This past year, we showed *Football Fever* — a pre-evangelistic, entertaining film — to all the football players at one of the high schools where we are working. We followed up most of those students who indicated an interest on their comment cards, and we started a varsity Bible study.

Due to lack of time, however, we did not fully follow up with the freshmen, only with the ones who had indicated receiving Christ. So a little while later, we decided to try to put together a freshman Bible study. There were 19 freshmen who had responded positively to the question, "If you have a Bible study, at least let me know about it." So we sent a post card to each one. At the first meeting, four guys showed up. It was a good meeting, but when we evaluated it, we asked, "Now where are the other 15?" Mike, the staff member in charge of this study, said, "I need to begin to get with these guys a little bit and see where they're at."

At the next meeting there were six. Mike continued to make himself available to these guys, going where they were and getting to know them. Within two weeks, he had twelve guys at the study. Mike's explanation sums it up: "I am finding that the quality of my discipleship — even at this lower level of discipleship — is directly proportional to the relationship that I have with those guys." By and large, it's true. If we are not building relationships, I dare say we are not making a lasting impact upon our disciples. We may be imparting   knowledge   or   content,   but   discipleship   without relationships is a contradiction in terms.

MODEL PERSONAL EVANGELISM

Another important part of leading a discipleship group is to lead them in personal witnessing. That is where we take students with us and go right out into the battle, exposing them to the needs of others. This is a two-pronged effort: some of the sharing is within the student's sphere of influence, the people God has laid on his heart; and some of the sharing is with people I am meeting.

One of the things I usually do to help a group of disciples begin sharing their faith is have them make a "Five Most Wanted" list. This is a list of five guys or girls whom they would like to see come to Christ, or at least have a chance to share with. Sometimes, then, on our appointments we may meet with those people or at least plan what we could do to make inroads with them. That way we are focusing on the disciple's immediate sphere of influence — somebody whom he cares about and is motivated to share with. Then, if that person comes to Christ, the relationship is already built, so he is a natural person to disciple.

At the same time, I always try to be kicking up my own dust by being with the athletes after practice or doing team meetings or speaking in classrooms or meeting kids on referrals. There are people with whom I want to share, so whenever I have a discipleship appointment and my disciple cannot think of anyone to share with, I can take him with me. "Hey, I'm going over to see Mac; do you want to come with me?" I am always trying to cultivate relationships with people so that I could feel free to call them on the phone and say, "Hey, I've got an hour to kill — are you doing anything? Could we have a coke?"

"Sure."

"Hey, I've got a friend with me whom I'd love to bring along to meet you. Can he come?" As much as possible, I never go anywhere alone. Take one of your students with you wherever you can, because that's how he gets to know you and sees how witnessing fits into your everyday life. I believe that if we are not doing that, we are missing an important dimension of discipling people. We may talk about the need to be sharing Christ, but if we are not doing it with them, it is just so many empty words.

HELP STUDENTS MULTIPLY

The ultimate goal of a discipleship group is multiplication, and this begins by helping students start a group. Now, this won't happen immediately. This is at the end of the process and may not occur until after students have graduated from high school. It is an important part of discipleship, though, and not just for the multiplication that takes place. Who learns the most whenever you study a passage — the teacher or the student? The teacher. And unless we are encouraging our disciples to get out there and begin to pour their lives into other people, they are not going to learn those principles in the same way. As a result of leading others, they begin to develop convictions and commitments. They have failures, but as you know, God works through those, too.

For all of us, God uses the discipling of others as a key method of discipling us. As we are growing together, God begins to reproduce our efforts in the lives of others. Then they will grow to the extent that they will reproduce, and on and on, from generation to generation. That is the essence of discipleship — discipleship which will multiply to reach the world for Christ.

That dynamic is so strategic that the last words that Christ ever said on earth were, "Go therefore and make disciples of all the nations. . . ." I pray that, no matter where you are in this process of discipling others God will enable you to be increasingly effective in investing your life to fulfill His mandate.

PUTTING THIS CHAPTER TO WORK

1. Since selecting the right people is such a pivotal element of discipleship, list the people in your ministry who meet the qualifications discussed in this chapter: faithful, able to multiply, committed to evangelism, and available.

2. If you had only three goals for your disciples (or potential disciples), what would they be? Think through how you can achieve those goals in relation to the students you are seeking to disciple. (Consider the approach Daryl proposes under the section entitled "Personalize Your Goals.")

3. If the long-range purpose of discipleship is multiplication of mature believers throughout the world, what is the *one* most important thing you can do *now* to begin strengthening the role you can play? When can you start? What barriers might you face, and how can you overcome them?

13

RECRUITING AND DISCIPLING ADULT VOLUNTEERS

by Dan Smythe

The young youth pastor sat at his desk with his head in his hands. Even though he was serving at a strong church with great potential for youth ministry, he was ready to quit. His eyes fell on the note he had just found on his desk which had surfaced this discouragement again — the resignation of another of his volunteer leaders. The job was just too big; he certainly could not do it without help. He was frustrated with the battle he faced almost weekly with his volunteer leaders. They showed so little willingness to serve. At times he felt that he would even be better off without them. And if the past was any indication, most of them would quit sooner or later anyway. He breathed a heavy sigh and managed a weary prayer, "Lord, if I could just get some help I could count on . . . ."

EIGHTEEN-MONTH BURNOUT

The scene just described occurs all too often. It surfaces over and over again in the youth ministries of our nation. It is known as the "Eighteen-month Burnout" — the ministry expectancy of the average youth pastor. Then, it's pack the suitcase and move on to "greener pastures" (one hopes). Often it means getting out of the ministry altogether. A major cause of burnout is the youth pastor's feelings of being overwhelmed and undersupported. I believe that Satan is using this destructive cycle of leadership turnover to inhibit the growth of God's kingdom.

We want to focus our attention on some proven solutions that will give us more and better leaders — people who will multiply the

Dan Smythe is the minister of counseling and discipleship at Northwest Community Church in Phoenix, Arizona, where he also served as youth pastor for four years. Previous to that, he was a youth pastor in Huntington Beach, California. Dan received his bachelor's and master's degrees from Pepperdine University, where he graduated summa cum laude. He and his wife, Debbie, have one daughter.

leadership base and give the youth pastor the kind of support he needs. We are talking, then, about recruiting, discipling, developing and training adult volunteer leaders. I believe they are the people upon whom a youth ministry must ultimately be built, and they are the key to discipling students. Why do I believe that? Why should we invest significant amounts of time in developing volunteer leaders? Because it fits in perfectly with our primary objective in the ministry.

PRIMARY OBJECTIVE

The *ultimate* vision of Jesus' ministry was to reach the world with His claims so that people could have a personal relationship with Him. In Luke 19:10 Jesus said, "For the Son of Man has come to seek and to save that which was lost." But though His ultimate vision was broad, His primary objective was smaller by way of initial numbers — to build discipled leaders who could carry out the ministry. As you study the Gospels, you can see how this objective works itself out in Jesus' life. *The Master Plan of Evangelism*, by Robert Coleman, summarizes Jesus' rationale.

> Why did Jesus deliberately concentrate His life upon comparatively so few people? Had He not come to save the world? . . . Jesus was not trying to impress the crowd but to usher in a Kingdom. This meant that He needed men who could lead the multitudes. What good would it have been for His ultimate objective to arouse the masses to follow Him if these people had no subsequent supervision or instruction in the Way? . . .
>
> Though He did what He could to help the multitudes, He had to devote Himself primarily to a few men, rather than the masses, in order that the masses could at last be saved. This was the genius of His strategy. . . . Here is where we must begin just like Jesus. It will be slow, tedious, painful and probably unnoticed by men at first, but the end result will be glorious even if we don't live to see it. Seen this way, though, it becomes a big decision in the ministry. One must decide where he wants his ministry to count — in the momentary applause of popular recognition, or in the reproduction of his life in a few chosen men who will carry on His work after he is gone.[1]

If we are to "begin just like Jesus," then we also must invest our lives in building discipled leaders who can multiply our efforts.

Let's say our ultimate vision for our ministries is to expose all of the students on the campuses within the sphere of our influence to the claims of Jesus Christ so that they can come to a personal knowledge of Him. Then what is our primary objective? I would suggest to you that our primary objective is to recruit, disciple, develop and train *adult leaders* who can, in turn, disciple the students from our campuses. If we are not discipling adult leaders to work with us, we are going to be limiting our discipleship of students to the few individuals with whom we can personally spend time. I know many youth workers who are slugging it out alone in the ministry, and though God may be blessing them with growing numbers of kids, they are saying, "I don't have people to spend time with these kids." I believe that is because they have lost this perspective.

THE FIVE-YEAR TEST

The ultimate test of our ministries is not how many flashy programs we have or how many kids show up on a Friday night. The real test of our ministry is seeing what will be left after five or ten years. What will the students be like five and ten years from now? What kind of adult leaders will there be to carry on the work? (And it will have to be *volunteer* leaders in most cases, because most churches are very limited in their resources to hire staff.)

My father is a university professor. Several summers ago he had a heart attack. They were able to treat him quickly, and he is doing very well today. But for three months, he was unable to work. What would happen if you were removed from your ministry for three months? Would it stop? Would the church have to hire someone quickly to replace you because you did not have adults to take on the ministry? The test of our ministry is the kind of students and adults that we are developing into disciple makers. That is why it is so important that our primary objective be the development of adult leaders. That is the way our ultimate vision of seeing students coming to Christ can be fulfilled.

TURNING OVER THE TURNOVER PROBLEM

Eighteen months may be the average ministry expectancy of the professional youth worker, but the average turnover rate among volunteers must be about six months. Maybe you have seen the need to develop adult leadership, but what do you do when they come to you every six months or less saying, "Here's the quarterly; I've had it, I need a break, just give me some space"? Either we are tempted to quit, like the youth pastor in the opening illustration, or we beg, we plead, we encourage and we say, "Oh, it's going to get better, just hang in there a little longer." But it doesn't get better, and they don't hang in there, and all of a sudden we're left with no one to run the programs. We have to grab someone here or rob someone from there and shove him into the program to keep it going.

The Most Important Quality in a Volunteer

How can we avoid this ridiculous cycle? We avoid it by *developing* our leaders. But if we are going to develop our leaders, they must be leaders with some foundational qualities already apparent in their lives. If I had to narrow it to only one quality for which I was looking, it would not be their experience, their spiritual gifts, their age, their looks, or their charisma. It would be their *commitment*. Are they committed to being developed and discipled in order that they might have a spiritual impact upon students? It is not necessarily a commitment to a time frame. It is not a commitment to a program of completing a certain number of work/study sessions or training lessons. It is a commitment to becoming a disciple maker.

Commitment was obviously an essential quality in the mind of Jesus. When He called His disciples, He said, "'Follow Me, and I will make you fishers of men.' And they immediately left the nets and followed Him" (Matthew 4:19-20). Jesus' first challenge to His potential volunteer leaders was a challenge to demonstrate their commitment. If they were not willing to follow Him, guess what? They would never become fishers of men. Jesus explained commitment further by saying:

> If anyone comes to Me, and does not hate his own father and mother and wife and children and brothers and sisters, yes, and even his own life, he cannot be My disciple. And whoever does not carry his own cross and come after Me cannot be My disciple. For which one of you, when he wants to build a tower, does not first sit down and calculate the cost, to see if he has enough to complete it? (Luke 14:26-28)

I think these passages, among others, underscore the necessity of having a high level of commitment from our volunteer leaders.

Building an Environment of Commitment and Love

I am sure you would be glad to have that kind of commitment from adult leaders — who wouldn't? But how do we get it? We get it by giving. I believe that if two foundational qualities are present in *our* lives, then we will be successful in developing volunteer leaders.

First of all, if we want commitment from our volunteer leaders, then we ourselves must show commitment to them. We must be committed to their growth and to their needs, as adults, regardless of their ministry to students. That means being willing to commit a large portion of our time to invest ourselves in their lives on a weekly basis. You may feel that you are so spread out ministering in programs to students that you do not have time left over to build into the lives of adult leaders. But if Jesus spent all His time healing or preaching the Sermon on the Mount every day, I don't believe He ever would have been able to say as He did to His Father, "I have accomplished the work which Thou hast given Me to do" (John 17:4). He ministered to the masses, but He also invested significant time in His disciples. That was the key to His ministry. It is so simple, yet so profound!

The second quality needed for successfully developing our volunteer leaders is love. We must love them as people. We do not merely use them to help us do *our* ministry. Rather, we see our ministry as a team effort, as we work alongside one another and under the Lord Jesus Christ to meet the needs of students. In the process, we demonstrate love for our adult leaders of the kind the apostle Paul described in 1 Thessalonians 2 — caring, encouraging, exhorting, urging.

To summarize, we get the kind of adult leadership that is needed by creating an environment of commitment and love in which they can develop. Proverbs 3:3,4 (NIV) shows what happens when that environment is present: "Let love and faithfulness never leave you; bind them around your neck, write them on the tablet of your heart. Then you will win favor and a good name in the sight of God and man." Our leadership teams will be affected much more by the quality of our lives than by our gifts or our training. They will be motivated when they see you communicating verbally and nonverbally, "I love you and I am committed to your growth."

The Exciting Results

As a result of demonstrating your love and commitment to adults through discipleship, you will see at least two results. First, a team of leaders will be raised up to serve the needs of your students. Adults will reciprocate the commitment you have demonstrated to them if they are true disciples. And they will know how to commit their lives to kids because they will have seen it modeled in your life first.

The second thing that will happen is that God will begin to multiply your ministry in ways you never would have dreamed possible. So much more can be accomplished through the 45 volunteer leaders we now have than when it was just my wife and me three years ago! Discipled adults can multiply your ministry. We share the hope the apostle Paul had in coming to the Corinthians: "Our hope is that, as your faith continues to grow, our area of activity among you will *greatly* expand" (2 Corinthians 10:15b, NIV).

DISCOVERING YOUR VOLUNTEER LEADERS

In a practical sense though, how do you find committed people? You need to find a way of bringing to the surface the right people into whom you will pour your life as your volunteer staff. There may be many ways to do this, but the one God used in our ministry was a meeting called Youth Worker Orientation. It was a method of "throwing out the net" by describing our ministry and seeing whom the Holy Spirit would raise up to make a commitment to our leadership team.

Throwing Out the Net

First, I went to our pastoral staff and asked them to help me come up with a list of people who might be interested. I added to that list anyone else I knew and other recommendations I had received. Then I sent a letter to all those people. It was very upbeat and motivational. I briefly described the need for people like them in youth ministry and the benefits of involvement. I gave the particulars — dates, time, place, etc. We offered the orientation at two different times to ensure the greatest possible total attendance. We made it clear that attendance did not obligate them in any way and that our primary purpose would be to share about the direction and plans for our youth ministry.

After sending out the letter, I telephoned each person to answer any questions. To be sure the word got out to everyone in our church, we also put up posters, made announcements and put together a multimedia presentation made up of slides, testimonies and songs about students which briefly depicted youth ministry in our church and its importance. We showed it in our church services the week before, announced the Youth Worker Orientation and invited anyone interested in knowing more about our ministry to come.

Presenting Our Ministry

The meeting itself lasted about three hours, and we held duplicate sessions on Saturday morning and Sunday afternoon. When the people arrived, we gave each one a syllabus so that he could see where we were going and take notes if he so desired. There were five different subject areas that we addressed. We began by depicting the *importance of youth ministry* and the need to minister to youth today. We utilized some contemporary songs, examined the lyrics and discussed them as a means of sensitizing the adults to the problems kids are facing today — even kids in our own church. These included such problems as self-image, loneliness, despair, troubled homes, etc.

Next, we discussed the *need for adults* in youth ministry. Due to the break-up of the home and the neglect of children even in Christian homes, there is a need for adults who will come alongside to help — paraparents. Even though it was early in the program, we challenged them to consider becoming paraparents to kids in our ministry and even to kids not yet in our ministry.

The third section focused on *understanding the teenager*. We had them break into small groups and discuss the question: "What feelings and problems did you experience as a teenager?" That was a good exercise and served to remind them of the tremendous need of ministering to students. We underscored that by sharing some statistics about the needs of youth; we hoped that as they saw the complexity of students' needs we could dispel the myth that all you need for youth ministry are popcorn, peanuts and balloons. Finally in this section, we talked about some of the characteristics of students — social, mental and physical.

The fourth subject area related to the *type of person* that God can use in youth ministry. Though the syllabus dealt with this topic more fully, basically we said that there are four kinds of people who will do well in youth ministry: the one who feels inadequate but is trusting the Spirit's power; the one who loves kids more than programs; the one who is stable, yet flexible; and the one who has stick-to-it-iveness.

The final aspect that we covered was our *ministry strategy*. We talked about our philosophy of ministry. We laid out our plans for the year. We talked about the activities and programs we are utilizing in our ministry and how we are using them to evangelize and disciple students. Finally, we talked about our volunteer leaders and the discipleship that we make available to them.

Commitment — Without a Quarterly?

At the conclusion of the meeting, we tried to clarify how they could be involved specifically, if they were interested. We presented three possible responses. First, we made it clear that it was okay to say no. Some had come only as interested parents; some had come out of curiosity; some knew after listening that this kind of ministry just wasn't for them.

On the other hand, there were some people whom God was prompting to be involved — people who were feeling the burden of helping kids, people who were interested in pursuing further. To those people there were two other possible responses. I call them *less time* responsible ministry and *more time* responsible ministry. I realize there are some people in our church who want to help but do not have a lot of time to give. They can be in our "less time" ministry. They will do behind-the-scenes things — helping with details, programs, etc. They will not likely work directly with the kids, however. But I make it clear that the greatest need in our ministry is for people who can serve in the "more time" area, because we need people who could give hours of their time to relate personally with kids. We tell them that if they choose to be involved in the "more time" area, they also must be willing to make the commitment — to meet every week with all of our volunteer leaders and staff for ministry to their own personal needs first.

We explained that that meeting was important for two reasons. First, if a person doesn't have the time to meet with us weekly to be discipled, then he doesn't have the time to minister to the lives of students. Second, we want to make sure that the adults we put before our kids are adults who have something to give — that there is an overflow in their lives because their own needs are are being met.

In addition to being committed to meeting together weekly, we also ask those in the "more time" area to commit themselves to come to some of our activities just to get to know the kids. They will have no other responsibility until they tell me they are ready for it, until they sense the prompting of the Spirit toward a certain area of ministry. The response to this challenge has been excellent — in fact, even fun to watch! They were so *surprised* that I asked for that type of commitment! I am sure they expected me to say, "Here's the quarterly; we have a Sunday school class you can start teaching two weeks from today!" When I didn't give them some specific area of responsibility, they were simply amazed. They had never been approached like this.

DISCIPLING YOUR VOLUNTEER LEADERS

Let's assume that you have gathered a group of potential volunteers, challenged them, and now there are a number who have agreed to be on your team. How do you train them? In many ways, it is much like a student discipleship group. I will focus here on the discipleship meeting, but let me hasten to add that you must not view discipleship as a program. You do not disciple people in a meeting room with a Bible study booklet and a verse to memorize. Those things may be elements of discipleship, but we are talking about a lifestyle. It is a daily process. But the meeting provides a setting for corporate discipleship, and it is an extremely valuable time for all involved.

We meet together every Thursday night for two hours. There are three basic elements to the meeting. The first element is *the role of expression*. This is our opportunity to express to the Lord what is happening in our lives through songs, praise, and prayer. We do not talk about youth programs, we do not talk about students, we just talk to God.

Another element of our evening involves the *role of impression*. That is a time of Bible study and learning. The format of this has changed over the years. When there were only eight or ten of us, we would do our Bible studies together. Then as we grew in number, we separated the junior high from the high school and the college workers. There is quite a bit of flexibility now. Sometimes we all come together for a part of the meeting; sometimes we divide the men from the women, or the singles from the married couples — whatever meets the needs best.

The content of this time varies a great deal, but in the initial stage we focus especially on two areas. The first is a quiet time — many of our leadership people do not have good quiet time patterns. Second, we help them in the areas areas of establishing priorities, setting goals and managing their time. We also focus Bible studies in the felt-need areas — marriage, communication, needs of singles, identity. And we will often select a key Christian book to read and study together.

As we learn, we utilize the third element of the meeting — the *role of accountability*. We target specific needs in their lives and challenge them to action. They have to come prepared. They must study and complete the required assignments. We hold each other accountable because we view the discipleship meeting as a serious time of growth.

INVOLVING YOUR VOLUNTEER LEADERS

Part of the initial agreement to be a volunteer leader is a willingness to come to some of the student activities. This allows the person to observe the students and begin building relationships with them, but in a protective atmosphere free from any risk of responsibility that goes with leadership. It also gives him an "incubation period" during which he will get acclimated to what is going on in the ministry. If, during that period of time, a person has any second thoughts about working with high school students and feels the desire to drop out, it is no problem. My kids or my program have not been hindered, because the volunteer was not carrying any area of responsibility. If, on the other hand, God has called him to minister to any of the students he has met, this is a very informal and natural way for him to begin.

Needs Surface Interest

The process of involving our volunteer leaders in student ministry is very individualized and spontaneous. We have found that as we let it happen naturally, the commitment and ownership are so much greater. Usually enough time has passed that by then they have demonstrated their level of commitment to Christ and their faithfulness to the group — which is absolutely essential before any leadership role is given.

There is no hurry to get started on some big training program.

We don't train everyone for everything. By being involved in our ministry, in our programs and with our kids, volunteer leaders start seeing what the needs are. Soon, they will actually come to me and say, "Dan, I'd love to be in a student discipleship group," or "I'd love to teach Sunday school," or "I'm interested in being a camp counselor." And we say, "Okay, we will train you specifically for that." We gather them together periodically. We don't meet every week to train them for programs; rather, we meet in cycles throughout the year. When we have a camp coming up, we will spend six weeks preparing them for that ministry. The weekly commitment is to build them personally; and as the need arises, we train them for the programs and the ministry to students.

This method works well for us, since volunteers have such a limited amount of time. If I had them out weekly for discipleship and student activities, as well as ministry training meetings, they wouldn't have any time with their families! But this way, we can both meet the needs *and* keep our priorities in approximately the right place!

Student Discipleship

It's exciting to see the system work. As you can imagine, volunteer leaders handle practically all the discipling of students. It is being accomplished in two different ways: We have a structured discipleship process called "Root Groups," in which the volunteer leaders use specified materials and lesson plans. There is also another very relational, non-structured system in which the volunteers just reproduce the types of things we are doing in the adult discipleship meeting. This primarily takes place in groups of two or three students, and then the volunteer meets individually with each of them sometime during the month.

MULTIPLYING YOUR VOLUNTEER LEADERS

Over the years, we have consistently had more and more leaders coming on our volunteer leader team. Basically, we have solved the turnover problem — the people on our leadership team rarely ever leave. In most cases, you can't pry them loose, because it is one area of their lives where their needs are being met. We're not *using* them, we're *building* them, and then God is using them to minister to kids.

Divide as You Grow

At first we had only eight or ten leaders. When we grew to about 20, we felt the group was getting too big to meet needs adequately, so we divided the junior high volunteers from the high school and college volunteers. But those groups continued to grow as well. So we challenged several of the volunteer leaders to help us lead the groups and to have as the primary focus of their ministry the discipleship of other volunteer leaders. Of course, that meant they would have less time to minister to students.

Today we have six multipliers — three men and three women. Their responsibility is to pray for, train and equip the other volunteer leaders, to be ready at the Thursday night discipleship meeting to lead their cluster of four or five men or women, and to keep in contact with them during the week (by phone, socially, etc.). My wife meets every week with the women multipliers, and I meet weekly with the men. Our approach is similar to our other discipleship meeting — we share, pray for students and each other, and then study together.

You Can't Keep a Good Thing Quiet!

God is blessing, and it is exciting! We are seeing people hungry to serve the needs of students because their needs are being met, and they are ministering out of an overflow. Since we have begun this approach, we have never had to "scrape" for new leaders. Our leaders are recruiting for us! They are telling their friends, and we are developing more leaders as a result. God is building something here, and we praise Him for it.

The principles outlined here definitely work. As we have studied Christ's life, it seems apparent that He used this same basic pattern in discipling His closest followers. First, He challenged people to make a commitment. Then He spiritually developed those who were willing to make such a commitment. In the process, He established a strong relationship with them. Only after they had been ministered to in such an environment did He finally train them and give them leadership responsibility. In our youth ministries, we would do well to follow the pattern that our Master has set for us. It is our only hope of having enough laborers for the enormous harvest field of young people that is ready and waiting.

PUTTING THIS CHAPTER TO WORK

1. Are you a candidate for "burnout"? (Congratulations if you have made it past 18 months!) Would having a more effective volunteer leader program make a difference in how you might answer this question?

2. As you look back on your past ministry, what students and adults have passed the "Five-Year Test" or are likely to in the future?

3. If the average volunteer quits after six months, what are you currently doing to minister to your volunteers and increase their longevity?

4. Review the principles and methods Dan discussed for discovering and developing your volunteer leaders. List the two or three ideas that you want to incorporate and determine what action needs to be taken.

NOTES

[1]Coleman, Robert E., *The Master Plan of Evangelism,* Old Tappan, N.J.: Revell, 1978, p.33.

COMMITMENT

14

COMMITMENT TO CHRIST

by Dawson McAllister

The American high school student is in trouble. Though we are helping him some through our youth ministries, it is safe to say that we have not significantly altered the trend of spiritual ignorance and moral decay. We love God. We want to serve God. We have seen some miracles take place. Yet America continues to slide further and further away from the Lord. God is sovereign. God is working. God is going to build His Church. Still, America seems to be on a self-destruct path.

THE BATTLE RAGES

Homes are not healthier. Drugs and alcohol are not decreasing. The sexual revolution may have declined somewhat, but that is due primarily to a fear of herpes and AIDS. Self-centeredness and rebellion toward authority are part of the American tradition. The average Christian student more often reflects the world around him than the Christ within him.

What should our response be? Sometimes I get depressed. I feel like it is just too much for me — sin is too rampant; it is out of control; we are losing so badly. But somehow, I don't think that God is shocked; I don't think He is depressed. I think that God has seen it all before.

Jesus said, "And just as it happened in the days of Noah so shall it be also in the days of the Son of Man" (Luke 17:26). How would you like to have been a youth worker in the days of Noah? Or in the days of Jesus? The prophet Isaiah said that Jesus was "like a tender shoot, and like a root out of parched ground" (Isaiah 53:2a).

Dawson McAllister has been a popular youth speaker for many years, speaking to 100,000 students annually. A graduate of Bethel College and Talbot Seminary, he has authored five books on discipleship and student relationships. He is founder and president of Shepherd Productions and resides in Bailey, Colorado, with his wife, Ruth Hill, and young daughter.

197

Most scholars agree that there couldn't have been a worse time for Christianity to spring up than when it did 2,000 years ago.

Dawson Trotman, founder of the Navigators, illustrated this point. My father was highly influenced by this man — in fact, I was named after him. Dawson Trotman told the story of his meeting with 25 Christian leaders in Germany right after World War II. His goal was to give them a greater vision for evangelism and discipleship, helping them fulfill the Great Commission throughout Western Germany. One day one of the men stood up and said, "Mr. Trotman, that is nice that you are challenging us, but many of us do not even have New Testaments."

And Trotman found himself saying, "Well, in Christ's day they didn't have New Testaments, either."

A little while later another man stood up and said, "But Mr. Trotman, you have evangelical books in America, and we don't have any evangelical books."

Another said, "You have radio; we don't have radio."

Someone else complained about the difficulties with transportation; another noted the risk to their own safety.

Each time Trotman answered that they didn't have those things in Christ's day, either. Dawson Trotman made this evaluation of that experience: "It dawned on me in a way I had never considered before that when Christ sent the eleven out, He let a situation exist that was so bad there could never be a worse one."[1]

Let's get our chins up off the floor. Let's remember that God has been here before, that He was victorious before, and that we can still have an awakening in America. We must get serious about our ministries and determine, in the power of the Spirit, to reach and disciple young people for Christ as never before.

THE APOSTLE PAUL — AS A YOUTH WORKER?

In order to win this battle for the lives of students, we need to learn from the example of others. If you could bring back anyone from the past to serve alongside you as a youth worker, who would you pick? I would choose the apostle Paul. Wouldn't it be great to find out how he would approach youth ministry?

EGO IN ITS PLACE

I believe that if the apostle Paul was to give us advice about youth ministry today, he would expand upon at least three principles found in Scripture. First, I believe he would say that *our egos must be in the right place*. I think that Paul would give immediate attention to our character. I don't think he would train us how to share our faith first, although he would do that. I don't think he would teach us how to use all the discipleship materials first, although he would do that. Techniques and plans are powerless if our hearts are not pure before God. And let's face it — so often our egos stand in the way of lives being changed for eternity.

We All Have Our Lists

Galations 6:14 starts out, *"But may it never be that I should boast, except in the cross of our Lord Jesus Christ...."* Some translations say "glory." What does it mean — to "glory" or to "boast"? Literally, it means to give praise, honor or worship. Let's be honest — you and I have strong egos. You are where you are because you have a strong ego. And we are going to praise someone. We are made to boast, and the Bible seems to indicate we are going to praise either the Lord or ourselves.

Do you think the apostle Paul had a strong ego? Probably. He certainly had reason to boast. You know the list of his attributes as a nonbeliever (Philippians 3:4-6) and the list of his sufferings for Christ later (2 Corinthians 11:23-30). Paul had reason to boast, but in the above passage he said, "May it never be."

You have reason to boast, too. We all have our lists. Maybe they aren't much in comparison to the apostle Paul's, but we definitely have our lists. Youth workers are fairly well educated, gifted with many skills, and have a wealth of spiritual insights. Some of you are incredible communicators. You have a following. You can help kids in their needs and hurts.

The Feeling of Power

As I work with students, sometimes I think I am walking through the wounded and dead on the battlefield. Kids are crying out, "Please help me! Please help me!" There's power there. Not too long ago I met a runaway at a fast food restaurant who found out I was a preacher and asked, "Would you please help me?" We sat down, and with a little bit of Bill Gothard and a little bit of Dawson McAllister, I blew her away in twenty minutes.

There is a feeling of power, but often we give ourselves credit for the things that the Holy Spirit did. So often the problem with a strong ego is that we are not glorying in the cross. We are glorying in *ourselves*, and we are *using* the cross. It is a treadmill. We church-hop and brag about numbers; we use people; we are proud of our spirituality; we compete with the youth leader next door. And through it all we seem to be blind to what is happening.

The Great Divide — The Cross of Christ

There is nothing glamorous about glorying in the cross. The cross was the ultimate proof of Christ's servant-spirit and humility. I remember learning a graphic lesson about this in the later years of the so called "Jesus Movement." I was speaking at a large student conference along with Chuck Smith, the well-known pastor of Calvary Chapel, a unique church in Southern California that draws hundreds of youth to every service.

Chuck had just finished speaking, and we were going to have a march with those 1,000 students through Santa Barbara, California. I went up to him and said, "Chuck, are we going to lead this march? Do you think we think we ought to march at the front?" — which I thought was a logical place for us.

He said, "No, Dawson, let's do something different. We'll let somebody else march in the front; let's march in the back." So we did, and as he walked behind the crowd, he picked up pieces of paper the kids were dropping.

The world says, "Glory in money." But we say, "No, we are following Someone who had all the money in the world yet allowed Himself to be stripped naked." The world says, "You had better be successful." But we say, "No, we want to follow Someone who was so 'unsuccessful' that when He first preached to His home crowd they tried to throw Him over a cliff, and then they crucified Him." The world says, "Don't live for anybody but yourself — get all the gusto you can." And we say, "No, I want to learn the discipline of Jesus Christ who sweat drops of blood in the garden for the sake of others and who was willing to hang in there even though it cost Him His life." This is the kind of character that separates us from those who are trapped by a dying world. The cross is the Great Divide.

Why do 70 percent of our teenagers drop out of church after high school graduation?[2] There are a lot of reasons, but I will tell you one. They do not see enough people living on the other side of the Divide — the side of Christ. If they did, they couldn't stay away, because Jesus attracts. *The real Jesus attracts.* When our kids look at us, what do they see? Do they see us glorying in the cross? Or do they see us glorying in power, ability, charisma, gifts, success, being culturally relevant, and being with it? What do they see?

Paul said, "May it never be that I should boast, except in the cross of our Lord Jesus Christ." We must get our egos in the right place, and that's a constant battle, is it not?

SHAPING OUR WORLD VIEW

Second, I believe the apostle Paul would tell us that *our world view must be shaped by the right priorities.* Paul would say, "If you are going to reach this country, you are running out of time; so you are going to have to abandon yourself recklessly for the sake of Christ and the gospel."

Death Brings Perspective to Life

The apostle Paul was amazing. When he wrote Philippians, Paul was in jail. He was facing death. There were people bad-mouthing him and even preaching the gospel out of jealousy. But observe Paul's view of the world in the midst of all this as recorded in Philippians 1:19-21:

> For I know that this shall turn out for my deliverance through your prayers and the provision of the Spirit of Jesus Christ, according to my earnest expectation and hope, that I shall not be put to shame in anything, but that with all boldness, Christ shall even now, as always, be exalted in my body, whether by life or by death, for to me to live is Christ, and to die is gain."

Paul faced death. It's tough to face death, isn't it? It really is, because when you face death, all the superficial things of life seem to disappear. All the cotton candy of this world and all the things you thought were important are just stripped away. That's why non-Christians have such a hard time at funerals. The apostle Paul was facing death, and I think his philosophy can be summed up in the lyrics of a song we used to sing often with high school kids: "If I live, well, praise the Lord! If I die, well, praise the Lord! If I live or die, my only prayer will be 'Jesus in me — praise the Lord!'"

Now Paul was not some masochist. He was not some weirdo saying "I want to die, I want to die" because he was mentally ill. No, it wasn't that at all. It was hard for Paul to die,too. He expressed himself in 2 Corinthians 1:8 and 9:

> We do not want you to be unaware, brethren, of our affliction which came to us in Asia, that we were burdened excessively, beyond our strength, so that we despaired even of life; indeed, we had the sentence of death within ourselves in order that we should not trust in ourselves, but in God who raises the dead.

Becoming Dangerous

Paul put himself on death row. In 2 Corinthians 4:11 he said, "For we who live are constantly being delivered over to death for Jesus' sake...." You know something? *You are dangerous when you are no longer afraid to die.* Terrorists have done some major damage to our embassies overseas, haven't they? Do you know why? Because the people who drove the vehicles full of explosives were blown up with the bombs. They weren't afraid to die.

Shaming Christ or Exalting Him

Paul could face death because he was motivated by his "earnest expectation and hope" (Philippians 1:20). Literally, this phrase pictures someone sticking out his head as far as possible to look expectantly. What made Paul sit on the edge of his seat? What was his eager longing? What was he intently looking for?

He was consumed by one thought: "That I shall not be put to shame in anything." Now this is very interesting. Paul was not saying, "Oh, I hope they don't humiliate me; I hope they don't make me look stupid; I hope I don't say something that would make me look dumb." Rather, Paul was saying that his concern was that he would in no way embarrass Christ; that he would never back off from his commitment to his Lord and Savior.

Paul was saying, "I just want to — with all boldness, unfailing courage, and complete outspokenness — *exalt Christ.* I want people to see Jesus Christ in my entire personality. I want them to see *pure Jesus.*"

He went on to say, "For me to live is Christ, and to die is gain." In other words, "If I keep on living, that will be fine — I can keep on preaching. But I am so consumed with Christ, I so want to imitate Christ, I so want to commune with Christ, I so long for Christ, I so want to talk with Christ, I so seek Christ, that if I die, it would be even better." "Gain" is actually a banking statement, implying that he would get the *principal* plus the *interest*!

Are We Really in the Battle?

You know the old song, "Turn your eyes upon Jesus, look full in His wonderful face, and the things of earth will grow strangely dim in the light of His glory and grace." The apostle Paul looked to Jesus, and I think he would say to us, "Do you mean business or don't you? Are you serious or aren't you?"

If I am on death row, I really don't care what others say about me, as long as I am lovingly trying to live for Jesus Christ. I am not trying to be "odd for God," but if I take abuse from someone because of aggressive evangelism, I really don't care because I am consumed with exalting Christ. And if some gang intimidates us or someone beats our faith into the ground, we have got to get beyond that. If we are not willing to get on death row, if we are not consumed with not embarrassing Jesus Christ, if we are not committed to clearly showing what He is like in our entire lives, then we are not really in the battle. The world will laugh at us.

We must get dangerous. We must step over the threshhold. We must be willing to be humiliated. We must be big enough to let our critics take shots at us and to keep on going. We must let the carnal Christian parent take shots at us and keep doing what God has called us to do. We have got to get beyond these things. We are on death row.

THE MESSAGE IN PERSPECTIVE

Finally, the apostle Paul would tell us that *our message must reflect the right perspective.* To understand what I mean, let's look at 1 Corinthians 2:1-5. The Church at Corinth was a lot like the youth of America are today. They had it all, folks. They had their great speakers, their great poets, and their great philosophers. They may not have had Pac Man, the *Return of the Jedi*, and 3-D movies, but I tell you what — they were a spoiled group of pagans! How did Paul communicate the gospel to them? Observe his perspective:

> And when I came to you, brethren, I did not come with superiority of speech or of wisdom, proclaiming to you the testimony of God. For I determined to know nothing among you except Jesus Christ, and Him crucified. And I was with you in weakness and in fear and in much trembling, and my message and my preaching were not in persuasive words of wisdom, but in demonstration of the Spirit and of power, that your faith should not rest on the wisdom of men, but on the power of God.

Razzle-Dazzle

The apostle Paul was probably not a brilliant orator like Apollos. 2 Corinthians 10:10 reports that "his personal presence is unimpressive and his speech contemptible" — which means they thought he looked bad and his sermons were worse!

Of course, I believe that it is important for us to communicate well. But I would rather hear some fumbling, bumbling idiot tell kids the truth about Jesus and the cross than to have some "el slicko" razzle-dazzle them and not tell them the truth. When you are dying of thirst and someone gives you a glass, do you stop and say, "Oh, isn't this a nice glass! Is it an antique?" No, when you are dying for water, you don't ask about the goblet, you go right for the water.

Paint the Grand Canyon?

Do you know what amazes me as I speak to thousands of students each year? It is the number of "Christian" kids that become *Christians!* One of the greatest mission fields in America today is the evangelical Christian kid. And I want to tell you something. He doesn't know what Jesus did for him. Here are these kids, sitting in Christian churches across America, and *they don't get the clear message of the cross!* I am convinced we have become so cool, we are uncool. We are so relevant, we are irrelevant. If we are going to make a dent, we must go back to the cross. Just tell the story. The story is good enough.

On my last plane trip, we passed over the Grand Canyon.

Everybody was straining to look out the windows and was raving about the tremendous beauty. Wouldn't it be something if somebody went to the government and said, "Hey, I've got an idea. Let's paint the Grand Canyon!" He would be put in the "loony pen." Just let the Grand Canyon speak for itself — it's beautiful enough.

Get Them to the Cross

Paul said, "I did not come with superiority of speech, or of wisdom." Now, Paul knew the philosophy of the day. But when he came to Corinth, he didn't say, "Tonight my lecture is going to be on Jewish law and tradition, sculpture and the Greek world, decadence in the Roman empire, the whereabouts of Zeus, and Jesus as an example." He would not do that. He said, "For I determined to know nothing among you except Christ and Him crucified." You say, "Well, Dawson, wouldn't he talk about the weather?" Yes, if it would get him to the cross. "Wouldn't he talk about sports?" Yes, if he could quickly get to the cross. "Wouldn't he talk about politics?" Yes, if he could point his listeners to the cross. "Wouldn't he talk about philosophy?" Some, if he could lead them to the cross. But his determination was *to get to the cross*.

That's the way Billy Graham does it. And that's why he has been around all these years. I don't care where he starts, he always ends up at the cross.

I have seen a lot of styles of youth ministry. What you are doing is great for the most part. Have your slide shows, have your rock bands, relate, get the pagans in, throw out the net. But while you are doing all this work, whatever you do, hurry! Get to the cross! That's the only thing that is going to make any difference. The cross is the greatest demonstration of God's love. The cross is the greatest demonstration of man's sin. And the cross is the greatest demonstration of God's power over sin. The students of today are jaded, but when they really understand the cross, it will get their attention.

I'll tell you one thing — the cross preached in the power of the Holy Spirit will blow Pac Man right out of the room. The cross proclaimed in Jesus Christ will make video-rock look like garbage. I think we ought to help kids with those things. But they are all symptoms. Our number one priority is not to be an expert in football, counseling, or the social scene. Our number one priority is just to tell the story — the story about Jesus at the cross.

Reflecting On the Jesus Movement

The apostle Paul went on to say in 1 Corinthians 2:3, "And I was with you in weakness and in fear and in much trembling." Do you know why Paul was afraid? He wasn't afraid people would laugh at him. I believe he was afraid that he wouldn't clearly communicate the story of the cross. Paul continues in verses 4 and 5, "And my message and my preaching were not in persuasive words of wisdom, but in the demonstration of the Spirit and of power, that your faith should not rest on the wisdom of men, but in the power of God."

The thing that broke my heart the most about the "Jesus Movement" was that I'd talk to some of those kids three years later and they would say, "Hey, man, I tried that stuff, and it didn't work." That was the worst thing a kid could say to me. Do you know why that happened? There are a lot of reasons, but I'll give you one. Some razzle-dazzle youth speaker got in front of those kids and said, "Hey, are you lonely? Jesus will be your friend." "Hey, have you got heartaches? Jesus will solve your heartaches." "Hey, do you want Jesus? It's easy." And the speaker never got around to the cross. He never got around to repentance. He never got around to brokenness over sin. And he never got around to true converts. So if you go out and try to talk to those people about Jesus now, it's tough. I would rather give them a chance to hear about the cross from a screamer on the street corner and risk them rejecting that than to let them get "vanilla," accept it, and call it Christianity.

Breaking Through to Hardened Hearts

I am not saying we have to go to either extreme. But if I had to err, I would rather err being "odd for God" and telling the truth. Who cares if we had 500 kids four years ago? Where are they now? That's the bottom line. I can come in with my charisma, or you can come in with your charisma, and tell them some long story about a kid who was killed in a car accident. We can get them all crying and invite them to come to Jesus. But when someone else comes along with a little better story, they will follow him. Why? Because their faith rested on the wisdom of men and not on the power of God. Only the power of God can break the hard heart of the American high school student. You can't compete with the *Return of the Jedi*. All we've got is the basic gospel, and *that's all we need*!

IT'S WORTH IT!

I've been in youth ministry a long time, but recently I felt like quitting. I came very close to leaving a few months ago. I think I became bored because I didn't have a big enough vision anymore. We tend to make our dreams out of what we think we can do in the flesh. And those dreams will always bore us because God doesn't care about what we can do in the flesh; He wants to know what we can do in the power of the Holy Spirit.

Since doing some thinking and praying along those lines, I made a commitment to go around the track another three to five years. Since then, I have had some incredible moments. Recently I spoke at a Texas camp. After the altar call, a little girl walked up and stood by me. She was probably 11 or 12 years old. She struck me as being so young — she could have been my daughter. She said, "Mr. McAllister, I want both worlds."

I said, "Hey, I'm not going to play games with you. You are old enough for us to talk straight. Want to hear it? There's no both worlds."

She said, "Well, I want my friends and drugs, too."

I said, "You can't do that."

She said, "I want Jesus, but I want my friends."

I said, "I'm not going to pray with you [to receive Christ.] You know why? That would be a disservice to you. I want you to go out and think about it. When you are ready to come to Jesus Christ, you come to see me, because there's no two ways."

To make a long story short, three nights later she came forward to receive Christ. This confused 12-year-old girl had already had sex and drugs. But she was totally changed. I watched her the last day as we were singing,"We are the reason that He gave His life." We were all holding hands, and she was trying to lift up her arms with everybody else, but she was too short. Yet she was beaming and beaming! And when the tears came to my eyes, I said, "You know, Lord, I can do this longer. This isn't so bad, this isn't so bad!"

I was in Tijuana recently. There were 1,500 kids — and many came to Christ. It was exciting. A girl came to Christ one night, and the next morning she drowned. It reminded me how important it is to reach kids now while they are in high school — they are more open now than at any other time. I said, "Lord, I can do this. This is where it is at." And the Lord said, "Yes, I know. I can use you, Dawson. But you had better make sure you glory in the cross. You had better make sure you get on death row, and just tell the story, son. I'll take care of the rest."

PUTTING THIS CHAPTER TO WORK

1. Review Dawson's main points and ask the Lord to search your heart.
    a. Is your *ego* in the right place?
    b. Is your *world view* shaped by the right priorities?
    c. Does your *message* reflect the right perspective?

2. Consider offering the following prayer as an expression of your heart:

> God, if I'm on an ego trip and I'm glorying in anything other than the cross, take it away. I just want to glory in You. I want to step on the other side of the Great Divide. I want kids to see me as "different."
>
> I want to be crucified to the world. Lord, help me to get on death row in my attitude. Make me "dangerous." And, God, give me the courage to forget the razzle-dazzle and get to the cross with my message.
>
> Oh, Father, I don't know how much more time I have, so help me make every minute count. I want to glory in You. I am nothing, Lord, nothing apart from You. Yet I know You can use me, and I am willing. Bring spiritual awakening to my young people, to America, and to the world. But Lord, let it begin in me. Amen.

NOTES

[1]Dawson Trotman, "The Need of the Home" (Taped message, available through NavPress, Colorado Springs,CO).

[2]Dennis Miller, *Moody Monthly*, September 1982, p.200.

15

COMMITMENT TO YOUTH MINISTRY

by Bill Stewart

Francis Schaeffer's mother was visiting L'Abri — the well-known Christian community and study center in Switzerland that her famous son founded. One day she drew another guest aside and asked, "When do you think Francis is going to stop all this and get a job?" I have met a number of youth workers who have had the same question asked of them. Some people question the maturity of a person who would give his life to young people. I believe this is especially true in the local church. A number of years ago another minister said to me, "You will never be an executive staff-level person, you will never be a full minister. In effect, you will never be on the level of senior staff if you just work with young people."

Why should it be so difficult for some people to understand how reasonable it is for someone to invest his entire life in reaching and discipling young people? There is no question about a person who gives his life to teach high school or elementary school. There is no question about a person whose life work is with the YMCA, the Boy Scouts, or the state juvenile authorities. There is no question about a person who makes a career out of being a public school administrator or a teacher in a Christian college or seminary. But often, there is a very definite question, though sometimes subtle, about a person who says, "I want to give my life to young people in the church of Christ."

GOD'S CALL

In Biblical Times

Throughout history, God has called people to be His represen-

---

William H. Stewart has served for 16 years as the minister of youth education at First Baptist Church of Modesto, California. His 30 years of youth ministry experience also include ten years with Youth for Christ. Bill received a B.A. at Northwestern College in Minneapolis, where he graduated cum laude. His M.A. was earned at the Mennonite Bretheren Seminary in Fresno, California. He and his wife, Jan, have two teenagers.

tatives to each generation. God called people in the Old Testament, like Abraham, Joseph, Moses, Deborah, Ruth, Samuel, David, Esther, Daniel, Isaiah, Jeremiah and Hosea; He called people in the New Testament, like the apostles, Mary, Paul and Timothy. Likewise, God is calling people today to represent Him to this generation.

God's Call Today

In the past, when God called people to minister for Him, they were not all called to fill senior pastor-type positions. There were many different roles to play. Now don't misunderstand; I am convinced that we must have strong senior pastors if we are to have great youth ministries. But I am also convinced that many individuals are receiving a specific call from God the Holy Spirit to work with young people.

My own call to the gospel ministry came when I was 14 years of age, sitting in a Sunday school class as a new Christian. A layman spoke the Word of God, and my heart was touched. But it took 10 years for me to understand that my call was to youth ministry. I didn't know anyone in youth ministry. I didn't know anybody did anything in the Lord's work except be a pastor. I knew I was not called to the pastorate, but I did not understand what I was supposed to do. Initially, I started a career in radio, thinking that I might someday go into missionary radio. But gradually, over a 10-year period, God showed me my calling. Students asked me to work with them, pastors asked me to help them on campuses. Through these and other circumstances, God made it very apparent that youth ministry was what He wanted for my life. And 25 years later, it's still what I love to do! I didn't think you could have so much fun in the Lord's work. I really didn't! I thought it had to be some kind of a drag. But it's been just the opposite — ever since I found out that this is where God wanted me to serve.

YOUTH WORKER QUALITIES THAT SUCCEED

Many people have a stereotyped image of youth ministers.

Unnecessary Qualities

A youth worker is not necessarily a person who wears trendy clothes, has a flashy personality, and uses all the latest lingo. He may not drive the hottest car on the block (I'm sure of that — I bought a Corvair once and then traded it in on a Vega). Youth ministry takes all kinds of people with different personalities, different gifts and different backgrounds. Yet, God blesses all kinds of youth workers because there are just that many kinds of young people. I want every kind of person possible represented on my youth staff because young people in my town will relate to them. If we have only one type of youth worker, then we don't recognize the importance of the whole body of Christ.

Extremely Necessary Qualities

There are a number of things that are far more important than the above superficial qualities. The person in youth ministry must be a person who loves Christ, loves Christ's Word and loves the church of Christ. Interdenominational youth organizations serve a real purpose, but we must also have strong youth ministries in local churches if we are ever going to see the kind of effectiveness we need to reach the youth of our cities.

One of the most essential qualities for the person working with young people is a willingness to play the role of a parent to the young people under his care. When God calls a person to youth ministry, He has not called him merely to be a recreation director or a babysitter. He has called him to be a *parent* to the students with whom he works. Paul reflects this kind of family relationship with Timothy and the church in Corinth.

> I do not write these things to shame you, but to admonish you as my beloved *children*. For if you were to have countless tutors in Christ, yet you would not have many *fathers*; for in Christ Jesus I became your *father* through the gospel. I exhort you therefore, be imitators of me. For this reason I have sent to you Timothy, who is my beloved and faithful *child* in the Lord, and he will remind you of my ways which are in Christ, just as I teach everywhere in every church (1 Corinthians 4:14-17).

The person in youth ministry must also love young people, be transparent and have a sense of humor. One time I asked a mission agency executive what made the difference between success and failure on the mission field. Though he listed several qualities, he said that a sense of humor was one of the most important.

A man or woman in youth ministry must also learn to communicate the Word of God effectively. Paul said, "I solemnly charge you ... preach the Word." Some people I know leave youth ministry because they want to preach to a crowd. In one denomination I am aware of, the average church has a membership of 140 people. I didn't always have this many kids, but today I could preach to more people than that in my junior high group alone. You stay in one place for a while, and you'll have a big crowd to preach to!

Finally, a person in youth ministry must be willing to work hard and handle administrative tasks. I believe that men and women lose professional acceptance in youth ministry because they do not follow through in detail. If we expect God to use us fully, we must prove ourselves trustworthy. Jesus said to the wise servant who invested his talents, "You were faithful with a few things, I will put you in charge of many things, enter into the joy of your master" (Matthew 25:21).

YOUTH MINISTRY TRANSITIONS

The growth of a youth minister takes many forms through the various periods of life. When I was 18, I was an older peer to the youth I led. I could motivate a lot of people to get involved — especially the girls in the high school group!

From College to Career?

Once college is completed and you are married, you sometimes wonder if you can still motivate people as you did in your early ministry. It is a time of transition. Many who were in youth ministry in college now leave to pursue another career. I did. I went on to radio and television school in Hollywood. I didn't even consider youth ministry as a vocation at that point. I was ready to have an "important" position. That is another transition that some of us must make.

Is There Youth Ministry After 30?

Then there is the age of 30! Some feel that a person cannot relate to kids effectively after that age, so they bail out. A lot of thoughts go through a person's mind when he is 30. Daniel Levison, a researcher at the Yale Medical School, stated: "When a man gets in his 30's or late 20's, he is concerned about building a satisfactory life structure and has powerful forces at work within him for stabilization, status, professional pride and accomplishment."

Position is important to men going into their 30's. Often a man will have pressure from his family, his wife's family, or even his own children to excel or achieve a certain status. Some of us have pressure from our employment — we question what our life's work should be. Some of us want more material wealth.

Many of us struggle with ministry at age 30. But we need to bear in mind that many outstanding people did not even begin ministering until that "ripe old age." C.S. Lewis, the British writer, began his spiritual pilgrimage and return to Christianity at 30 years of age. Albert Schweitzer left his professorship in Europe to spend his life working as a medical missionary in Africa at age 30. John Wesley was 30 when the sense of religious conviction came over him and caused him to go out as a missionary at age 34. John Knox was 30 years of age when he embraced the teachings of the Protestant Reformation and began his ministry. Martin Luther was converted on his 30th birthday; at age 33 he wrote the 95 theses. The apostle

Paul, according to scholars, was 30 years of age at conversion. John the Baptist was about 30 years of age when he became a wilderness Elijah.

Finally, it is significant to note that even Jesus of Nazareth began his ministry at 30 years of age. It is ironic that some of us leave youth ministry just when we are able to accomplish something, just when we are getting a little bit of wisdom, just when people are beginning to trust and respect us. That is no time to leave the ministry!

Forty and Beyond

Youth ministry is not limited by age. I don't have my 30's to spend again. In fact, I am well past 40, but as I look back, I think of the young men and women in whom I have invested my life — some are in ministry today. If I had it to do over, I would again spend my time in ministry with young people. I don't know anything else I would rather do with my life.

What do young people need today? They need parent figures. They need fathers and mothers. That's why you can be over 30, 40 and beyond and still be so effective with youth.

STUMBLING BLOCKS OR STEPPING STONES

There are a number of pitfalls in youth ministry that we need to be aware of and guard against. There are some things that I must consider in evaluating the young man or young woman who comes to work with us. First, what is his *attitude toward secular work*? Does he know how to work with his hands? This is a good test of diligence, which will be needed to succeed with youth. If there is a person in youth ministry who has not learned to work hard, he might as well clear out; youth ministry is not designed for people who are just there to "put in their time."

Second, *financial discipline* is essential. Every time you turn on the television, the advertisers want you to buy something! It becomes a real problem, especially for those new to the ministry. One young man who came to me had an income of $200 a month, a wife and two children, and debt of $4,000. They had their last child on MasterCard! Since then that young man has learned discipline in that area of his life. He had to in order to be successful in anything, especially in some kind of ministry to people.

Third, *discipline in academics* is important. In some universities, people look at the education department as the people who didn't make it in engineering or medicine. Sometimes people look at youth ministers in the same way. They are the guys who don't do well academically so they spend all their time with kids. But I want people who work with me to be the best students. Some of our staff members do as well as or even better academically than some of the men who are preparing for the senior pastorate. I believe that is the way it should be. One fellow who worked with me was a little lax in this area, so to motivate him, I posted his grades on the wall at the junior high building where he worked. He got motivated!

Fourth, a youth worker's *relationships* will greatly affect the ministry. The atmosphere with his family or roommates is an indicator of his ability to succeed in ministry. If a person cannot get along with those he lives with, that problem will reflect in every part of his ministry. Personal relationships with fellow staff and students are also pivotal.

Discipline in human sexuality is a very, very important area. Probably more people have been put on the shelf due to failure in this area than any other. We must develop more transparency here so that we can help each other before a point of no return is reached.

Allowing a *root of bitterness* to surface is so very destructive. There will always be someone who upsets us, disappoints us, or mistreats us. Allowing bitterness to fester will cause a critical spirit, lack of blessing and lack of growth. It will divide the body and will eventually destroy a ministry.

Finally, a *humble spirit* is non-negotiable. The opposite, of course, is pride — one of the deadliest of all pitfalls. It can be manifested in an overt attitude: "I'm great, my program is great," etc. Or it can be more subtle: "We are the only ones who are doing anything in this church"; "We are the only ones who are seeing anybody saved"; "We are the only ones who are bringing visitors." This attitude is like a cancer, bringing division and damage to the entire body.

BEING THERE

For the Homecomings

If you stay somewhere long enough, you will see many homecomings. People who have strayed spiritually will come back to the Lord and, because you have persevered, you have the privilege of welcoming them home.

I think of a girl who dropped out of our youth group when she was in her senior year in high school. She was away from the Lord for four and a half years, but when she got ready to come home, we were there.

I can think of another young man who hated me, and I didn't even know it. I did some classroom speaking at one of the local high schools several years ago. Jim was in some of those classes. Now he is in our college/career ministry, but then he was very antagonistic. He told me not too long ago, "I used to come to those classes. In fact, I cut other classes just to come and hear what you had to say because I was so upset with you. I used to listen to you every Sunday night on your radio talk show, and I knew you were always going to turn the conversation to Christ. It used to make me so mad. I hated you." Jim "came home" about one year ago; he came home to Christ. I was still there, and the group was still there, and the Word of Christ was still there. There are not many places like that.

Are you going to stay? How long are you going to be there? Six months? Two years? Five years? In some cases it took me five years to see results from the things I had been working on. Had I left earlier, I would not have known what accomplishments were possible.

Christianity Today reported that a study from Concordia Seminary indicated, "Ministers that remain in the pastorate for less than four years are less effective in all areas of their ministry." In the early Christian church, a priest who left his first parish was thought to be as bad as a man who ran out on his wife. In Puritan times, it was common for a pastor to stay in his church his entire life. Even the apostles, for the most part, stayed a long time where they were.

As a Parent

It takes time to be a parent, because parents stay. At least they used to. A girl recently told me about a youth pastor who had been in their church. She said, "Just when we found out he loved us, he left." Another friend of mine said that their youth ministry had been through four or five youth pastors in as many years. That is tragic, because for some young people there is as much trauma in the loss of a youth pastor as there is in a divorce.

Some time ago, a ninth grade girl came to me from a Christian home that had tragically broken up. She said, "Bill, will you be my father?" I assured her that I wanted to be that for her. Today she has a successful career and is the wife of my college/career director! Thank God I had the time to be her parent. Now this girl is helping other college/career girls in an outstanding way. That's discipleship, but in the spirit of being a parent.

Many years ago, a singer I had invited to our group brought a black pianist named Dave. Before they left, I put my arm around him and said, "Thanks, Dave. I just wanted you to know I really would like to have you come back." I didn't know that he had been involved in the Black Panthers. Later he said, "That's the first time any 'honky' ever put his arm around me." Since then, our relationship has grown, and today Dave is involved in running two halfway houses in our town. He is 30 now and has three kids. I find it a little strange when he calls me Dad, but I love it! Being a father in the ministry — whether you are 22, 42, or whatever — is exciting!

BUILDING A TEAM OF PARENTS

"Countless tutors" but "not many fathers," Paul said in 1 Corinthians 4:15. In this generation of transiency, let me encourage you to build a ministry team that can play a parenting role to young people. Build a family where you are. Build men and women who will team up to reach young people — people who will work with you, who feel called to the ministry, and who will support themselves. We will never reach every young person we need to reach if we wait for enough full-time youth ministers.

The person who had the greatest influence on my life as a new Christian was a factory worker who had given his life to youth ministry. He and his wife had no children — God gave them other people's children.

Roots in the Community

Today we have multiplied that influence through the laymen who have worked with me. One is a parole agent with the state. He went to seminary and has now given his life to young people. Another is a real estate man — the most fantastic people-person I have ever met. Another is a representative in our area for the California Almond Growers. Another one is a restaurateur. Another owns a tire shop.

Another man who worked with us in our youth ministry for several years was interested in politics; he ran for the school board and won. Now that's one way of solving problems with the schools! Somebody actually tried to throw him off one of the campuses one day. In fact, a new vice principal took him into the principal's office and announced, "I found this outsider on our campus."

The principal almost died; he said, "I'd like to introduce you to the chairman of the school board!"

The party moguls tried to get him to run for Congress, but he declined. One said to him, "Well, I guess after you've worked for God, you can't work for anybody more important!"

Saving a Child

Will you be a parent — a father or mother — to kids? Will you surround yourself with a team of people to be a stable influence in an unstable world? As we team up with parents and laymen in our communities, we can make a difference.

Recently I read an article about a policeman in San Diego who was out on a new beat and hadn't learned the area. He received a call on his police radio, "Code 3 — child choking." He drove faster, feeling the urgency. When he approached the approximate area, traffic was everywhere and he couldn't get through. People wouldn't pull over. So he drove his car up onto a freeway that was not yet opened. The officer hurried down the freeway and came to the place where he had to get off, but there was only a huge ditch and no offramp. He felt trapped and panicky as time was running out. He got out of his car and cried, "Oh God, help!"

In answer to his prayer, he turned around and a man was right there — sitting on a huge earth-moving machine. "There is a child in trouble," the officer blurted out, pointing across the street, "and I've got to get over there." The man instantly took off with his earth mover, driving across the shoulders of the freeways and up into the traffic. The traffic stopped immediately, allowing the officer to get through. He quickly found the address a few blocks away and rushed in the front door. The child was already blue. In seconds, the officer managed to turn the child upside down and strike him, releasing a button that was caught in the child's throat. The officer breathed a sigh of relief; it does not always turn out that well.

The next day, when the officer was in the same area, he saw the workman on the earth-moving machine. The officer stopped the man and said, "Thank you so much. You helped me save the child's life — you helped me!"

The man replied, "I know. He was choking to death. But when I helped you, I didn't know that it was my own son."

STANDING IN THE GAP

The need is every bit as urgent with our young people. As we work together, we can be a parent to kids who have nowhere else to turn. Can you think of anything more important?

Where to Start

"But, Lord, You know I'm nearly 30 years old — what can I do?" "But, Lord, You know I'm nearly 40 — do You have a place for me?"

God is saying, "You are finally worth trusting to some young person."

"Lord, You know I am single. What can I do?"

God is saying, "You have the resources and the time to give, and I will bless them."

"Lord, You know my wife and I have no children, and we don't know how to work with kids."

God says, "You will have My children and I will teach you."

You and I live in a strategic time in eternity right now. Picture an hourglass. The sand represents our entire culture, and the bottleneck represents the high school — the institution virtually every young person in our culture will pass through. You and I stand at the bottleneck, where we have the opportunity to help fulfill the Great Commission. The student must pass by you. Will you reach out?

God said, "And I sought for a man among them, that should make up the hedge, and stand in the gap before Me for the land, that I should not destroy it: but I found none" (Ezekiel 22:30, KJV). Will you stand in the gap — the gap of a generation without God and without hope? Will you become involved in the lives of young people? Loving them, believing in them, supporting them like a parent through their problems?

Are You Willing?

You may already be sure that you have been called to youth ministry. Maybe you are not sure. I would like you to consider prayerfully the role God wants youth ministry to play in your life. If God made it clear to you saying, "I want you to commit your life to young people for the rest of your life," would you be willing? Would you say yes to the call of God? "Yes, God, I'll do whatever it takes. If I have to go to work in some far city and support myself, or if I have to give everything I have to see this generation reached for Christ — if You have called me to that, Father, then I will do it."

That's a pretty radical-sounding commitment for a generation that is so laid-back and noncommittal. But Jesus Himself said, "For unto whomsoever much is given, of him shall much be required. . ." (Luke 12:48, KJV). What Mordecai said to Esther may also apply to us, "Who knoweth whether thou art come to the Kingdom for such a time as this?" (Esther 4:14b, KJV).

We are alive at a very strategic moment in history. God has a special purpose for your life. He has chosen to give you some very special opportunities. Some of you have relatives and friends who cannot do what you can do. But God has called you.

I have a brother who will spend the rest of his life as an invalid. Somehow, in our heredity, he got a genetic disease and I didn't. There are just two of us; I'm living an active life, but that is impossible for him. I don't know why God allowed that, but I do know this: God has given me a tremendous opportunity, and I want to be found "standing in the gap," faithfully investing my life for eternity by ministering to young people. Will you join me?

PUTTING THIS CHAPTER TO WORK

1. In the context of Bill's challenge to "stand in the gap," are you *willing* to commit your life to a ministry to young people? If so,

after adequate thought and prayer, you may find it meaningful
to sign the following covenant:

MY COVENANT WITH GOD

*Before God, under His guidance and empowering, I submit
myself as His servant, willing to serve Him through a
lifetime of ministry to youth, as He directs.*

_____   _____
Signature   *Date*

---

2. How has God led you toward making this kind of commitment
   (or how is He leading you)? List circumstances, meaningful
   Scriptures, convictions, etc.

3. What barriers make it difficult to keep such a commitment?
   (Review the "Stumbling Blocks" Bill listed, and consider if any
   need special attention. Does youth ministry after age 30 or
   40 present problems for you?)

4. How can these barriers be overcome? (Consider how a team of
   parents could help.)

5. In order to keep such a commitment, what changes will be
   necessary in your life?

16

COMMITMENT TO MARRIAGE AND FAMILY

by Barry and Carol St. Clair

Carol and I took our kids to the Barnum and Bailey Circus some time ago. We love the horses, the elephants and everything else. One of the climactic moments was when Elvin Bailey got on his balancing wheel. He started at the bottom and ran up to the top of the wheel. When he began to lose his balance, he'd run down and then he'd run back up, then down, then up. Finally, he got to the top and his feet were just flying around that wheel. The crowd gasped just watching him try to stay in control on top of that balancing wheel. Sometimes Carol and I feel that this is a picture of our lives as we seek to strike a balance between our marriage and our ministry. It is a "balancing act" that requires tremendous concentration.

In today's world, we have found that one of the greatest platforms for ministry is our marriage. Young people desperately need to see Christ-centered marriages and loving relationships. They need to see how Christ can provide unity, security and nurture within a Christian home environment. But it doesn't come automatically — there are no "quick fixes" here.

We've been working at this for several years now — thirteen, as a matter of fact. I met Carol in the seminary library and knew just three days later that she was the one for me. During the nine months before we were married, we didn't have one single cross word. We didn't have one single conflict. We didn't have one single difficulty in our relationship. It was marvelous. We had a wonderful, wonderful time. And then we got married.

ADJUSTING TO MUTUAL MINISTRY

When we got back from our honeymoon, things came down to

Barry and Carol St. Clair were married in 1970. Carol focuses her attention on their two sons and one daughter, while also assisting Barry in his role as pastor of Christ Community Church.

earth — especially the morning we were supposed to leave for California to work in a church for the summer. Carol tells it like this:

> I lost a contact lens — and then I lost my composure! We were getting ready to board an airplane which would fly me away from my family and friends to start our new life together. But when I lost my contact, I just "lost it" entirely. I think I cried all the way from my house to the airport and all the way to California. Barry assured me that things would seem better when we got to California. But, ironically, when we moved into our little honeymoon apartment, we found it had bunk beds!
>
> We began learning how to minister together. Barry was Mr. Gung Ho — he had just worked with Campus Crusade for Christ the year before, and it seemed that he knew all the right things to do. But I didn't feel like I knew a thing. I knew I had a heart to want to serve God. I had grown up in a pastor's home, and I saw God's working in our family. But I didn't know what God wanted *me* to do.
>
> Now here we were in this little church, and we were everything. I was the secretary and had to type out the little bulletin and run it off on the ditto machine. I do not type! I spent all day Saturday and Saturday night picking out this little thing on the typewriter. We didn't have any members. This was a new little mission church we were trying to get started, so we literally had to round up people to come to church. I was also the janitor, and every week I'd have to clean out the bathrooms and make sure everything was just right.
>
> We didn't have anybody to play the organ, and since I had played hymns in Sunday school while growing up, I got to be the organist, too! And I tried so hard! I had worked up this little prelude of some hymns and I just thought I was doing great. After the first service, Barry tried to say it kindly to me, "Hon, you really did a nice job on the organ. But you know what, we've got some records back here and a stereo..." and so from then on we had beautiful Mormon Tabernacle Choir music for the prelude! That was the beginning of this business of our working together.

After graduating from seminary, I became the director of Youth Evangelism for the Southern Baptist Home Mission Board. It was a traveling ministry. I would go away to minister, and Carol would stay home and do her thing around the house. I would come back telling these wonderful stories about how God was blessing, and she had been home scrubbing floors, washing dishes and eventually having babies and taking care of them. As you can imagine, we have had a number of adjustments to work through.

Balancing marriage and ministry isn't easy, but over the years we have come to see that things go more smoothly when there is balance in three essential areas: developing vision, meeting needs and setting goals. This balance comes as both the husband and the wife assume their unique and vital roles. In Ephesians 5, the classic passage on marriage, Paul speaks of the role of the wife and the role of the husband and how they balance each other. With that in mind, let's address these essential areas, noticing the unique role both husband and wife can play in achieving this balance.

A FAMILY-ORIENTED VISION

The first essential for balance is to *develop a vision for ministry that includes the family*. Both husband and wife must discover their call to the ministry. Without that, we flounder, we don't go anywhere, and we have no real feeling of accomplishment or sense of intensity.

The Husband's Leadership

For those of us who are husbands, there are six things I want to mention here. First of all, think through your call to the ministry. Write it down so that you can know *specifically* what God has called you to do. I think that's a real difficulty for many individuals whom I encounter. Quite often I counsel youth workers who ask all kinds of questions about what they should do, when in reality the difficulty is that they have never thought through the answers to two very basic questions: (1) Has God called me to the ministry? (2) If so, what has He called me specifically to do? I think that writing down the answers to these questions will help.

Second, ask God to give you a vision for that call. Ask Him to help you *picture* what your ministry will look like when it is at its peak and what some of the steps will be along the way.

Third, develop the vision to include your wife and family. The definition of success for the average American businessman rarely ever includes his wife and family. I think there is also a tendency within the church to fall into that same trap. Our definition of success and the vision that God has for us must include our wives and families.

Fourth, communicate your vision to your wife continually. Don't just write it out and share it with her once and then forget it! Instead, as you're living out the burden of that vision in your own life, continue to communicate it to your wife. Pray with her over your concerns, talk to her about your dreams, expose her to the things you are doing, and involve her as much as possible. These kinds of things will help you communicate your vision to her.

Fifth, within your vision, help your wife discover and implement *her* gifts of ministry. It is essential that she experience fulfillment and not just be a "tag-along." I have a tendency to impose my ideas on Carol and and expect her to tag along. Because I have very definite ideas about what the ministry ought to be, I tend to think she should fit in with those ideas. I'll never forget the first time I tried to integrate Carol into what I was doing. We had been dating about two weeks, and we went to speak at this little church in Oroville,

Kentucky. The pulpit stood behind a big pot-bellied stove in the middle of the church. As I was preaching that morning I told the people "Now if you'll come back tonight, the young lady I brought with me is going to sing a solo for you!" We had been dating such a short time that I didn't even know whether she could sing or not! That's one illustration of imposing, right? Fortunately for me, she did sing. She graciously "tagged along." In fact, it was great! But that certainly wasn't the ideal way to help her discover her gifts. Involve her in your vision *naturally*.

Sixth, be willing to modify the focus of your vision to accommodate your family. A short time ago, I accepted the responsibility of pastoring a small church in the Atlanta area. One of the primary reasons motivating us was to help involve our family as a unit in ministering together. At first, we were hesitant to take our children out of the good program they were part of in our established church with the traditional choirs and all the things that we thought were so good. But it has been so exciting to see our children respond — they see this church as their project. They have *ownership* in this church, and they communicate that vision to others. In fact, our son has friends who are twins. On their tenth birthday they asked their mother if they could come to our church — that's what they wanted for their birthday! Our kids feel that they're a part of what we're doing, and they are really enjoying it.

The Wife's Complementary Role

The wife also plays a vital part in the couple's call to the ministry. The first thing she must do is to really listen to what the husband is saying about his ministry calling. A lot of times the husband's vision may not be the same as the vision that the wife has for herself. Carol comments:

> Barry is a real visionary. He comes up with these wonderful ideas. My immediate response is to tell him all the ways they won't work, just because my temperment is much more that way — pragmatic. I like to say I'm pragmatic — really, I'm negative! I need to have a listening ear. As I listen to him and understand where he is coming from, I begin to catch his vision.

Second, as the wife begins to identify with her husband's vision, she needs to discover how she can help him fulfill it. Carol continues:

> This has been a struggle for me. As a teenager I felt that God was calling me into ministry, but I never knew exactly what role I was to play. So all these years that Barry has been traveling, I've been primarily at home, which is what I wanted to do — I love being a

mother and a wife — but I always felt that I wasn't doing quite enough.

God has recently freed me to see that our home is the means by which I can help Barry the most right now in our lives. If I can help make our home a place we all can enjoy, a place where others feel welcome, a place where our children can be trained, then I have played a tremendous role in enhancing Barry's ministry and in freeing him to do what he does. And as our children get older, I have more time to get together with people one-to-one and to do many of the things that I just haven't been able to do in the past. God is confirming that I am fitting in with Barry's ministry — but my role changes all along the way.

The third thing a wife can do is to discover how her strengths and gifts fit with her husband's. Carol observes:

I don't have to be a Barry St. Clair, thank goodness, because my gifts are so different from his! But I've seen how God uses us to complement each other. Barry can sit down with somebody and exhort him to action, but at times I have been able to smooth a few ruffled feathers. Barry can have some great idea, and in talking about it, I can help him plug out the practicalities of how it's all going to work out. So I feel that God will combine our strengths and our weaknesses if we'll allow Him to do it. A lot of times we resist that because those strengths and weaknesses are differences that sometimes cause conflicts. But the things that cause conflicts can also be the very things that can draw us together, if we allow God to combine our gifts.

There are probably no two other people who have ever been married who are as different in temperament as Carol and I. I am a pusher and a driver, a person who is goal-oriented and always going after it. In the process I may leave a lot of messes in my wake. On the other hand, Carol is sensitive and loving and merciful, and she comes along and cares for all those people that I've wiped out somewhere along the way. I hope that will be an encouragement to some who may be wondering, "Did I marry the right person? We are so different." I just think how unbalanced I would be if I didn't have Carol to offset some of those strengths and weaknesses in my personality.

MEETING EACH OTHER'S NEEDS

The second essential for balancing marriage and ministry is to *make the meeting of needs within the family a high priority*. Not only do we need to fit our marriage into our vision for ministry, but we also need to see that part of our ministry is a ministry to one another's needs, and that must be a huge *priority*. It's hard, isn't it? We're always juggling those priorities, always trying to keep things straight, and always trying to work in time for our family. And who usually bites the dust first when it comes to priorities in our schedules? Our family, right? That's wrong. I do it, you may do it; but God is not pleased with that.

Think From The Other Person's Perspective

When we consider meeting the needs of our spouses, we need to consider needs from the other person's perspective. When I look at Carol's needs from my perspective, I think, "Well, she needs this and this and this and this." Usually about 90 percent of my assumptions are wrong. I need to learn to see what her needs are from her point of view so that I can begin to meet those needs. An example would be the time I bought Carol a guitar. I like to hear her sing, but she didn't want a guitar. I felt she needed it, but I had failed to consider her perspective!

Recently we went on a vacation to Florida. I was relaxing and having a good time, while Carol was going to the store and buying food and cooking it. I was on vacation having a great time, and she was still doing all the stuff she always does at home. She wanted a break, so she made a few subtle hints, which I didn't catch. Then the hints kept getting stronger and stronger. Finally she said, "Hey, we just need to go out and eat!" Alert fellow that I am, I began to pick up on that, and we went out to eat — but it just took a while for me to see the picture from her perspective.

Meeting the Husband's Needs

There are a number of universal areas of need which are part of the wife's ministry to her husband. One of a man's primary needs is to feel accepted. You may look at somebody who's "up front" and think that he may not have as much need for that warm acceptance from his wife. The fact is, however, that he probably needs it as much as — if not more than — any other person. Gordon MacDonald, in his book *Magnificent Marriage*, points out that especially with those of us in ministry there tends to be an "integrity gap." A wife sees her husband teaching and preaching about all these wonderful spiritual truths and giving insight into how to live life, yet she lives at home with him and sees the nitty gritty. Sometimes that nitty gritty does not measure up to the things she hears him teach, and that discrepancy may keep a man's family from really accepting him, loving him and trusting him as a leader. That attitude starts building a barrier which prevents the wife from receiving from her husband, especially in the spiritual area. But neither of us is perfect, and we need to ask for God's grace to accept each other as we are.

Another thing the wife can do is help set her husband free to do what he needs to do. We have already established that the family must be central in the vision for ministry. But the wife must not be jealous of the time the husband spends apart from her. She has a tremendous ministry if she can set him free to do those things which enable him to do what God has uniquely called him to do.

A third thing a wife can do to meet her husband's needs is to monitor what is happening with him — for instance, to realize when he's getting too tired. When that happens, encourage him to take a day off. As strange as it might seem, he might not know how much he needs it. Those in ministry tend to minister around the clock. He may need to hear you say, "Honey, you're just pushing yourself too hard; we've got to set aside some time to get away and rest." A man also needs somebody to really listen to him — somebody he can bounce his ideas off of and get a different perspective. As the wife graciously gives feedback, she can often provide insight that will make a real impact on their ministry.

A husband also needs a warm atmosphere at home. Many times when he comes home at night he is ready to relax and do nothing. But the wife is ready for a break, too. Here is an area where there needs to be balance — juggling the circumstances to meet each other's needs and thereby produce a warm home atmosphere.

The husband also needs the wife's warm physical response. In the ministry, men are giving, giving, giving. They often face sexual temptation. Research shows that the same brain load that controls our spiritual thinking also controls our sexual desires. Talking about these things and meeting each other's needs in this area are important in making a couple's marriage a solid foundation for their ministry.

Meeting the Wife's Needs

One of the primary needs of a wife is to feel worthwhile. If you have read any of James Dobson's material, you know how significant self-image is for women. Women must have positive reinforcement from their husbands — they may not get it from others. I'm out all day dealing with people, and I can get those positive strokes in the things that I'm doing. On the other hand, so many times my wife has been home battling the kids all day, keeping them out of trouble, cleaning up the messes, and she needs those positive reinforcements from me that cause her to feel worthwhile. It is this encouragement from me that can help her develop to her maximum potential.

Second, a wife needs sacrificial love. Ephesians 5 says that the Spirit-filled husband "nourishes and cherishes" his wife. I need to make sure that I hold Carol in the highest honor and esteem in our home, in my own mind, before our kids and out before others. So many times husbands and wives play this little game of cutting one another down and making little snide remarks — things that show lack of esteem and respect for the other person. It should be just the opposite. It is my responsibility to feed Carol, encourage her and give her those things that will stimulate growth in her response to me, her response to the Lord and her response to life in general.

A third need of the wife is to feel that her husband is in charge, that he is the protector, as the Scripture charges us to be. I get irritated in dealing with small details, so when I get into things like finances, it drives me nuts! Yet I see that handling our finances is my responsibility because it is part of being Carol's protector and taking care of her in the way I should.

A fourth area of need is communication. We need to communicate not only about the broad visionary things, but also about the nitty gritty of everyday life. This is one area about my relationship with Carol that I really enjoy. We talk, and we talk a lot. One of the things I have always appreciated about her is that always, in every situation, all the cards are on the table. And that's good. That has helped me to be more in touch with my feelings. It is easy to communicate the facts, but often our communication leads us to ask, "Hey, how do you really *feel* about this? What do you *really* think about this?" It is so healthy and helpful to move through to some deeper levels of communication.

Fifth, a wife needs a husband's undivided attention. I'm a moving-toward-the-future kind of person, and so I tend to focus on those things in my day-to-day life. It is so easy for me to become preoccupied. But when I'm at home, Carol needs to have my full attention. Even though I share some of my ministry burden with her, there are times when I need to move off that hobby horse and begin to spend time listening and paying attention to the things that she's involved in within her world.

A sixth need is for a wife to have time away from her family. That's interesting, isn't it? When was the last time your wife just went off by herself and took a little vacation — just her, not even the two of you, but just her? Carol did that recently. It was tremendously refreshing for her. Her parents invited her to come to the beach. I took care of the kids, and she spent a week with her folks, enjoying herself and having the chance to spend a lot of time alone. It was very positive for our relationship because she came back refreshed and out of the grind of doing the things she does every day. It was good for us at home, too. Katie, my seven-year-old daughter, was my main cook. One night she was helping to get some stuff together for supper and a friend asked, "Katie, are you doing all the cooking?" And Katie said, "Oh, yeah, my Dad's not worth a flip in the kitchen!" It was a real memory in every way!

Seventh, a wife needs emotional love and warmth — not just physical warmth, but emotional closeness. Sometimes, because of my intensity, I can tend to be harsh and make harsh statements and not even mean them. My verse is 1 Thessalonians 2:7. "But we were gentle among you like a mother taking care of her little children" (NIV). God is working on that in my life. Carol doesn't need those harsh responses. She doesn't *ever* need them. I'm praying that God will give me the ability to be more gentle and to give that emotional love and that emotional warmth that she needs.

Summary Thoughts

To summarize, there are three things that a couple must be willing to do to make the meeting of mutual needs a priority. The first thing that comes to mind is to talk, talk, talk, talk, talk. Most of the things we've referred to are just a matter of communicating back and forth to one another about what your needs are and how you feel that the other person can help meet them.

For our vacation this summer, we had two weeks in Florida, a wonderful time away from everything. After we had slept for about the first two or three days, we started reading a number of books. In the process, a lot of needs in our relationship came to the forefront. At first, we hesitated about getting too "heavy" on our vacation. But these were areas in our relationship that we knew we needed to talk about, areas that we had just been sweeping away because of lack of time.

I remember one night we sat up late just talking out these issues that had come up from the books we had read. We got back to some things in our early years of marriage that had been hidden under the rug — things that we didn't even realize, but which kept cropping up over the years. After that conversation, it seemed that God opened up a whole new awareness of who we were to each other. There is no substitute for consistent communication with one another. It is a key to balance in marriage.

Second, be willing to compromise and adapt. There are always areas of give and take, like on days off. Carol comments:

> How I want Barry to spend his day off may be very different from the way Barry wants to spend it. I have two pages of projects I want him to do around the house! And that may not be exactly how he wants to spend his day off! We have to compromise on issues like that.

Finally, strive to be accepting and loving. Treat your spouse and family as you want to be treated and as you want to see your children treat one another. Give each other the freedom to fail, and love each other with the same degree of mercy that you constantly receive from Christ.

GOALS, PRIORITIES AND SCHEDULES

The third essential for balancing marriage and ministry is to *set goals, priorities and schedules for your family and your ministry.* It helps tremendously to get these down on paper. Putting it in writing helps you to think through more effectively what will be pleasing to the Lord and constructive in developing your relationships.

Clarify Simple Goals

Define your personal and family goals clearly. They don't have to be difficult or even long-range, but when you communicate with your spouse about your week-to-week schedule, be sure that what you do reflects your personal and family goals. If you don't have any goals, if you don't have that planning time set aside, there is going to be slack. If your goals don't include the family, then you're going to have the wrong goals. You need to sit down and ask, "What do we want to accomplish in our family? What are some of the things that we desire to do?"

Carol and I did this as we prepared for summer. To avoid feeling that the summer was wasted, we decided to put together notebooks for the kids and we worked out a "contract" for each of them. In the notebook we wrote down several goals that we all agreed they would try to accomplish during the summer. We included goals for mental, spiritual, social and physical areas. At the end of the summer, we would reward them with something they would really like to do if they fulfilled the contract. We sat down with them and said, "Okay, what do you want to do?" We had some ideas, but we involved them. We chose some books to read, some verses to memorize. We decided they would learn to ride a bike, etc. It was hard on us sometimes to keep them at it, but generally it worked out very well, and the kids were excited to check things off as they accomplished the goals.

Schedule Time as a Couple

It is also important that your goals include realistic time slots for the family — starting with your time as a couple. You need to plan times to talk. Occasionally those spontaneous times come up and they're great, but few couples have enough of those times. There needs to be some scheduled times to talk, times to work on your schedule, times to work on business items, times for romance, date times. We always look forward to those times when we know we're going to be able to go out and be together, just the two of us.

Sometimes you need a weekend away, or two or three days during the week, if you're in local church ministry. Recently, Carol and I took off up to Sapphire Valley, North Carolina, for a couple of days by ourselves. We had the best time reading, relaxing, talking, going out to eat, and just "hacking around" together. It was a marvelous time away. These days away are so valuable, but be willing to make the effort to arrange the details. It will be worth it! Maybe you can trade babysitting with another couple who may want to do something similar in the future.

Involve Your Children

Of course, time with your family also means time with your children. One of the things we do is try to make a habit of eating our breakfasts together. I round up the kids, everyone gets his bowl of cereal, we sit down around the breakfast table, and we have a time together as a family. We talk a little bit, we pray, we share Scripture verses, and we read out of the Bible. We recently finished outlining the book of Philippians on a big poster board, and everybody made his own contribution. It probably wouldn't win any scholarly awards, but it's a great time with our family to interact — a kind of discipling time.

Carol and I also try to take individual time with the kids. Often when I travel I try to take one of them with me. Recently I took Katie with me when my trip fell on her birthday. We went a day early and stayed in a motel. I took her out to eat, and she felt like a queen! It was so much fun, and meant so much to both of us. So attempt to plan those individual times with your kids — not just on a week-to-week basis, but some special things that will help them feel how significant and important they are to you.

It's also important for the children to be involved in your ministry. This means that you don't just take them on trips — which, of course, is very special — but you can also take them with you when you run errands or let them help you set up at church on Sunday. Our son, Scott, just loves to put flyers in the seats or set up the hot chocolate. He likes to be involved in what his mom and dad do.

Entertaining has also been a great thing for our family. Our kids have always felt a real openness to the people who have been in our home. When Katie was about four, Carol's cousin came to visit us, and Katie hadn't seen him for a long time. It was getting late, and we sent all the kids to get their pajamas on, but Katie came back and cuddled right up where we were. Carol said, "Katie, it's getting time, you just scoot on to bed now."

Katie just sat there and adamantly said, "Well, Mother, don't you know this is how little people learn?"

And Carol said, "Well, I guess so!" And still, to this day, whenever we have people over to our house, Katie is right in the middle of the conversation. Our kids love it, and we're so excited that they want to be a part of what we're doing.

THE RESPONSIBILITY FOR BALANCE

You may be wondering how you could ever set up all these times with your family. Obviously, you won't be able to have all these times with your wife, your kids, and your whole family every week. But if you make it a priority to put these times in your overall schedule, then it will happen much of the time. We try to schedule in at least one night a week when we're all going to be home. Our kids are young, but they're already involved in their own activities. We have soccer one night, ballet one night, piano one night — we're running back and forth with them, in addition to going to all of our own meetings. So last year we tried to hold Monday night as a family night. We tried to have a nice dinner together, and then we played games or did something else that was fun. It may not always work out the way we plan, but at least it is a goal worth shooting for — especially in today's society when we all get so scattered.

It certainly is not easy to balance marriage and ministry. We must work at it diligently, but we must also be careful not to take the burden on ourselves in a legalistic way. Carol illustrates what I mean:

> Not long ago I took the children to the library. Somehow things got a little hectic, and by the time we left, we were all a little frazzled. When we got back in the car, they all *had* to sit in the front seat. So we were all in the front driving home with this stack of books. On the way home, some of the books fell over, and Scott and Katie got into an argument about who was responsible. Finally Scott said, "Katie, you know you did it, and God knows it, too." Then I said, "Let's not bring God into this argument." And Jonathan, our four-year-old philospher, said, "Why not? Don't you know God's responsible for everything?"
>
> His question stopped me in my tracks, but as I thought about that during the day, I thought, "He is so right. God is responsible — He is responsible to enable us to work out the difficulties and the details of our lives."

If you think about all these things, you get somewhat overwhelmed — meet the needs, work out the vision, set your schedule. How can we ever do all that? We do our best, but ultimately we rest in the knowledge that God is responsible. We can trust Him to enable us. Proverbs 3:5,6 says, "Trust in the Lord with all your heart, and do not lean on your own understanding. In *all* your ways acknowledge Him, and He will make your paths straight."

Carol and I do not have it all together, but we know that God is working in our lives to make us more and more into the image of Jesus Christ. He has put us together to sharpen us and to take off the rough edges, and we need to be sensitive in allowing Him to do that. As we begin to understand our call, meet each other's needs and plan our schedule according to goals, God will make us like Him and give us fulfillment in ministry. In the process, God can use our marriages as a platform for ministry. Young people desperately need to see loving relationships that demonstrate how Christianity can work itself out in daily living.

PUTTING THIS CHAPTER TO WORK

1. What has God called you to do specifically? How do you envision that will be accomplished in the next five years? In the next two years?

2. What are some of your mate's strengths and gifts that might complement your call?

3. What do you think your mate would say his/her needs are right now? How can you help meet some of those needs?

4. What are your goals for your spouse and children in the coming year?

17

COMMITMENT TO THE CAUSE

by Dr. E. V. Hill

In Psalm 11:3, the psalmist asks, "If the foundations are destroyed, what can the righteous do?" When this text was first recorded, the idea of foundations being destroyed was farfetched. The people of Israel were tutored in the concept of protecting the godly foundations upon which they stood. They would not touch the ancient landmarks. When I was a child, the idea that our foundations would be destroyed would not have attracted anybody's attention because we believed that a time never would come when mankind would concentrate on destroying foundations. We just assumed that everybody would always be brilliant enough to know that a building or a family or a society cannot exist if you destroy the foundation upon which it is built. But in our time, there is no need to emphasize the "if" in verse 3. You and I are living in an age of crumbling foundations, an age in which the society has set out, with aim and direction, to deliberately and intentionally destroy the foundations upon which we — as Christian families and as a country — were built. The activities of many organizations in our nation — highly financed and promoted — are dedicated to destroying the foundations.

THE NEED FOR COMMITMENT

There is intense activity today to destroy the home. There is little appreciation any more for a father who looks out for and provides for his family. It is no longer popular to be a wife who, with tender grace and sweetness, is the refreshment that a man needs when he comes home after he has been at labor. It is considered unimportant by many to be a mother who takes care of her children —to be one who nurtures, leads and brings children up in the fear and adoration of God. There is an intense, organized, international conspiracy to destroy those concepts.

My own daughter, after finishing college, got way into this idea

235

that a woman has much more to offer the world than being a wife, than being a mother, than taking care of the children. We used to have long discussions about that issue. She would say, "Daddy, it's all right for Mother, but don't look for me to do that. I love you as a Daddy, but I am *not* going to marry a chauvinist male like you!" Everybody knows I am president of the International Chauvinist Society! Ironically, it just so happens that the man she selected as a husband I am nominating as vice president of the International Chauvinist Society! He is a great fellow. I couldn't have picked a better husband for her myself. They have really made a wonderful home, and the only debate now is whether they will have six children or nine!

So I am thankful that things have turned around. But there are those who are seeking to stab a fatal wound into the very body of the foundations that have sustained us as a people and as a nation. And so today, Psalm 11:3 could easily say, "the foundations ARE being destroyed."

We are hearing a great deal these days about the so-called "alternative lifestyle." In the city of San Francisco, 30 percent of the population now claim to be homosexual. They boast of having a fair amount of pressure and influence over the city and county governments. People view what the Bible says about homosexuality differently than in the past. In my time, we felt that if you did any sinning, you should repent. We believed that people would always recognize the Bible as the inerrant Word of God. We had no difficulty that an all-powerful, no-error God could write a book of the same. But some people don't accept that, so the foundations are being destroyed.

I recently returned from Europe. It occurs to me that America seems to be intent on emulating Europe and bringing the customs, patterns and beliefs of Europe to the United States. Just look at Europe. There is a land where the foundations for the most part *are* destroyed.

I am a great lover of health spas. The first thing I do when I get into a new city is to find out where the health spa is. So when I was in Amsterdam recently, I told my wife, "I have to go find my health spa." I found one, but it was a confusing experience. First of all, there was a female receptionist. Then the girl who took me to my room had nothing but a towel wrapped around her. I said to myself, "Well, it's all right; you'll finally get to the men's section back here somewhere."

We found the sauna, and it was empty. It was just like I like it — real hot. So there I was in the sauna, fully enjoying it. And about that time, a beautiful young lady walked in — completely naked! She put her towel right down beside me and, with nothing on, just lay down. All of a sudden things got too hot in there for me! Later my wife said, "You sure got home early." I said, "Yes, it was quite hot down there!"

THE CALL TO COMMITMENT

The foundations ARE being destroyed. Wherever you look — the school system, the home, politics, to name a few — we are living at a time when the foundations are being destroyed. And today's youth are suffering because of it. You are dealing with young people today who know nothing about the steadiness of life.

Focus on Christ and His Finished Work

How can we help our young people in light of the fact that the foundations *are* being destroyed? What should we teach them? What can we do? First of all, 2 Peter 1:10 says that we ought to make our "calling and election sure" (KJV). There is no place for doubt, especially with those who are leaders of young people. There certainly is no place for any who may not be completely sure where they stand with God.

When I say, "Make your calling and election sure," I certainly don't want to send you out on any exotic hunt for some type of physical evidence or Pauline experience. I am not referring to anything that comes from within you. I am not referring to any amount of righteousness that you have seen in yourself or anything which you have achieved. Those things are so fickle and changeable. You can be feeling like the apostle Paul one day and then like Judas the next.

One way that I *know* I am saved is to remember the finished work of Jesus Christ on Calvary. That's my whole confidence. If He didn't accomplish what He said He accomplished, I am lost. But if He has arranged it so that "whosoever believeth in Him should not perish, but have everlasting life" (John 3:16), then I am saved. I'm in Him. I'm saved because I have believed Him for salvation. I trust in Him, I lean on Him, I'm relying on Him, and if He and the Father are right, I'm in the kingdom. That's my whole confidence. I don't look inward to make sure that I am saved. I'm trusting the complete work of Jesus Christ — that He has done what He said He would. He said, "Whosoever will may come" (Revelation 22:17), and I am a part of the "whosoever will."

So re-examine your faith in the finished work of Jesus Christ and help your youth to do the same. Young people have the tendency to examine God's work in *you,* and you have the responsibility to cast the attention off of yourself and onto Jesus Christ. As you continue in ministry, there will be people who will come running to you — as soon as they see you help somebody, as soon as you go through a crisis with someone. And that is wonderful, but focus their affection on Jesus Christ.

Make your calling and election sure, and make sure that your young people's faith is not in you but in Christ Jesus. Because in these days of falling and crumbling foundations, they are going to need somebody better than you. They are going to need Jesus! The certainty that we want to give our young people in these days of crumbling foundations is the certainty that Jesus Christ accomplished all that He said He did and that they can trust Him and rely on *Him*. Throw the spotlight off of yourself. Don't let them make you their hero. Let Jesus be that hero.

Put On the Whole Armor of God

In these rough days when the foundations are falling and the walls are caving in, we must also teach our young people how to put on the whole armor of God. Ephesians 6 talks about the helmet of salvation; it talks about the sword of the Spirit; it talks about girding ourselves; it talks about the breastplate of righteousness. We need to teach young people the importance of the Word of God, the importance of faith, the importance of Jesus Christ as our breastplate of righteousness. And we have to get them into the Word.

One assumption rampant in the United States today is that to get the ear of young people you must have some unusual amount of fun, giggles, foot-stomping/hand-clapping entertainment and socials. It is not so! I pastor a church. In 1966 after the Watts riots, it was declared that E. V. Hill wouldn't have any young people if he didn't change his mannerism to fit the times. I lived right in the heart of the south central ghetto — the ghetto that was gripped by "blackism." During that period, my life was often in jeapordy. I was theatened; I lived with bodyguards. The men of our church had to protect my life and the life of our church, but I preached the Word of God.

And guess what! Today we have more young people in our church than just about any other church in our area — and they were not won by gimmicks. They were won by doctrinal preaching and by the stubbornness of the gospel that we faithfully preach and teach. And today these young people are enthusiastically involved in the many ministries of our church. Young people are eager for the Word, but we play them too small. They want to know about the assurance of their salvation. They want to know how to put on the whole armor of God. They want to know how to be strong in the Lord. And they can, as we equip them with the offensive weapons of the armor of God.

One offensive weapon is the Word of God. The other offensive weapon is prayer. Let me encourage you to pray for yourself.

Youth workers often permit their work to drain them completely as they try to meet the challenges of young people — answering their questions, living with their problems, and being another mother and father to them. You can come up drained and burned out at a very early age. So pray for yourself, and organize a group of people who pray for you. I have people whose ministry is to pray for me as I travel. We have a 24-hour prayer clock at our church so that people are praying every 15 minutes, around the clock.

One more thought on prayer. I know that there are times when you get down on your knees and nothing will come out. You can force prayer out, but the best thing to do is to pick some prayers from the Bible. I hang in there with Psalms 51 and 71. Those are my two great prayers. And then if you can't find a prayer in the Bible, pick up a song book and go to the prayer hymns: "Thou, my everlasting portion, more than life to me; all along this pilgrim journey, Savior, let me walk with Thee." Any night you can't get to sleep there are two things that will put you to sleep — reading the book of Revelation and reading prayers from hymn books. The devil doesn't like it, and he will say, "Go on to sleep. Don't be up studying this, go on to sleep!"

Report for Duty

We must help young people with the assurance of their salvation. We must teach them how to put on the whole armor of God. Then what? Most Christian young people are sure of their salvation and completely dressed with the whole armor of God for the purpose of going to bed! Or for the purpose of spending one hour a week in church! The whole armor of God for a one-hour performance! So the third thing we must do is to *report for duty*. Report for duty! All leaves are cancelled. All furloughs are out. Everybody must report, and the churches must include their young people in their warfare against sin.

The problem we have among Christians today is that we have this whole army of folks completely dressed with the whole armor to do *nothing*. At the average church, the person who joins is asked, "Can you sing?"

"No."

"Can you usher?"

"No, I've got bad feet."

"Then sit down."

And the whole Christian army has been rocked into complacency because there seems to be nothing to do! With all of these foundations being destroyed, these walls falling, and Satan on the attack, there seems to be nothing to do but usher, sing, or tithe.

It is for that reason that at the church where I pastor I have 62 committees on evangelism. I have a separate committee for every way you can be lost! I have 62 organized committees in order that young people, with their talent and energy, can report for duty. One of my committees is called the Fantastic Committee. All of my radicals are on that committee. They get together and think of something fantastic, unbelievable, or out of this world that we can do to shock south central Los Angeles to believe in Jesus Christ. Their favorite project was when they decided to do skywriting. They picked the soccor tournament, when there were 55,000 people in the Coliseum. At half-time they had a plane fly right over the Coliseum and write, "Jesus is coming." Fifty-five thousand people looked up and said, "What? Jesus is coming?" Now that's fantastic! And then my Tract Attackers, which is another committee, were at every gate after the game, and they passed out 18,000 copies of *The Second Coming of the Lord Jesus.* There was something to do — something very important!

A young lady came to our church one Sunday night. Generally we have more men than women in attendance on Sunday night, and this lady saw all these men and said, "I want to talk to the pastor."

An usher led her to my office, and she said, "My name is Dorothy. I am a working girl."

She looked the part that she was, and I said, "You mean you are a prostitute."

"Well, you can call it whatever you want to call it, but I'm a working girl."

I said, "And you saw all of these men over here and thought that maybe you could do some business."

"Well, I am in business," she said.

I said to the usher, "Will you go get Barbara for me?" Now Barbara was a prostitute for eight years. She is chairman of my Prostitute Committee! Barbara came, took Dorothy to her home across the street, and 45 minutes later Dorothy returned all cleaned up and in a dress. She came weeping and accepted Jesus Christ as her Savior.

After it was over, she said, "Pastor, I have a great big problem."

"What is it?"

"My pimp. When I go home tonight, I don't have the $300 to give him, which is my quota per night. When I tell him I got converted, he'll kill me."

"No, he won't," I said. "Hold it, Dorothy. Somebody go get Lee for me." Well, who is Lee? He is the head of my Pimp Committee!

The night Lee joined our church, he had nine working women. A few days later he said, "Pastor, what do I do with my women? That's my livelihood. I take care of nine women, and they take care of me."

I said, "What has the Spirit said to you?"

"It's wrong."

"I agree with the Spirit. Now what else has the Spirit told you to do?"

"I don't know," he said.

"Wouldn't He tell you to win the nine to Christ? Wouldn't that be like Him?"

He said, "That's exactly what He would tell me."

The next Sunday he had four of them on the second pew, and three of them got saved!

We have another committee for unmarried girls who are pregnant. We have an Alcoholic Committee, a Drug Committee, a Blackism Committee, a Jehovah's Witness Committee. We have many committees and opportunities where our young people can become involved. Report for duty! The church must not be complacent, stuck away, sitting in the dugout, waiting for the Rapture! We must get on the field. Play!

Four years ago, we had 647 in our Vacation Bible School, and everybody in the church was tired, worn out. I was on a plane flying to Mobile, Alabama, and the Lord said, "You didn't reach enough young people." And I said, "Well Lord, I will turn it over to the committee for next year." He said, "You didn't reach enough. When you get back from Mobile, reopen Vacation Bible School, and this time have Backyard Bible Studies." I said, "Lord, everybody I know is tired. Ain't no way in the world we can have Backyard Bible Studies. I don't even know what it is! But we will turn it over to the Christian Education Committee to work it out for next year." The Lord said, "No, I want to have it this year." I said, "I told you, Lord, I'm tired; everybody else is tired; it's the middle of July."

The next Sunday when I got back home, I went into my office before I went to the pulpit. The Lord said to me, "Call for 100 people to have Backyard Bible Studies. You didn't reach enough young people." I said, "Lord, I'm tired. Everybody in this church is tired. It's the middle of July. We are entering now into our social period when we relax!" And the Lord said, "Call for 100." I said, "What about 50?" I actually did! He said, "I said call for 100." So I went out, preached the sermon, and I almost announced the Backyard Bible Studies as if I weren't behind the idea. No sooner had I made the appeal than 96 people stood up to say, "The Lord would have us do it." At the end of two weeks, we had enrolled 2,600 and 500 young people had indicated they received Christ — in people's backyards! One 13-year-old girl enrolled 40 in her backyard. Thirteen years old! These kids don't need to be entertained. These kids are not to be chaperoned and babysat at 13, 18, and 19. They are to report for duty! Our young people are an untapped world of energy and excitement.

There are 11 teenagers on the High School Committee. One day they announced, "We want a Christian school — let's build one."

"Oh, no, we're not going to build one," I said, "but let's *take* one!" And that got them excited! I said, "Now, where do you all go to school?" And I found out that most of them went to the same high school. So I got them together and said, "Now we are going to have a 'church' right next to the school. We are going to meet before school and after school. Now go find out how many Christians are already there." They brought back 69.

Then I said, "Now go to the principal and ask him what you *can* do on that high school campus."

The students came back and excitedly reported, "The principal said we could have our meetings in Room 101 every Tuesday and Thursday, and we can have Chapel once a year!"

In less than two months they had more than 300 in Bible studies on Tuesdays and Thursdays! When they had their Chapel, they explained the plan of salvation, and 85 students accepted Jesus Christ. The foundations are being destroyed. The walls are falling. So everybody report for duty! All hands on deck!

Keep on Believing

Finally I would remind you that in times like these we must tell young people — and tell ourselves — *keep on believing*. Keep on believing. The old devil's trick is to test us with time. He will cause delays and stumbling blocks in order to test us with time. Remember when Jesus raised Jairus' daughter (Luke 8:40 ff)? Jesus was told that she was sick, and later a messenger came running to report, "She's dead."

Jesus' reply was, "Keep on believing."

I'm sure people were thinking, "What is there to believe? She's dead. The mourners have already gathered; the pallbearers have already been selected; the preacher is already preparing his sermon; what is there to keep on believing?"

But Jesus said, "Keep on believing."

You and I, my friends, are living in a day when the pallbearers have already assembled to bury this nation and to bury the church. The death throes are supposedly heard by some already. But our message to our young people and to those with whom we work is to say with Jesus, "Keep on believing." Don't give up on God so fast. You can't hurry God. Keep on believing.

Remember that ultimately the battle is the Lord's. Don't count your victories or your defeats too quickly. Having been a pastor for thirty years now, I am beginning to understand that some of the things I once thought were failures have actually turned out to be victories. Young people who left my church and seemed to follow after the world are now back in the church and are doing great. Sometimes I wish I hadn't grieved all those days when I thought they were out there totally lost. So don't count your victories or your defeats too quickly.

Keep on believing. And keep on believing what? The simple story — that He was born of a virgin, that He was God in the flesh, that He lived a perfect life, that He was baptized in the Jordan, that He did all the miracles that are recorded in the Book, that He died on Friday and rose on Sunday, that He has all power in His hand, and that He will save all who will come unto Him. Keep on believing! Some glad morning God will answer our prayer. Some glad morning God will come through. There *is* a bright side somewhere. We keep on believing.

So, my beloved friends, believe and teach the assurance of salvation. Believe and teach the putting on of the whole armor of God. Demand that everybody report for duty. And encourage everybody to keep on believing. Do you know what will happen one of these days? Revelation 19 says that the heavens shall roll back like a scroll, and a great white horse shall come bearing the King of kings and Lord of lords. And the armies of Heaven will be with Him, and the Bride will be with Him. Every knee shall bow and every tongue shall confess that Jesus Christ is Lord, to the glory of God the Father (Philippians 2:10, 11). In this age of crumbling foundations, keep on believing. KEEP ON BELIEVING! God is going to do it! And He is going to use *you*.

We are in a battlefield, and we can expect a fight. But if you have a burden to reach and disciple young people and God's Spirit has affirmed that calling, then keep on believing. Dr. Martin Luther King, Jr., stood on the porch of his home in Montgomery, Alabama, after the Ku Klux Klan had dynamited his home. In one room his children were crying, in another room his wife was crying, and out in his yard four hundred men were gathered with rifles, knives and pistols, ready to fight the Klan. And Martin Luther King said to the men, "Here is a box. Bring every pistol, bring every knife, because we are going to win this battle of time. We aren't going to give up. We are going to wear down hate with love." Twenty years later in that same Montgomery, Alabama, the Joint Legislature welcomed Jesse Jackson with a standing ovation. I have often wondered what would have happened had Martin Luther King gotten mad and looked at his crying family and told those four hundred men, "Go do what you want to do."

Keep on believing. There's a bright side somewhere. God has shown it to you, and you have affirmed it of the Spirit. Hang on to it. Rest in the joy and peace of the Lord as never before. Ask Him to dispel your fears. Call your young people to report for duty, and remember that the battle is the Lord's.

PUTTING THIS CHAPTER TO WORK

1. Campus Crusade for Christ studies indicate that 50 percent of the body of Christ does not have assurance of salvation. If that statistic holds true for your youth group, what specifically could you do to help a greater percentage make their "calling and election sure"?

2. Dr. Hill emphasized the need to make the Word of God more central in our ministry to young people. He said, "We play them too small." Is this an area which should be improved in your current ministry? Summarize your thoughts about action you could take.

3. The average Christian young person is underchallenged in relation to spiritual things. If many in your youth group responded to your challenge to "report for duty," how would you utilize them? List ways your youth can enlist in "active duty" for Christ.

4. All of us need to "keep on believing," remembering that ultimately the battle is the Lord's. What are some areas that you need to keep on believing God for as you presently engage in the battle for youth? As you list them, trust God to carry the burden and give you new power to be "committed to the cause."